SHOY

Aandi Greenway

This book is a work of non-fiction. Names of people and places have been changed to protect their privacy

© 2004 Aandi Greenway. All rights reserved.

No part of this book may be reproduced, stored in a retrieval system, or transmitted by any means, electronic, mechanical, photocopying, recording, or otherwise, without written permission from the author.

ISBN: 1-4140-4438-0 (electronic)
ISBN: 1-4140-4439-9 (softcover)

Library of Congress Control Number:2003099350

This book is printed on acid free paper.

Printed in the United States of America
Bloomington, IN

1stBooks – rev. 12/31/03

CONTENTS

Flashbacks 1

Watching And Waiting 7

A State Of Mind Or Is It? 19

New Arrival 32

'Special' Moments 46

New Beginnings 60

Someone To Love Me 81

Stranger In The Night 112

Footsteps Of Friendship 146

No Entideno El Español

(I Don't Understand Spanish) 179

Battles Of Degradation 222

A Masked Escape 228

Again 275

Looking For What? 311

Fingertip Love 342

Knowing What You Want 390

Nightmare In Paradise 418

What The Heart Wants 455

The Worth Of Life 460

A Forgotten Milestone 508

Mini Mansion 514

Confessions Of The Heart 521

The Truth Will Set You Free 529

FLASHBACKS

It was very early in the morning. The sun had just come out of hiding and the air was damp, but to a child this was outside playing weather. I stood at the window behind these huge brown curtains that hung all the way from the ceiling to the floor and looked up and down the road. There was nothing in sight, not a car parked, not a person walking, not a child playing – nothing, it was so quiet. The clock making that racket it always made, when the hands reached the twelve and whatever number the other one was on, broke the silence. Mum was always telling me to count with the dings – did she think I was clever? I moved from the cur-

Shoy

tain; what was I going to do now? My face lit up as I remembered my new bike. The bike of my dreams, a bike of my own, my new bike was calling. It had a red frame with a blue seat, on which it had a picture of a teddy bear and at the ends of the handlebars it had white rubber with tassels hanging down in colours of red and blue. There was a large front wheel and two smaller ones at the back.

'Come play with me Shoy,' it was saying to me. 'Come on, there is no-one around.' How could I refuse such an invitation? Here I was in my flannel pink with white daisy pyjamas and the rest of the house asleep in their beds. Smiling at the thought of riding my new bike, I unlocked the back door and tried to manoeuvre my bike around the door. For something that had wheels it did not move too easily around the heavy door, with its blue interior and yellow exterior. Nice colours, I thought as I scraped the wheels along side it, but it was closing in on both of us. My foot was now stuck in between the back wheels of the bike and the door and I could not move. I was now building a temper and I pushed the bike outside as hard as I could and it fell with an almighty bang, but hey, it was out and my foot was now free. I pulled the door in, trying hard not to close it, as I would not be able to get in again. I was free and so was my bike. I pushed it up the path and pulled it up the step, passed the shed, the pear tree, which had no leaves

Flashbacks

on it at all, and finally, arrived at the apple tree. Panting, I turned it around and got on. It was a long way down, but this was going to be fun, and I was going to enjoy it. I began to peddle. The grass was uneven and I bumped up and down. It was hard keeping the handles straight and I kept going off the edges into the patch where my dad would plant the carrots and cabbages.

'You stupid bike.' Keep still, go straight!' I kept shouting at the bike. 'That's better.' Just as I got to the bottom of the garden just before the step, my mum's head appeared around the door.

'Shoy?' Oops – the shout of trouble.

'Yes mummy.' I replied, trying to concentrate on where the bike was taking me.

'You have no shoos, no coat arn, you feel say it summer? Bring the bike here now and come in the howse. Mine the step.' I stopped short of the step and looked at it. It was small and I knew I could ride right over it. I totally ignored my mum, who for some reason did not come out of the house. I got off the bike, turned it around and pushed it up the garden, only half way this time. Going all the way to the apple tree was too far. I was exhausted now, but I managed to turn it around again, jumped on and started to

Shoy

peddle again.

'SHOY, did you hear me chile – come in di howse now, ess di bike is going back to di shop and you will not see it again.' My Aunt Shirley now had her head out of the bathroom window, which was opposite the step. I was going really fast now. I raised my legs off the pedals right up in the air along side the handlebars.

'Whee............'

'SHOY stop!' It was all too late; I left the bike at a rate of knots. The front wheel had gone over the step and got stuck, the handlebars went one way and I went the other, head first, straight onto my mouth. I was caught, well trapped under the bike. Blood! Bright. Dripping red blood. Everywhere. What had I done? Well, I knocked my front teeth out. That's what I had done.

Memories of childhood are funny things. They come and go. Flashbacks? Or are they?

Anyway, the day came to go to the dentist. How many days since that fatal day of knocking my front teeth out that were 'so precious,' as I was always told – who knows? I was seated in a chair that went up very high, and was being approached by the man in the white coat who had implements in his hands that he was trying very hard to get into my mouth, but I was not having any of it. I began rocking vigorously almost to the point of throwing myself out of the chair, so another injury would have not have made much difference, but I wanted out of there.

'Shoy, di man is trying to fix your mout, keep still chile, come on, daddy coming to get you when he finish.' I looked at her. My dad was the best. He was tall and very, very strong and he loved me. He would always carry me, even though I could walk, he would lift me on to his shoulders where I could see the world, but mostly I did not have to walk; and get my legs tired. He was great. I was now calm, but the dentist with his white coat came towards me with a mask, which was hissing. So where did he think he was going with that?

'Come on, Shoy; that is such a beautiful name. The nice man is going to look at you to make you better.' I don't think so. 'Hey, Shoy; take a look at this doll. She needs to be mended. Would you like to fix her?' I stupidly took the doll and before I knew it there was this rubber contraption on my face, and it was horrid-smelling and I could not get away. Can you believe it? They gassed me. Next thing I was being carried home by my dad. Why was I so sleepy? My mouth was hurting, and there were streaks

Shoy

of bloody dribble running down my dad's back. I had cotton wool stuffed in my mouth. How could they take me home through the streets looking this way? No good for street cred!!

WATCHING AND WAITING

The morning was cold and I was dressed in brand new clothes. I had shiny black shoes, green thick tights (lovely), green pinafore, white shirt with a very stiff collar around my neck (this type of top I had not worn before), green/blue striped tie, green jumper with a V-neck so my tie would show, and a warm coat and hat (the description of which I cannot remember), but I remember the hat came down over my ears and tied in a bow under my chin (very nice). Now breakfast was always a very stressful time in our house. My mum would sit me to the table and put this bowl of cornflakes in front of me with warm milk, which would make any normal person heave with disgust. I hated cornflakes and w-a-r-m milk.

'Come on Shoy, open your mout.' She would position the spoon tightly against my mouth, which I would squeeze together as tight and as long as I could. The force of this spoon would be almost to the point of pushing my teeth in. As it began to hurt, my mouth would shoot open and in went the cornflakes and w-a-r-m milk, which promptly came back into the bowl.

'Shoy, don't do that, cause you know you gwan eat every bit before you leave for school, eh?' Now my mum was not as tall as my dad and she was cuddly and warm, except when she was angry or trying to get me to eat. She had short black hair, which was always plaited, and she always wore glasses except when she was in bed, and her teeth were lovely and white. Sometimes I would sit on her and count them. Tears were now rolling down my cheeks, but this did not deter my mum from force-feeding me every morning in the same fashion. Once that ritual was over, (of which my mum always won), I would end up feeling really ill. So here I am dressed to kill and all excited. Why was I dressed this way and where was she taking me? We left the house and walked all the way to the end of the road, down the hill (just as if we were going shopping), but instead of going all the way down to the

Watching and Waiting

bottom of the hill, we turned into another road that I had never been along before. There were trees along both sides of this road, unlike ours, which only had trees on one side. It was quite dark as the road was not as wide as ours, but hey, it was a new place I had never seen before. We came to the end of the road, crossed at the top and walked into this strange place; a large building with a lot of people (my height), some running around, some sitting very quietly, some crying, some even screaming, some holding on to their mummy's and daddy's hands just like I was and wearing the same clothes. What was this place? A lady called Mrs Coleman pinned a pink tag to my new green jumper. Had I been naughty? Mrs Coleman was a tall, thin, white lady who never really spoke much, but was always smiling. Her hair was short and greyish and she always had brown shoes on which made her silent as she walked along the corridors of the school. She would always appear in the classroom whenever it got noisy and we had to do our work in groups or when we were having PE. At the thought of leaving my mum, the tears began to form in my eyes and out they fell, streaming down my face like a river flowing from the highest point of the mountain, first as a trickle and then as a torrent.

'Wave bye, bye to mummy.'

Why? I did not want to. Did she not want me anymore? The lady

Shoy

who had pinned the tag on my jumper took me by the hand, and there was my mum waving good-bye to me.

'See you later darling. Have a nice day and mummy will see you later, okay?' Well I suppose it would have to be okay, no choice really. Here I was in a room full of others; black, white, light brown, some crying, some smiling, some talking, some being naughty and some not saying a word like myself.

Suddenly, there was a voice from a very tall and large lady with brown short curly hair wearing glasses (just like my mum).

'Okay class, please be quiet. My name is Mrs Wren.' She then held up a picture of a wren. 'This will help you to remember my name. Every time you look at the wren bird you will remember my name – okay?' That was so clever. She then stuck it up on the wall behind her chair. Mrs Wren was a very large lady with dark brown curly hair, dark, thick-rimmed glasses that seemed to take up the whole of her round, red face. She was always in green and brown knitted suits, which felt quite itchy to touch, and brown shoes, almost the same as Mrs Coleman's, but she was always smiling with her bright red lips. 'Now, children, I am going to call out your names from this book and when you hear your name I want you to answer – Yes Mrs Wren – is that clear?' Well, what were we supposed to say? She started, and one by one everyone would answer as she had instructed. When she got to my name I did not know what I was supposed to say. Stupid really, because she had told us and I heard everyone else saying the same thing. Some of the other kids turned and looked around to see who was not answering. The boy who sat next to me knew I was supposed to be answering. He nudged me:

'Go on, say Yes Mrs Wren.' I looked at him and then answered,

'Yes Mrs Wren'. She smiled at me and moved on. I smiled at the boy, the very first person, the same as me in height, to talk to me, well sort of. His name was Wayne.

'Well, hello children and welcome to your first day at school.' School. I had heard it mentioned before by my mum and dad, but never knew I would have to leave home to attend such a place and with so many others, but it was looking good. We played with toys. We learnt how to tie shoelaces, and once again helped by another boy called Dwaine. Funny - I do not remember any girls that day.

The day was almost over and we had a story sitting on the classroom floor. Some of the other kids fell asleep, but I didn't. When

Shoy

the story was over, we put our chairs on top of our tables, put our coats on and went outside. There she was, my mum, where had she been. She had missed all the fun. I suppose I must have told her all about that day. Well that was it; school over and done with. What next?

Of course it was not done with; it was just the beginning to an end. Didn't care for it much. Why should I? Why did I have to write? Why did I have to add up with plastic coloured bricks? Why did I have to colour in? Why did I have to play with plasticine? (Secretly, I did like that). Oh, Why? Why? Why?

I was now getting older and I had a new teacher - Mrs Sutherland. Mrs Sutherland was a slim, tall lady with long blond hair and she always reeked of perfume that would gag you as you stood near her at the desk waiting to get your work marked or reading. Her fingers were long and thin and her nails were always painted red. On every finger there was a ring. Some had brightly coloured stones in them and others were just gold with designs. She always wore the same necklaces at varying lengths and these would jangle together as she moved. They were always a distraction to me, as she would constantly play with them. Periodically, she would disappear from the class for a cigarette and on returning would pop a couple of mints in her mouth. I did not like her, as

Watching and Waiting

she did not seem to like us too much. She was always shouting and sending someone out of the class, or putting them to stand in the corner facing the wall for the whole lesson. Mrs Sutherland came in today with a new book. It was all about animals at the zoo. This was a fantastic book. There were big animals, smaller animals, scary animals and creepy crawlies. Mrs Sutherland was going to take us to a Safari Park to see some of these animals – how brilliant was that going to be? She gave us a letter to take home to our mummies and daddies. This was the very first trip I was going to go on and it was exciting. I was now aged six, and still quite small for my age compared with the others in my class and would be teased about it. My hair was very thick and a brownish/black colour and very hard to comb, and as a result, my mum would always keep it plaited, changing the style every week after giving it a good washing, greasing with hair grease and tugging. My nose was flattish (which I hated and would not linger around in front of a mirror). Everyone else seemed to have noses that left their face somehow, but not mine; it was just there, spread almost from cheek to cheek. My teeth were now missing which meant I did not smile a lot, as I did not want to show the huge, gummy gap. My eyes were big and stuck out almost like frogs' eyes, and of course some of the other kids would call me 'frogs' eyes' or 'bug eyes'. I would constantly bite my nails until there was hardly any left. Hmmm. What a mess. Anyway this safari

Shoy

trip was going to cost seventy-five pence. Now you would think that that little sum would not break the family bank, but boy, did it create some arguments and they seemed to go on and on. The upshot was that I was not going, as they could not afford it. Why? How could they not afford for me to go? It was just a few more pence than my weekly dinner money, which was sixty pence. This was not fair. The whole class went except for me. I had to stay with another class. Why did my mum and dad do this to me? At six years old this was not understandable. Why could they not afford it? There were other children who got free dinners. They should not have gone. They could not afford it, but they all went. I hated them from that point on and had a downer on school. This episode started other troubles for me in that some of the other children (not all of them) would tease me and not let me join in with their games. When they were doing projects about the zoo they did not want me in their group as I did not know what they were talking about, and so they would not talk to me and I was totally lost. It was more interesting to look out of the window at the world going by – the trains anyway. When in the playground they would not let me join in their games. They would sometimes pull my hair or undo my ribbons (which I could not do up again and so would get into trouble for undoing them from my mum). They would push me around and call me names. I was so alone.

Watching and Waiting

There was one thing I enjoyed about going to school: the dinners. They were great. My favourites were the roast dinners and this delicious pudding, which was pastry with a layer of jam and cornflakes on top, baked. It was out of this world. Whenever I could I always had seconds, but I always ate slowly, whether at home or at school. I never ate fast. Many times I got into trouble at home. I would get the occasional lash or have my food taken away and would be sent to bed hungry or without a drink. I was sorry, but I could not eat faster. Some people are made that way. And anyway, what was the hurry? We had nowhere to go. It seemed I was destined not to be able to please anyone. I felt as though no one loved me.

Since starting school I created this aversion to using the toilets. It's as if I had a phobia about them. I would use them but somehow I was very frightened of being locked in and not being able to get out – why? From that very young age I trained myself not to use toilets unless they were at home or in someone's house that I knew. They just used to smell so much. How could I use it?

As I got older, I eventually made friends and they would let me join in with their games. They were mostly boys though, but at that age what did it matter – friends were friends. We were now older and had moved from the small playground to the larger one.

Shoy

At the bottom of the playground there was a high fence made of wire and beyond that there were bushes (in which occasionally we would see a small brown snake slither by) and the railway track, which was always a distraction to me. In class, every time a train went past carrying cars, trucks, huge metal containers and carriages with people, my eyes would follow and keep looking until they had all passed by. I would stare out of the window and not listen to the teacher – of course this meant trouble again and I was moved from the window and put right over the other side of the classroom. At the top of the playground there were some arches up against the main building of the school, and we always played in and amongst them. To the side of the playground there were outdoor toilets (both boys and girls); these were separated from the main building by a huge tank, which held all the fuel for the school. These toilets were horrid and cold and I never ever used them. Whenever it was raining, if you wanted to go to the toilet you would always get wet, as you had to go outside the building to get to them – no chance of me ever doing that.

One day of many, a group of us that always played together (Ingrid, Camilla, Brenda, Leo, Lionel, Laura and another Laura). Were under the arches, we were playing kiss-chase as you do, but in those days were you supposed to? It just so happens that a lodger who lived at my parents' house was passing by the school

Watching and Waiting

on the road that ran alongside the school, which led to the town centre. The lodger's name was Roger, he was a very light brown colour, and his hair was black and very straight, not like mine. He was podgy and quite short. In fact, he was about the same height as my mum. He was very hairy and you could see strands of hair poking out of the top of his collar, and on the backs of his fingers he had bits of hair, thicker on some fingers than others. He had this laugh that was so weird. It was the kind of laugh that just stayed in your head. Whenever he was laughing, he would hold his stomach and stick his head back. He was like a character out of a Walt Disney cartoon.

Roger had stopped by the wall of the school playground and was watching our game. Quite often we would hang over the wall, look down towards the town, and say hello to anyone that walked past – how carefree we were. Whilst this game was going on (all high spirited and happy), Leo (who was very dark and had the whitest smile you ever saw and two large dents in his cheeks and was always laughing and getting into trouble with the teacher as he was always talking and quite loud as well) lifted up my skirt. I chased him, laughing. I caught him and gave him a kiss on the arm (well it's a start). I was happy. It was a brilliant game. The whistle went and we returned to our classroom. My fun was spoilt. I hated classes with a passion. I found it so hard and I felt

Shoy

like an idiot. It always seemed to take me a lot longer to understand what was being taught.

A STATE OF MIND OR IS IT?

One evening, my mum and dad went out. I can't remember where they went, but it was very unusual for them to be out together; it was just the way things were for them. Roger's wife, Agnes, had gone to one of her prayer meetings. She was well into religion. She would sing hymns at all hours of the day in her bedroom and she would be reading the Bible all the time. I never once saw her read a magazine or a book of any description except the Bible, which she had had for a long time. It had a black, floppy, and leather cover and when the pages were closed, the edges were lined with gold. There was a tiny red string attached to the

Shoy

inside somewhere that she used to mark the page she had got to. So, me (still age six and a bit by this time), and my brother Clarence (who was a baby just crawling about and making a nuisance of himself), were left, being looked after by Roger.

Roger was being nice to me.

'Go get your favourite book,' he said. The only book I had at the time was a library book from school, so I got that one. 'Here, sit on my lap and then you can read it with me, okay?' So I did. This was nice. He started reading the book to me. He got to the end, closed the book and gave me a big hug. 'Do you like school?'

Still looking at the cover of the book, I replied, 'yep, I like it very much. I have lots of friends to play with.' Well that was a lie if ever I heard one, but I did like the 'playtimes' as I was never alone.

'Do you love your mum and dad and your baby brother?'

'Yes, except I don't like when Clarence cries and makes a lot of noise in the night as he wakes me up and he is very smelly as well.'

A state of Mind or is it?

'Okay up you get. Let's get you something to eat now and get you off to bed as you have school in the morning.' So up I jumped and followed him to the kitchen. Clarence was left in his cot, rolling around and making stupid noises with his teddy. Roger made me some dinner and sat at the table watching me eat it (very slowly), but he never shouted at me to eat up like my mum did. 'Did you enjoy your dinner?' He asked.

'Yes it was very nice.'

'Okay, its time for bed now.' He took me by the hand and lifted me up the stairs to my bedroom. He watched me undress and put my pyjamas on and get into bed. My bedroom was very small and overlooked the road where I would stand for ages, just looking out at the hills that were far in the distance and the occasional car that went up and down the road. There were not that many cars in those days. Finally I would get tired, get into bed, and drift off. So here I was in bed now with Roger sitting on the edge of my bed just looking at me. He leaned across and tucked the blankets in around me. 'Why don't you give me a kiss like you do your mum and dad? You could pretend that I am your mum or your dad tonight as I am tucking you in.' Where was the harm. After all he was tucking me in, and my mum or dad always did that.

Shoy

'Okay.' I kissed him on the cheek. He looked at me and smiled. I smiled back.

'Why don't you kiss me like this?' I looked at him. What did he mean? 'This would make us special friends.' He showed me his tongue. 'Go on, stick your tongue out as well, like this.' I was laughing now, but I did as he said. 'Now touch my tongue with your tongue.' It felt and tasted funny, but I kept touching his tongue. It was fun. He was making me laugh. Suddenly he jumped, which made me jump. 'Okay, come on, lie down, quickly. Come on, close your eyes and pretend to sleep otherwise your mum will be very cross with you for being awake still at this time of night, okay?' He turned out the light and left my bedroom, closing the door quietly behind him. It was dark and I did not like the dark, so I threw my head under the blankets, under which I began to get very hot, almost to the point of suffocation, but I did not want to come out as under the blankets I was safe from the dark and all the funny faces and creatures that were around me on the wall and on the curtains. You see, the curtains had huge red roses on them and in the night these came alive and moved. The wallpaper was of Thomas the Tank Engine and the eyes would follow me all around the room. Finally I must have fallen asleep. Before I knew it there came this voice.

A state of Mind or is it?

'Shoy? Time to get up.' It was my mum calling me to get ready for school (again) and so the ritual began, the washing of me from head to foot, the brushing of my teeth, the brushing of my hair over the plates, which had been plaited the night before with all the pain and tears. Every morning after brushing them, my mum would add in an array of ribbons; at least three (it was the in thing - the more the better). Then she would petroleum jelly me all over, which made me very slippery, and then dress me and everything was laid out in the order they were being put on: first the vest, knickers (of course matching), socks (white, up to my knees, always too long and had to be folded over at the top), white shirt, tie, pinafore, jumper and then a bib, which led on to the breakfast thing. Breakfast finished, the bib would come off, mouth would be washed again, petroleum jelly applied, shoes on, coat on, hat on (which always flattened the hair) and then out of the door with Clarence in his pram. He was so lucky that he did not have to walk anywhere. He was always in this huge pram which had four big wheels and a little basket which was underneath and mum would always put the shopping in it whenever we went shopping. There was a green cover and a hood that matched, but these were only put over him when it rained, which was often, and he would then be warm and dry. Me, I would be wet and cold even though I had an umbrella of my own. Still I would change places with him any day.

Shoy

'Here we are Shoy, at school. Give mummy kiss and I will see you later, okay?' Did I have a choice in the matter? No. So I kissed her goodbye and ran down the little hill that led to the playground. The whistle went and we lined up in our class groups and were then led into the classroom by our teacher. Once inside the building the chatter would start and we would hang our coats and hats up on our pegs that had our names on with a little picture that we had chosen and make our way into the class. We would sit at the same desks. These were our own desks. The register would be called and then someone was called out to prepare the milk. MILK. Why oh why did we have milk? I hated milk, which we all had every morning before assembly (this was where all the children from all the other infant classes came together in the big hall and sang songs and if someone had a birthday they would go out to the front, we would sing them happy birthday and they would blow out the candles on the pretend cake, make a wish and then they would be given a birthday badge which was either Birthday Boy written on a blue badge or Birthday Girl written on a pink badge. I never got to do this as we were never at school when it was my birthday). So the milk was now ready (to prepare the milk all you had to do was put a straw in each bottle through the silver top) and we were called table by table to go and get a bottle, bring it back to the class and of course drink it, ALL of it. What

A state of Mind or is it?

torture. I would sit there and pretend to drink it, but it was going nowhere. It made me feel sick, and I would heave and cry, but the teacher would always make me drink it, every time reminding me of the only way I would get out of drinking it, saying, 'The only way you will get away from not drinking the milk is if we get a letter from your parents saying you are not to be given the milk at all.' This I knew would never ever happen, as at home I had to drink milk as well. 'It is good for you.' Whoever made that one up? I was of course always last to finish my milk, but my saviour was at hand. I used to sit next to a boy called Alex. Alex was thin, tall, and very, very chatty. His hair was always cut short, which he hated as all the other black boys had quite a lot of hair compared with him. He was always smiling and getting into trouble with the teacher, pretty much normal for our class. He loved milk and he would always finish his in a whoosh. 'Are you going to drink that or would you like me to drink it for you?' Without saying a word I pushed the full bottle in front of him and grabbed his empty one. Yes, yes, yes, this was the answer. Alex would always drink my milk, I would have his empty bottle, and everyone would be happy. And so this went on and no one was any the wiser, Alex was happy, the teacher was happy, my mum was happy and I was over the moon. Success.

One weekend (probably a Saturday as Sunday was the most bor-

Shoy

ing day ever, everything was closed and you either went to church, Sunday School or just played in the garden if it was not raining), there was no one in the house when I woke up. (By no one that is my mum, my dad or Agnes) only Roger and my brother, still crawling about the place, but by now adding in the 'holding on to furniture' stage and pulling everything in sight on top of himself and then having the nerve to cry when he himself had caused the injury. He was always doing something just to get attention, and that he always got.

'Shoy?' It was Roger calling me.

'Yes Roger.' He appeared in my bedroom and looked at me.

'Go and wash your salt fish.' Salt fish? I hear you say. This was his term for your vagina, fanny or whatever you call it, but I knew exactly what he meant. So off I went down to the bathroom, yes down to the bathroom as this was all the way down the stairs, past the living room, through the dining room and through the kitchen and finally you arrived at the bathroom, which was at the back of the house. It was painted blue (blue was a well loved colour in our house) and it had blue plastic tiles which came in blocks of eight and were stuck on with some sort of adhesive which never kept them on the wall as they would fall off periodically. My

A state of Mind or is it?

mum would always shout at my dad to put them back up so there were always gaps everywhere where they had fallen off and were waiting to be put back up. Anyway, Roger followed me. When I got to the bathroom he was right behind me so I could not close the door.

'Show me your salt fish.' I stood there and looked at him not saying a word. 'I will help you to wash it properly.' I was now screwing my face up not wanting him to help, not even my mum helped me now I knew how to wash myself. He glared at me. I had never seen him look like this before. I was frightened and, knowing he was not going to leave the bathroom, I was beginning to feel embarrassed. How could I let him help me? My mum would hit me if I even attempted to scratch it occasionally, so why should I show him and let him help me have a wash? 'If you do not show me, then I will tell your mum what I saw happen at school.' I looked at him, puzzled. 'You don't remember the day when I saw you playing with all those boys and NO girls?' I was still looking at him, but there were girls: there always were, it was our group and there were loads of us. 'Your mum will send you away because girls who let boys look up their dresses are always sent away, do you know that?'

'No.'

Shoy

Roger was very close to my face and I started crying.

'Shut up.' He started to pull my nightdress up. I was now in nightdresses instead of pyjamas, maybe a grown-up thing. 'I promise I will not say anything to anyone if you be nice to me.' What did he mean? I was always nice to him. I was never horrid. Well, he did not tell me. He took the bottom of my nightdress and wiped my eyes. 'Pull your knickers down.' I did. He was now touching my fanny with his fingers. His voice was very quiet and his eyes were shut tight and he just repeated, 'your mum and dad will send you far away because girls who let boys look up their dresses are always sent away.' He was so close to my face and he was breathing on me. 'But if you are nice to me and do as I show and tell you to do, it will be our little secret.' He pulled away from my face. I answered quickly.

'Okay?' He closed the bathroom door, locked it, and sat himself on the floor. He was now undoing his trousers.

'Don't look so worried; I am just making myself comfortable. Here, I have something to show you, something special and it is all yours. You can love it and it will love you. Here, come touch it, I will show you how it loves you.' He pulled me down to the

A state of Mind or is it?

floor. 'Come on, sit there.' He patted the floor next to him. I sat down. 'Now, do you remember how I showed you our special kiss with our tongues?' I looked at him and nodded. 'Well, now you can do the same to our friend with your tongue.' He knelt in front of me with this thing straight in my face. He pulled my head towards it and held my head between both his hands. 'Lick it, come on, just the way our tongues were licking each other.' So, I did. Again and again and again. Over and over. 'This is your very own lollipop and you can lick it anytime you want, you just have to say. Okay?'

I was licking and sucking this so-called 'lollipop' for ages. Suddenly, he held the back of my head very hard and stopped me licking it and he started to move his hands up and down very quickly along this thing, his breathing getting faster and faster, then all this white stuff shot out onto my face. It was horrible. He sat on the floor against the bathroom door, panting, with his eyes closed. I took my hands and wiped my face, mixing the tears with this stuff. He opened his eyes and looked at me. 'Go on, get washed and make sure you brush your teeth properly.' He watched me brush my teeth, wash my face and my 'salt fish'. He never helped me; he just kept on smiling and looking at me.

My life had become non-existent. School never existed anymore.

Shoy

I can't remember anything I did. Any parties I went to, if any. Whether I got into trouble at school. Any trips I went on or not. PE. Playground games. Friends. Teachers. Nothing, nothing, nothing... Just Roger, Roger, Roger, Roger and his white stuff, which happened quite frequently, either in his bedroom, my bedroom, my mum's bedroom. (Once in my mum's bedroom he had even dropped some of the white stuff on the floor near my brother's cot and he told me to clear it up, but I never did. I thought that my mum would find it and he would get into trouble for leaving it there, but she never did.) He would even sit me on top of the kitchen units, lick me, and play with my fanny with his fingers, making moaning noises. He would play with me in the living room on the floor. He would take me to the top of the garden by the apple tree. There were always lots of long bushes up there, he would make a little den, we would sit there, and I would carry out his little deeds of pleasure. In his bedroom he would sometimes squirt his white stuff on the mirror, which was on the back of the wardrobe, and then get me to lick it off slowly and he would watch. I hated him so much. I was always trying to avoid being left alone with him, but somehow I always ended up with him looking after me (us). Everyone trusted him and, as he did not work, he was ideal for looking after us, living in and all that. I hated my life, my existence, my brother, my mum, and my dad. In fact, I hated everyone. There was no one to help me and

A state of Mind or is it?

I so wanted to be caught so that it would all stop, because I knew it was not right to be doing these things with him, but what could I do? Who could I turn to? Who would believe me? To top it all, my mum went and got herself a job working as a nurse in the local hospital at night, so she was always away from us on a Friday, Saturday and Sunday night. Most Fridays and Saturdays my dad would go to the pub, Agnes would go to her prayer meetings and, yes, Roger would be left to look after us. There was no escape and no help.

NEW ARRIVAL

When I was eight years old, my older brother from the West Indies came to live with us. I was so excited I was getting an older brother and we were picking him up from the airport. We got up that morning. I got dressed in my new dress that my mum had bought, along with new shoes, socks, underwear and coat. This was special and of course my hair was plaited with numerous ribbons put in. I looked well smart. We drove to the airport. A friend of the family took us as my mum or dad could not drive and did not have a car. We arrived at the airport where you could see all the big planes taking off and coming in to land. I loved planes.

New Arrival

I would always run outside and look up in the sky whenever I heard one go over. They looked so peaceful and graceful in the sky and I so wanted to be up there on one. Anyway, here we were at the airport waiting for my brother. He took ages to come out. My mum and dad were getting quite worried as he had been spotted holding some lady's hand and they were walking around and around. Apparently they had lost his suitcase and were looking for it, and until they found it he could not come and meet us. My mum and dad were getting rather upset and anxious.

'So is what tekking dem so long? Dem jus a have him a waak rong and rong like some poppy show.' My dad wanted to go over and get him, but he was not allowed to. My younger brother started to make a fuss and he was given a bottle. This soon shut him up. He was so greedy. The milk would disappear in no time at all and then he would start to cry again, but there would be no more and he would be given his dummy, which was a poor substitute, especially for him, but he would be ignored and I would look at him and laugh.

'You greedy pig,' I would whisper in his ear and he would always look to grab me, or pinch me, but I was too fast for him and would move quickly out of his reach. Finally, here was my big brother. He was brought across to us with his suitcase in one hand and holding this lady's hand with the other. Everyone said hello and he said nothing. Well that went well, I thought. My dad took his case and my mum held his hand. She had bought him a new coat as well and she put this on him. He was hardly wearing anything. He had short trousers, these pointy shoes on his feet and a shirt that had short sleeves. I bet he was freezing as it had been snowing the day he came to England. Anyway, we took him back to the car and off we set home. I looked him up and down in the car. His haircut was very strange. It was short at the sides and the back, so short that you could see his scalp. From the back of his head to nearly the front, it was a bit longer, but not much, and right at the front of his head was this tuft of hair that was combed into a point. Although he was older than me, he was shorter. Hmm. My older brother shorter than me! But he looked stronger. There were no smiles from him at all. He just sat there in the corner of the car near the window looking out at the passing scenery. My mum kept talking to him, but there was no answer. He just kept looking out of the window. He was so sad, which in turn made me sad, because I was really happy to meet him at last and he seemed to hate all of us. We eventually got home and everyone got out of the car. (My mum was carrying Clarence on her lap next to us – that would never happen today). We finally arrived home and I took my brother by the hand, led him inside the house, and started showing him around. I took him up to what was now going to be

New Arrival

our room, as we were going to share. He was not taken by any of it, just made little grunting noises and rolled his eyes as if to say. 'Is this it?' He was cold and kept shivering.

'Are you cold Wayne?' My mum asked him (oh forgot to mention, his name is Wayne).

He replied.

'No.'

'Then why are you shivering?' I butted in.

'Wat is shivering, you taak some stupidness, me no wat you a say?'

'Well excuse me.' The day was cold and earlier it had been snowing, so I took him out in the garden. On opening the back door to go out, he disappeared inside. I grabbed him by the hand, we went out into the garden, and I showed him around. We had lots of chickens, I showed him where they would lay their eggs, and we would have to look for them. I showed him the fruit trees, which were bare at the time, but in the summer they would be full of fruit and the fruit was delicious. He laughed.

Shoy

'You tink this is big and you have plenty fruit, you nah see any ting. Where is the sea?' He asked.

'We are nowhere near the sea.'

'Wah, no sea to go play?'

'No.'

He turned and was making his way back to the house.

'Is all these yours?'

'All what?'

'Dees howse!' He was pointing at the backs of the houses. Our house was joined to three other houses, but from our back garden you could see almost the whole road of houses and their back gardens as we were all in a straight line.

'No, stupid!' This was now getting to be a very popular word in our house and Mum did not like it at all. 'Only this one. The one with yellow paint all over it.' Mum left us to play and get to know each other better and she made dinner. It smelt good.

'Come on. Wayne, Shoy, come get aal you dinner before it get cold.' She had done yams, sweet potatoes, English potatoes, dash-ine, green bananas, plantain, eddoes and dumplings in delicious light tomato coloured – gravy. It was my favourite.

'Can Wayne sit next to me, Mum?'

'Yes of course he can. Have you two been getting on good?'

'Yes.' There was no reply from Wayne; he was a brother of few words, for the time being anyway. I suspected he was getting used to being here and meeting so many different people all in one go. He sat next to me and looked at his dinner.

'Is wah dis?' My mum looked at him.

'It is not wah dis. Now you are in England you say 'what,' okay?'

'So nah dat me say?'

'No, you have to cut out that West Indian twang, because you will

Shoy

be going to school here and they will not be able to understand what you are saying to them.'

'Me nah go to any skool yah so, me don bin a skool and pass and me nah ha foo go again.'

'Well dat is wat you tink. Come Monday maarning you going to school wid your sister.' His gaze went back to the food that was steaming up in his face from the bowl.

'So aal you can get yam and dashine over yah so too?'

'Of course,' Mum replied, surprised at his statement. He tucked in. Whilst eating he came across a stalk from the fresh thyme that mum had used in the cooking. He promptly chucked this on the floor. I saw him, but no one else saw him. I did not say a word. I smiled and continued eating. It became apparent that whatever he did not like would end up on the floor quite quickly. When he finished eating he just got up from the table.

'Wayne, bring yourself right back here. You do not get up from the table until everyone has finished and we let you go, understand?' said my mum.

New Arrival

To which he replied, 'mammy never mek me do dat.' By his reference to Mammy, he meant my great, great grandmother. She had looked after him since he was a baby back in the West Indies, prior to his coming to live with us.

'Well it don't matter what Mammy bring you up to do down there. Here you do as I say, okay?' He sat down, not happy at all. My dad just looked at him, not too happy looking either. Of course Clarence just stuffed himself, oblivious to everything that was going on around him. Due to my eating habits, he was kept at the table longer. Anyway, I eventually finished and we left the table and went up to our bedroom to unpack his suitcase. This was the smallest suitcase I had ever seen, because the ones that my mum had on the top of her wardrobe were so much bigger, even though we did not go on holiday, but they were always there staring down at us collecting inches of dust as they were never taken down, or dusted. Our mum came up to help with the unpacking, which was not going to take very long at all. My mum turned the suitcase towards her, so she could open it.

'No, don't touch me grip. Mammy say no-one is to touch the grip or open it except foo me.' Grip, that was a new word for me. What was he talking about?

Shoy

'What's a grip?'

'Dis, stupid.' He slapped the top of the suitcase.

'Oh you mean the suitcase.'

'NO, grip, me say grip, you carnt understand, grip, grip because I grip it up in me han.' Well that made sense.

With that Mum told him,

'You must not call people stupid. It is rude and not nice, because people are not stupid, okay?' There was no response from him. 'Wayne I talking to you, okay?'

'Yes.'

'And it's alright; I can open it as I am your mother and you are going to live with me, okay?' He looked long and hard at our mum, but gave in. Just as well really. I think a sharp, swift slap would have been looming about his head otherwise. My mum opened the case. There was hardly anything in it; mostly papers, what of I don't know. There were a few sticks of freshly ground cocoa to make hot chocolate drink, which was delicious, and a bag of

New Arrival

bush. Now 'bush' is a funny thing. It is boiled in water, strained and sugared to taste. What sorts of bushes are in it? I have no idea. But there are various dried leaves and the bark of some sort of tree, and all of this together makes a good drink to help you get rid of colds, aches and pains, even stomach aches. It really works and it also tastes nice as well.

'Is wha Mammy send here with you. She nah send nothing, is better she did not send you with the case.' So much for pleasing people! Mum emptied the case and threw it away as it was wrecked.

'Don't cho way me grip. Is mine and me warn keep it.'

'This is no good Wayne and I am not having it in the house taking up room.' In the outside bin it went, waiting for the dustmen to collect it in their big dirty, smelly, dustcart.

Monday morning came and we were both ready for school in our uniforms. Wayne had a brand new uniform as it was going to be his first time in my school. I was going to have an older brother in my school to look after me and I could show him off to all my friends. I was so excited, much more excited than Wayne was. We arrived at school and I went into the playground as usual and

Shoy

Wayne was taken to the school office to meet the headmaster, Mr Jones, who was this round man with white/silver hair, lots of it, and he spoke with an accent. Mum told me he was Welsh. His voice was big and when he sang he would drown all our little voices. He was very good at singing and everyone liked him, unless you were bad and then you went to his office to get the cane across your hand. I told everyone about my big brother Wayne. Some of them did not believe me, but the ones that did wanted to be with me all day. I did not see my brother until lunchtime and he totally ignored me. He was too busy playing football with the friends he had made already. Well that was not right; he should have looked for me and played with me, but anyway I showed him to my friends and they thought he was nice. That afternoon, Mum came to collect us from school. Wayne had had a good time and was telling Mum all about his teacher and his new friends he had made and the food he had eaten at lunchtime, much the same as I was when I started school I expect. He kept walking funnily. Of course nothing ever got passed my m um and she asked, 'Wayne, what's wrong with your foot?'

'Nothing.'

'Show me your foot.' We stopped walking and Wayne lifted his foot to show my mum. Well, you have never seen anything like

New Arrival

it. He had only ripped the sole of his shoe off almost completely and it was flapping, hence the reason for not walking properly. 'Wayne, how de hell you manage to do dat? The shoo was new on this maarning. They look as doe you have dem for months and now your foot de ah doe, when it rain it gwan get wet. You tink I can afford to get you new shoos every day?' There was no reply, wise, really. I began to laugh at him. With a swift knock on the back of my head, my mum shouted.

'You can shut up. You tink its funny?' I shook my head. 'Wayne, why you doing this to your shoes?'

'Me don't like shoos. They squeeze me foot, but if I tek whey the bottom it give me more room and mek me foot dem feel better.'

'Wayne the shoes are a proper fit. Your feet were measured in the shop, so they should not be squeezing your feet. You just don't want to wear them, but here you have to wear them to protect your feet from the cold, the rain, the snow, the hard ground as this is not natural dirt you walking on. This is man-made tar everywhere and it is not good for your feet. There is glass everywhere and you can't walk bare feet here, you understand?'

'I don't want to stay here' came a reply. 'Me hate it. Me warn go

43

Shoy

back and meet Mammy. She would not mek me wear shoos and tie and trousers and belt and socks and shirt and all stupidness. She go let me wear wha me waan and go where me waan and do wah me waan.'

'You think I was going to leave you there to kill out my poor old mother? She too old now to look after you and that's why you are here now, so get used to it, otherwise you will have a very long and unhappy childhood.' We walked home the rest of the way in silence and mum stuck his shoes back together. The next day the same thing happened. This time the sole was cut in half; so Mum was unable to stick it back on, as he did not have the other half. She was furious. The next morning she made him put the shoe on as it was and went with him to see the headmaster and explained what he had been doing with his shoes. So every time he was in the class, his shoes were taken away from him and placed on top of the cupboard where he could not reach them, so he was unable to destroy them whilst in class. During break times he was to wear his plimsolls, which were less expensive. So his shoes were saved from his brutal wrecking. It was now warm and we played outside in the evenings every opportunity we got. I had a new bike now with only two wheels. Wayne was always riding my bike. I would have to run out to the shed to get it first; otherwise he would not let me have a go. Of course today was like no other; he was

New Arrival

first out and he got the bike as usual. He had plonked Clarence on the seat and was pushing him up the uneven garden. To the side of the garden there was a patch of nettles and as he went past, trying to keep Clarence on, he went into this patch and they stung him.

'Oh lard, cashy sting me foot.' He was still trying to hold Clarence on to the bike and not drop him and scratch his leg at the same time. This was so funny, but he was still determined to push Clarence up to the top of the garden. All the time he was scratching the side of his leg. He eventually gave up.

'Serve you right; you should let me have my bike and the stinging nettles would not have got you.'

'They are not nettles as you say, they are cashy, me know?'

'You think you know everything.' He pushed the bike at me and ran inside.

'SPECIAL' MOMENTS

The summer came and it was hot and everyday we would play out. Wayne now had friends of his own and he would be off up the road playing with them, and so I was alone again. On such a day, I was on my own in the garden. Mum had gone shopping (again with Clarence) and left Wayne and me at home. Well, we were supposed to stay in until she got back, but Wayne always had his own rules. Roger, the lazy bastard lodger, called me to his room from the window that overlooked the garden.

'No I am not coming.'

'Then I will have to tell your mum about you and that boy and how nasty you have been. Do you want that?' Of course I did not, so I went up to his room. He opened his bedroom door and I walked in very slowly. The door closed behind me and he locked it. He was naked and his thing was already sticking up in the air. 'I have been waiting for you; look I am all excited. Come on, lick him and lick him good.' He then laid me on the floor, and on his hands and knees, he kneeled over me. He was practically choking me, but he kept on pushing it further and further into my mouth. 'We are going to try other things today, because I am bored. Firstly, I want you to lick my arse.' What did he mean? Well, sure enough I found out. I was feeling sick and began to cry. How could this be fun? It gave fun a whole new meaning. Having had enough of that he then asked me to do the usual, licking him all over. My mind was blank. I did not think a lot. I was brain-dead. 'You know that you are my special girl and as you have been so good I have something extra special for you. Well, two things. I think you are a big girl now and you will like these better than what we have been doing. It will feel much better.' What was he talking about? He was lying on top of me. Squeezing me. I could not breathe properly. Before I could think about what was going on, he put his hand hard over my mouth and pushed something very hard and painful into my fanny. It hurt so much, so bad. I was

Shoy

crying, but his hands over my mouth drowned the noises into a muffle. The tears just rolled down my cheeks and into my ears. He was pushing harder and harder and he just kept on; it was going on for what seemed like ages. He released his hands from my mouth and told me to turn over, so I did. Who would have guessed that what happened next was ever possible? He had forced his way into my bum, again with his hands over my mouth. This time I really thought I was dying. I don't remember much about that. I probably passed out, but came round in time to his squirting all the usual white stuff all over my back and rubbing it in to my skin with his hands.

'You can now get dressed and go to your room.' I left crying.

Not long after that 'special moment' during the summer of 1973, I had this affliction; well, it seemed that way. I kept feeling as though I was wetting myself, but I was not. I kept looking at the inside of my pants, just to check. I was not wet, but I could feel dampness, so I took myself off to the toilet (as you do).

'Oh my God.' I looked away and looked back. 'Oh my GOD.' What was wrong? From the last time I looked to now, my knickers were really dirty. I quickly took them off and washed them in the hand basin with some soap. This was getting worse. I could not

'Special' Moments

get the stain out, the water had gone a murky, paint-water colour, and there was a distinct odour. What was it? I decided that my efforts were getting me nowhere and I hid my pants in the wash-basket that stood in the corner of the bathroom and was always full to the top, waiting for me to do my Saturday hand-washing over the bath. I had a wash, left the bathroom, went to my bedroom and put on another pair of clean pants. 'That's better,' I thought. A few moments later, I was back in the toilet going through the same routine. Well, this went on for two days, at which point I began to think this is it; I am dying because now I could see clearly that this was blood, fresh blood and it smelled disgusting. Where was it coming from and why? That night I finally plucked up the courage to try and explain to my mum what had been going on and that I was going to die. I did not want to die. One day she would come home and see me dead and would not have had the chance to tell me she loved me and that she was going to miss me (just like on the TV). Earlier on that day I had already had an argument with my brothers, telling them that I was going to die anyway and they would never see me again. It never got the reaction it deserved; they thought I was joking or over-reacting, they sucked their teeth and left me standing there. Anyway, I went up to my mum, who was getting ready to go to work.

'Mum,' I said very, very quietly, 'I am really sorry, but I cannot

Shoy

clean myself any more.' I was now hyperventilating and the tears were rolling down my cheeks and I could feel a panic attack coming on, (not that I had ever had one, but had seen them on the TV so I was ready for this; I should have been an actress really).

'What are you talking about?' I was crying uncontrollably now. 'WHAT'S WRONG?' Her shouting startled me, halting my growing wailing. I hesitated.

'I cannot keep my knickers clean. I have been washing properly but it just will not go away.' All said in one breath then sniffing all the snot back up into my head as though it had to come from my feet.

'Don't do that, it is disgusting.' She handed me a tissue. She looked at me. 'Show me your knickers.' I pulled my knickers down, which I had not put on too long before, and there, there was the evidence as clean as daylight and as dirty as night. She smiled. 'You are now a young lady.' What did that mean? She gave me a packet of these white, long, bulky pieces of what looked like cotton wool covered with a mesh to put in my knickers. 'Whatever you do, do not flush it down the toilet whole. You must rip it up first.' What was this? Obviously she knew what it was and I was not going to die - thank God. And when was it going to stop?

'Make sure that you change the pad frequently, otherwise you will smell and it might make you sore.' What was going to make me sore and why? She left it at that. 'I will talk to you further when I get home. Now that you have become a young lady, you are not to play with your brothers the way you have been any more, jumping around and climbing trees, or let boys touch you.' What did she mean, how could I avoid boys touching me when I had to sit next to one in school as it was always boy/girl/boy? This statement worried me no end. What would happen to them if they accidentally touched me? It was frightening. Of course, I never did let any boys touch me anyway, because if they did, Roger would tell her our secret and I could not have that. All these expectations that everyone was putting on me; why was it so wrong playing with boys of my own age? Anyway, the bleeding thing finally came to an end and life (existence as it was) went on.

Shock, repulsion; the dreaded episode returned again. Why? What had I done this time? Once again, this time a lot sooner, I told my mum.

'This is what is going to happen to you every month for the rest of your life.'

'What!' I forced a smile. I hated blood; I hated the smell, the mess, the padded, nappy-like effect, and the pain: the pain that just cut you in half as if you had rented someone else's body, and it was not sewn on properly and it was being rejected, as if an infection had set in, not to mention gangrene, was setting in and the only way out was to cut yourself loose from the whole thing. My legs would ache to the point where I could not stand up, just stooped over like an old woman. My stomach felt as though it were trying to escape from my body. I could not eat. I could not sleep. I always got diarrhoea followed by excruciating headaches. I would even throw up on occasions. I was an evil person and this was my punishment. Was it because I let a boy look up my skirt, was it because I let Roger do things to me and I did things to him that I could not stop, or was it because I was so stupid at school? With school in mind, it would not matter if I had a couple of days off to get over the pain then. I would lie curled up in bed. During these times (which were too often for my liking), I really could not do anything, and all my mum would say in her words of comfort was 'if you move around it would be much better.' What did she know? She had never suffered this way; she even told me that, so she could not appreciate the fact that I felt like I was dying and that was that. I had read in a magazine that if you cuddled up with a hot water bottle, the warmth helped to ease the pain. So I asked my mum to buy me a hot water bottle. She did, and whenever I had this 'young lady' episode I would curl up with it and go to sleep. It seemed to help too, to begin with, but then even that novelty wore off and I was back to square one again. I would almost overdose on painkillers, but even that stopped working. There was nothing to help me. I was going to have to grin, bear this one, and get on with 'life'. Life with this suffering was unbearable and, finally, my mum took some notice of the pains that I was getting and she took me to the Doctor to try and get some help. He gave me some tablets, but my mum would not give them to me. I remember her putting them on top of the wardrobe in her bedroom. 'There's no way I am giving these tablets to you.' So why had she taken me to the Doctor if she knew she was not going to let me have the medication? Looking back at it now, the Doctor actually gave me the contraceptive pill.' I thought she was heartless and she made me cry even more every time the dreaded episode came back. Getting a little fed up with 'my pains', and me she took me to see a private doctor in London. I knew it was in London because whenever we went to London, which was not very often, we always passed the white Hoover building (which is now the Tesco building) and I knew then that we were in London. Anyway, I saw this Indian doctor, who kept burping as if he was sick himself. He squeezed my stomach a bit and then gave my mum a prescription for me. This time (surprise, surprise), she got the tablets and gave them to me, instructing me on how to take them. They were huge and did not go down easily at all. I seemed to swallow gallons of water and they would still be at the back of my throat, now beginning to melt and the bitter taste escaping all over my mouth. Eventually they would go down and they worked. Relief. For a while anyway! Later on, I can't remember when, the pains returned even worse than before. Was my life ever going to be simple and pain-free?

I find it difficult to recall memories of this time; they are not clear. Were they memories, or were they dreams or thoughts in my head. All the same, I wanted to escape, escape forever, but I was not that strong. My torment continued from Roger; it just went on and on and I so wanted to be found out. I was now older and knew it was wrong, but now the boy-looking-up-my-skirt episode was a small and distant matter. Roger had me doing much worse things and they were disgusting. Who would love me now?

My parents had a funny marriage. Not funny ha, ha, but funny in that they did really love each other but they were always arguing and fighting to the point of blood being shed, mostly my dad's. By now our family had grown and I had three brothers and one sister and they were all pains; I hated all of them. There was never any privacy as we all shared one bedroom. One day, out of the blue, my dad came home and told the lodgers that they had to leave. Something was going on. There was a big argument and before

'Special' Moments

we knew it, they had all moved out. All these 'aunts' and 'uncles', who had been in three different bedrooms in our house for all this time, were now made to leave. They were leaving, but they were not moving far at all; two of them found other rooms further along our road and the other was on the same road as one of my friend's. We could actually see the house where he was staying from my mum's bedroom. Everyone had gone. I was free, free from that fiend and I would never have to see him again.

I was beginning to love my life. I was enjoying school, my lessons and being with my friends. My favourite lessons were dance, drama and humanities. Humanities looked at aspects of our lives, our bodies, hormones (and all those sorts of things) and what we wanted to be and achieve and how we could achieve those goals and aims. During one lesson of humanities we were asked to write a short essay about ourselves under the title,

'When I grow up I want to be…'

I wrote: 'when I 'grow up' I want to be an airhostess with the best airline in the world. I will be married with two children – a boy and a girl. I would like to have the girl first and then two years later have the boy. I will earn a lot of money and I will protect my children forever and make sure that they are happy, have everything they want and teach them about the different cultures of the world and about the people who live in all these different places. I will take them to visit some of the places that I have visited. If I do not become an airhostess (which I will one day), then I would like to be a secretary to a nice boss. Also when I grow up, I would like to be a nice person. I see myself as a very shy person, but inside I am full of fun and quite funny, once you get to know me. At home I am the loudest (when I have to be). I would like to have a lot of money and buy all the things that I want, like nice clothes and shoes. I have a part-time Saturday job at the moment and I am saving most of the money that I am earning to buy my mum a present for Christmas. I hope she will like it. Don't know what to get my dad, but it will be nice whatever it is. It will be the first present I have bought for them ever. Well that's it – not a lot is it?'

We then had to discuss what each of us had written and why, and ways in which we could go about achieving what we wanted. The teacher felt that I would have to change my personality to become an airhostess. I would be better off becoming 'an athlete' as I was very good at running, especially the one hundred metres, at which I was mostly timed at 14 seconds. I was also very good at the two hundred metres and also throwing the javelin. (My throwing was always practised with my brothers and friends that we played

'Special' Moments

with: we would hurl small apples at each other from either ends of the garden, so in order to catch each other, you would have to throw quite far and very powerfully). I held the school record for throwing the javelin the farthest for the girls. Obviously that must be broken by now. I was entered into the District Sports for the school that year in which I came fourth, just missing out on a medal, which upset me a lot, but there was always next year.

It was a nice hot summer's day and we had gone shopping with our mum. It was getting near to lunchtime and who should we bump into but Roger? My mum went to get us some chips and he stayed outside the shop to wait with us. I was now about 15 and fully aware of what was what. The hairs on my skin were on edge and I was very uneasy and tried not to look at him, grabbing on to one of my younger brothers to stay outside the chip shop with me, but of course they always let me down. So here I was outside the chip shop, with all the bags full of shopping and Roger.

'Have you got pubic hairs now?' I glared at him. 'I hope you are not letting anyone else touch you because I would know.' I turned and gave him the typical black disgusted look and through my teeth I voiced, 'Get lost.' He stood back and looked at me.

'So you think you're big now, and you can talk to me how you

Shoy

want?'

'Yes,' moving my head from side to side in the Arabian fashion.

'Well guess what? I am going to tell your mum our little secret.' I froze. He was still pulling that little number, but it scared me, even after all this time. He could see that I was worried. 'Come and visit me where I live.' He, at this time, lived in a rented room and he told me the address; it was close by to where we lived.

'Okay, I will.' But I never did. If ever I saw him in the town, I hid, or always made sure that there were others around if he was talking to my mum or anyone else, but somehow he always found a way to get messages to me or to talk to me alone. I really, really hated this man. Why could he not leave me alone? I thought of a way that I could possibly get away from him – I needed to get a boyfriend of my own. He would then have to leave me alone, otherwise I could get my boyfriend to beat him up, see how he would like that! Great, I thought. My mind drifted to Alex. He seemed to like me a lot, so I started to flirt with him. I was made a prefect at school and this would get us privileges such as jumping the dinner queue when you were on lunchtime duty. On the days that you were not on duty, you were allowed out of school. On such days a group of us (who were funnily enough all prefects) would go to

'Special' Moments

Ingrid's house, as her house was always empty during the day as her mum worked. This was a very dangerous act on my part as Ingrid lived along the next road, which was at the crossroads with our road, and you could see my house from her house and vice-versa, but excitement was the order of the moment. Here all sorts would go on, there would be older boys there from other schools, and they would pair off with some of the other girls and disappear in to one of the other rooms. I was always left, of course. I was ugly, I always dressed in last year's fashion, my shoes were always 'nursey' ones, I had 'Bugs Bunny' teeth (as I was called) and I was sure that I suffered with body odour (sometimes) as I was not given any deodorant to use at home so I would be washing under my arm quite regularly, even in school. Alex did like me, but the others always teased him, and being shy as well he never really made any attempt to even kiss me. We would just sit on the settee together and watch the TV or listen to music whilst there was laughter, ooing and haaring coming from all over the house.

NEW BEGINNINGS

At secondary school, our little group of friends was mostly split up into different tutor groups – depending on how clever you were. Ingrid was the cleverest of all of us and she was in the highest group. Ingrid was tall, slim, very athletic and very good at gymnastics and of course all the boys liked her. I loved hanging around with Ingrid just for this very reason, or so I thought. I always thought that if I hung around with her, someone would notice me and want me just like they all wanted her. She was a very popular girl, but she was a real friend to me as well. Whenever anyone called me names (as they still did from time to time), she would always stick up for me, like a big sister. She would always try to get me to stick up for myself, but I was never any good at it; I would try on occasions and it would work, but sometimes it just seemed too much like hard work. Ingrid would never walk to school without me. There were five of us that would meet at the cross-roads near the shop on the corner and we would walk the long walk to school which was about six miles, of which one mile was a hill that just stretched up in front of you like a summit and the prize was to get to the top and not sweat. (No prizes given out there.) We of course made lots of other friends, especially those of us that went to Ingrid's house at lunchtime, and because we were split up into different tutor groups, we made other friends in our own classes. So the group got larger and better and we were a happy bunch, never harming anyone, and generally enjoying life as we saw it, with no adults telling us how to conduct ourselves and sit up straight when you're eating and walk straight in your shoes and not slouch (what was that all about?)

During this time, my older brother, Wayne, went to another school (because of his behaviour); it was actually a boarding school, which was quite a way from our house. In fact it was in another county. I used to miss him when he was away, but I am sure he did not miss us; he seemed to enjoy it and when he came home (to begin with only on the holidays), he would meet up with the friends that he had been at school with in our town and just pick up from where he had left off. There was one particular friend, who I had my eyes on, but he was older than me and what would he want with me? Little did I know that he liked me just as much and had told my brother this, who took his time telling me. I was so excited. I told my brother to arrange for Clayton to come and play football with him outside our house and then I could get to talk to him and Mum would be none the wiser (how else was I going to get to see him as I was always with my mum – never out of her sight). This my brother did with some reluctance, given that he did not care too much about me. He was always slow to do whatever I asked. (Was this his caring, big brother act?). Well he could cut that out; I did not need any of it, and I had enough to contend with, namely Mum and Dad. So I got to talk to Clayton eventually. He was gorgeous, he had the deepest dimples you had ever seen and his skin was smooth and dark brown and his afro was immaculate, not a hair out of place. His legs were very muscular as he played football for the local team and he was an excellent athlete as well, and his smile was breath taking. How could he fancy me? I also knew that he was a very popular person and so many girls wanted to be his girlfriend, so if he was paying me attention; (which he was), when was the joke going to be revealed? But what did I care? He was here, outside my house, talking to me, playing football with my brother. Time went by and we got more and more friendly.

The doorbell rang and I quickly ran downstairs to answer it. I could not believe my eyes; it was Clayton. My smile grew a mile and he smiled back.

'Is your brother in?'

I hesitated, trying not to act as girly as I was feeling.

'No.'

'Okay.' He was turning away from the door.

'There is no one at home. They have all gone out to see my aunt and they will not be back for some time. Do you want to come in?' This I knew would not have been a problem with my mum if she had returned and he was in the house, because he was always in our house.

He smiled.

'Yeah, all right then.'

Shoy

I stood back and gave him room to come in. He walked into the front living room. (We had two living rooms: the front one was for visitors with all its fancy ornaments which had to be cleaned once a month and the pretty little doyleys all over the place with crocheted cushion covers that matched the chair-back covers and arm covers, but it all seemed to be too much. Always looked clustered, with hardly any floor space. In the back living room we had the television and would play board games, light a proper log fire and roast sweet potatoes and corn in it on winter days. We sat close together. All I wanted to do was kiss him; I had never kissed anyone my own age before and I was longing for this to happen. I wanted the experience, and not quite sure what it was going to achieve, but I wanted it to happen. I wanted to be grown up. Would I look different? Would any one suspect? Who cared? We never spoke a word to each other. Maybe our minds were on the same thought. We looked at each other and he came closer and closer. I could not breathe; what was I going to do? How would I kiss him? Would I do it right? Would I make a fool of myself? With all of this going on in my head, his lips touched mine and I melted. He was so gentle it lasted only a second, but his lips touched mine. He sat back in the chair and we talked for what seemed like hours. I wanted him to kiss me again and again, but he did not. After some time, my brother Wayne came home and they left together. Before leaving Clayton whispered in my ear,

New Beginnings

'Until next time!'

When was that going to be? I wanted him to come back now and kiss me again.

Not too long after that day, Clayton was back at our house and once again we were on our own. I wanted to have sex with him. I knew quite a bit (verbally anyway) from talking to Ingrid. Ingrid knew lots; she was not a virgin and she had had sex with loads of boys. We would talk about them for ages and what she had done and how. Her life was so exciting and I wanted to be like her, but her mother was always at work during the day so her house was always empty and she had somewhere she could take all these boys and have fun with them. My mum was always at home as she worked nights, so there was no chance of that). Clayton took me in his arms and kissed me, this time a lot longer. We were tonguing and this time properly; it felt so right and different. I had wanted to do this with him, but not with Roger. His hands were all over me and then he touched my fanny. What was I to do now? Should I move his hands or leave them alone to do whatever they wanted to do? I chose the latter. We slid down the wall to the floor and he lay on top of me (the floor was really hard against my back). He started to undress me. I stopped him and suggested that we go up to my bedroom, just in case my brother or someone

Shoy

came back and found us on the floor. He agreed. I led him up to my room. I was wearing a cotton flowered dress with tie straps on the shoulders which he undid and the whole thing just fell to the floor. He stood there and watched me. I had no bra on (as I only had one and it was in the wash) so boobs were just hanging around like they do. He looked me up and down and just said, 'Beautiful.' He got undressed himself, came closer to me, and hugged me and we started to kiss again and again. We lay on the bed together and he got on top of me. I was now feeling embarrassed because he was looking at me in such a way that I could not keep his gaze – what did it mean? He then showed me a little packet.

'What's that?' I asked breathlessly.

'It's a rubber Johnny.' Well that was crystal clear.

'Okay what is that supposed to do?'

'Well I wear it during sex and it stops you getting pregnant.'

'Oh yes, I have heard about them, but I have never seen one. Let's have a look.' It was small and circular, had all this lubricant on it, and had a very rubbery smell to it. I handed it back to him and watched him put this on, it looked quite difficult but he managed it.

'Are you a virgin?'

With some hesitation I answered, 'Yes, of course I am.' My voice drifted away, but he did not notice the pain in my eyes at that question. He did not know the signs of lying on my part; they were just words he wanted to hear. Was I ever going to tell him that I had been having sex of a kind since I was nine? Not likely. He smiled and very gently entered me. It did not hurt one bit. Having sex with Clayton was so gentle and it seemed to go on forever. He was sweating, I was sweating, and I was really loving it. He finally finished and lay besides me.

'I hope I did not hurt you?' He said softly, stroking my face.

'No.'

'Just one question though' he continued. 'How come it was so easy? How come you did not cry, try to stop me or even bleed?' What the hell was he going on about?

'I don't know. Why, am I supposed to cry and carry on?' He said nothing. We got dressed and he left, left me happy and content

Shoy

that I had had sex with the most wanted guy in town. Everyone wanted Clayton and now he was mine. I was having sex with him and in my bed. That day was the beginning of many such occasions. I would go to his house as he only lived along the next road down from ours. I would meet him in the cemetery, which was two roads up from ours (as you can imagine it was always very quiet there and not many people around) and we would have sex in the bus-like shelter that was there.

Music was my lifeline, the lifeline to my heart and soul. I loved it and could never get enough of it. The radio was always on in my bedroom and I was always taping my favourite sounds from the reggae show that was on at lunchtime, and then from the hit list that would follow every Sunday. I had my own little record player that had a cassette player. The songs I would tape I would sing along to, exercising my voice. I had quite a good voice (or so I was told by lots of other people), but I was too shy to sing in front of anyone. Some of Wayne's friends heard me sing a few times when they were in the house and told me that I should become a singer, because I had a 'Studio One' voice. (Studio One was a record company that was really big back then, and the girls they had all had a certain kind of voice to of which mine was similar, purely because I copied their style.) I used to model my voice on Janet Kaye who sung 'Silly Games', which was one of my favourite

New Beginnings

tunes at the time. There used to be this record-making shop down the road from where we lived and every time we went shopping there a man who worked there, who knew my mum, said he would find out what sort of tunes I wanted and he would get them for me, 'straight off the press' so to speak. He was a very nice person and he and my mum would always talk about me and how I was getting on or not, whatever was happening at the time, but he always gave me money and records, so my collection grew and grew very quickly, and my friends always thought I was lucky as I would get the latest hits before them. So at last I had something good that everyone envied me for. Sometimes my brother would ask me to ask him for various other tunes and he would give them to me for him. Music was my escape; whenever I sang, my life was happy and all the pain and trouble would go away. The days of the 'Roger Empire' would go away, far into the recess of my deepest memory bank. I would spend hours in my room just listening to music and singing. It also helped me to iron all those clothes that I had washed on the Saturday for the family a lot more quickly on the Sunday, which was my weekend routine. I did not mind so much because I would always listen to the pop chart countdown. I was always up-to-date on which records were doing what and who sang on them. Ingrid and I were good singers and would sing together in the playground, or at her house. We were in the school choir and even sang at the Winston Hall in a school competition.

Shoy

We would always sing in the school plays as well. These were happier times. We even sang a couple of times at school discos. Everyone liked our voices. People who did not know us always thought we were sisters and we never corrected them.

I used to belong to the St John's Ambulance Brigade and every Monday evening was St John's meeting night. All the junior St John's First Aider's would meet and practice first aid skills, working towards our badges. As this was another occasion where I was out of my parents' sight, on some nights I would arrange to meet Clayton. On one particular night I had made such an arrangement and we met at the St John's end of the alleyway, walked back along the alleyway, and stopped at the car park steps, opposite the train station. This alleyway was mainly used during the day as a short cut, so sitting on the car park steps seemed quite safe and no one would see us (no-one who knew us anyway). It was a lovely evening and we sat cuddling each other, talking and laughing. We had been there quite some time when there, right in front of me, was this apparition (or so it seemed). It was just unbelievable. Never in a million years would something like this happen, but of course my millionth year was up and tonight was that night, the night of all nights. Brimstone and fire would have been a better choice of execution. There in front of me was my dad. He had walked a few steps past us (of course, not expecting to see anyone

New Beginnings

there, I suppose). Did he recognise me? Well of course he did. He looked firstly at Clayton and then at me.

'GET YOUR ARSE HOME RIGHT NOW.' So was I going to stand up to him at this moment, at this very precise and calculating moment? To hell I was! With that I legged it, but instead of running home I thought I would run away, away from it all. There was no way I was going home to be beaten with a belt again, because that was the fate waiting for me the minute I entered the door, or my dad entered the door, as I would have got home much faster than he would have done. I ran all the way to the hospital. I had decided that I was going to tell my mum, but then thought against that as she would probably beat me right there in the hospital, so I turned and ran towards the shopping centre and went upstairs and hid. Whilst upstairs, these other boys that I knew came along and started asking a load of questions. They had even seen my mum and dad looking for me. I asked them, well, pleaded with them, not to tell them where I was if they saw them again. I had not even thought about where I was going to sleep that night and where I would find food the next morning, or have a wash or even get ready for school, but that was not important now, that was tomorrow. Right now I was here, scared, cold and frightened. After some time, which seemed like hours, I decided to walk around a bit. I headed back in the direction of the hospital

Shoy

and just as I turned the corner near the gas works this policeman came out of no-where and asked me my name. I was startled and told him. He then signalled to a police-car that was parked across the road and I was put into the car and taken home, crying all the way. When we arrived at my house, the door opened and there stood my mum. She took me – when I say took, she grabbed me by the collar of my jacket and shoved me into the house. There I was, being flung into the depths of no return, no recovery, tripping over the step at the front door as I went crashing to the floor.

'Get up, go in the sitting room and don't move.' I made my way to the sitting room, still crying, knowing what was to come. As I entered the room, my dad was already standing near the fireplace making vexing noises with his hands in his pockets. Obviously my mum had told him that she was going to deal with it, because he did not say a word to me. My mum spoke to the policeman and shut the door. Her footsteps were loud and thunderous as she walked towards the sitting-room door. As she entered I looked up at her, crying even more so now, bordering on a full-blown asthma attack; not that I suffered with asthma, but having watched my sister have one, the visual signs were getting the same way.

'Okay, young lady!' she shouted. 'Take your clothes off. Just leave your knickers on' (on which my dad commented that he was surprised that I had some on.) She then made me sit with my legs crossed underneath me. They then started on at me, both shouting at the same time and very loud. I was sure that the others were going to wake up and come down, but I bet they had been given instructions not to come down under any circumstances. They asked me question after question, and with most of my answers my mum would hit me with the belt that she had wound around her right hand. I was in pain as the belt lashed me in different places as I tried to stop her. It got to the point where I, very foolishly, decided in my not-so-large wisdom, that I was not going to answer any more questions, because it just encouraged her to hit me each time, but with that decision my dad hit me straight in the mouth. I placed my hands over my mouth and my hand filled with blood and also a tooth. This plunged me into hysterical crying with the sight of the blood and the tooth. My dad had knocked out my front crown (this crown had replaced my tooth that had been originally knocked out when I was younger on a netball post in the playground). I was toothless. How was I going to go to school? Of course, my mum said that there was no way that she was taking me to the dentist; I would have to live with it.

'Get up!' she shouted at me. I could not even stand. My legs were completely numb. She grabbed me and I tried so hard to stand, but I could not - I just fell on the floor. She made me crawl to bed. My legs were in agony, and my body was smarting all over. I eventually got to my bedroom and looked at myself in the mirror. I was a mess. There were weal's all over, but mostly on my back and on my arms where I had put my hands up to stop the lashes from hitting me and got caught on my arms instead. The sight of them started the tears rolling down my face. The tears of pain, anger and self-pity were very hot and salty. I stood there, watching the tears, wondering if my tears would ever dry up with the amount of crying I had done. I closed my eyes gently and I dried my face. My nose was now blocked, so I had to resort to breathing through my mouth, and my eyes resembled a blood red orange, not a milky white spot in sight. I was sad again. I wanted to die, but how was I ever to achieve this? I could never carry out the deed. How would I carry out the deed, whatever the deed was going to be? I was a born coward. I prayed that night and asked God not to let me wake up ever again, and then they would be so sorry for what they had done to me. I cried myself to sleep that night as I had done on many nights. I awoke some time in the night to find my face smothered by Stephanie's long black hair. She was so pretty with all this hair, not like mine which was short, thick, hard to comb and shrunk whenever it was washed, and took days to get back to normal, by which time it was time to wash it again. She was tiny though, and always hiding under beds and in cupboards whenever voices were raised. She had this little button nose with

New Beginnings

a dent in the end of it, but it suited her; after all, it was her nose. I swept her hair away and looked at her so peaceful and cute, just lying there oblivious to anything: the hardships of life, growing up and being loved. I kissed her on the cheek and whispered,

'I do love you, even though you get me in to trouble, but you're young. What do you know? Take care.' I turned away from her just to find a cold, soaking wet pillow. I turned it over, buried my head in it and thought: this is my last night in this bed; there will be no tomorrow.

'Shoy!' I jumped up. Where was I? But that voice was all too familiar. It was my mum shouting for me to get out of bed and get ready for school. I sat up in bed, having answered her and looked around the room. Even God had let me down. Even he did not want me. I was still here. Getting ready was a nightmare, my skin was hurting and my eyes were so swollen and, of course, the tooth: I had no tooth and I would have to go to school with this tooth missing and this was going to be embarrassing, to say the least. What was I going to do? Anyway, I left for school and reached the school gates. I was alone. I did not walk to school with the others as usual, because I was late and they had left without me. I walked into school and into the classroom. I was not smiling and I thought if I said as little as possible, no one would notice. It actually worked for a couple of days, but one day Alex

Shoy

was trying to make me laugh as he had not seen me laugh for a long time, and of course he did and he saw that my tooth was missing. With that he laughed and everyone found out about it. My girlfriends took me to the toilets and asked what had happened. I explained very slowly in between the tears. They were very sorry for me and stuck up for me against all the others that were trying to get me to laugh so that they could see it for themselves. Somehow the teachers never seemed to notice anything about us. Could they not see that my mouth was swollen, my tooth was missing? I would have belt marks on my skin where I had been beaten sometimes, having left weals, and we would be having showers??? Wayne and I would get beaten a lot for stupid things, things such as not tidying our bedroom, not putting the milk bottles out at night, not getting home on time (even when it was not our fault, especially if the class was kept behind for whatever reason), for not hoovering the house properly. For me, not washing the clothes properly. We would even get into trouble when the others, who were much younger than us, did things and we would get the blame because we should have stopped them. Life was not fair, but who cared? I started to play truant from school. I would leave school at lunchtime with some others and not always go back. We would go to Ingrid's house and she would call some of the other boys up and invite them over for the afternoon, and as usual I was always left watching the TV, but today was my turn. Alex apparently had liked me for a long time, but he was too shy to ask me out. Today he was looking at me and I knew what 'that look' meant. In no time at all, we were upstairs and in one of the beds. He was kissing me and I was kissing him back. He wanted us to have sex, which was fine by me. He was not very good, but what did I know? Well quite a lot really. I had had sex with Clayton who knew a lot. Obviously I was not comparing but Clayton was better. During the sex he kept telling me to 'move up' so I did. He then said it again. And once again I moved up the bed. So where the hell did he want me to move to? My head was already against the wall and I could move up no further. This request was so strange. He came and got off me (by the way, he was wearing a condom – as they were now called) and we sat and talked for a bit. These rendezvous went on for a while and I really grew to like him and slowly forgot about Clayton, who by this time had got someone else pregnant, so that was a close shave. I was now Alex's girlfriend, we would walk around the school holding hands, and everyone knew. I was happy, but this happiness was to be shattered. There was a rumour going around, which got back to me, that Alex had got someone else pregnant from another school. I confronted him and he admitted it, but said he loved me. He had not even told me that he loved me in the first place. I slapped him so hard that my hand stung and I told him that I never wanted to have sex with him again and that he was rubbish anyway. With that, he told me that I could not even move to excite him. (So that was the 'move up' thing - he wanted me to move to his movements to excite him more. Oh well, he should have explained himself better.) Everyone around us was silent, so now they all knew. We had been having sex, he was rubbish, and I was rubbish, a match made in heaven. I walked away and just thought about what he had said. Men are just pigs; they use you and then throw you away and expect you to be normal. Of course I still saw Alex everyday as we were in the same class for most of our lessons and in the same school with the same friends, and he tried so hard to get me back, but I was not having it. He kept sending me little written messages through other friends and he would even try to talk to me, but no, no way was I having it; what he had done was unforgivable. Mind you, I had another close shave. At least it was not me pregnant. For weeks the school was buzzing about us having sex, as if other people were not doing the same thing. It got so bad that we were both called up to the headmaster's office along with the deputy and we were both asked about the rumours and how true they were. Neither of us would say anything, so they split us up and questioned us separately. There was even talk of getting our parents up to the school. But they could not prove a thing. It was all rumours and we were not about to admit to having sex of any sort, not even kissing. They had only seen us holding hands and then we were told to stop by whichever teacher saw us. So we were saved, well I was anyway. I was now more appealing to the other guys who all thought I would let them have sex with me because I was no longer with Alex. What did they think I was? Like I said, just dogs sniffing at the wrong bitch. I knew what I wanted and it was not a dog.

My attention now moved to someone else who was in our group whose name was Ian. Ian was okay when I looked at him from afar, but once I got close to him, I did not fancy him at all. He could not kiss to save his life. His whole mouth would cover mine and he would lose all control of his saliva glands. It was like drinking water straight from the tap. It was disgusting. Needless to say, it went no further. One kiss was enough to put you off kissing for life. I was alone again, no boyfriend and no one looming on the horizon, so my friends and I just did girly things. They would always be at my house as my mum would not let me go to their houses, but they did not mind. We would sit in my bedroom for hours just talking and laughing, until my mum would come in and sit herself down and interrupt: So did she think that we would continue our conversation with her around? I think she was feeling left out, or she just wanted to be nosy. Whatever her reason, she was none the wiser. It would have been more beneficial to her if she had bugged my bedroom or just listened at the door, or got my sister to spy on us as she was always in the bedroom with us. I

Shoy

don't think she ever had a clue what we talked about, but she was now fun to have around. She was cuddly and cute and everyone liked her. She had long brown/black hair that was naturally curly and I would bathe her and comb her hair into all sorts of styles and dress her in her nice clothes, always colour co-ordinated. She would even choose her own clothes sometimes. She was quite nice so I would keep her around, even though we shared the bedroom, so I could not really kick her out even if I had wanted to.

SOMEONE TO LOVE ME

On this particular day, I got her all dressed up and I arranged for my friends to come down and had previously asked my mum if I could take Stephanie to the park, as it was a nice sunny day. Surprisingly my mum said yes, so off we went. Wayne came as well as he was bored, but he rode alongside us with his bike; he went everywhere with his bike. We were just sitting around and talking and watching Stephanie have a good time on the swings and slides, etc, when these two guys came over and started talking to my brother. Who were they? As they talked away, the rest of us took a walk up to the river and one of the guys followed us. He

Shoy came over to me and started talking to me.

'What's your name?' I looked at him and replied, 'Shoy.'

'That's a nice name. I've seen you before, shopping with your mum.' Wow, nice for him, but immense torture for me, as I hated shopping with my mum. It went on and on forever; we would go into every shop and leave without even buying anything, - what was the point of shopping?

'What's your name?' I asked. He replied,

'Denny.' We talked for a while before being interrupted by my brother Wayne.

'Leave her alone,' he said.

Denny's face dropped he looked at me.

'Who's this?' he asked.

'He's only my brother.' He sighed.

'I thought he was your boyfriend.' Boyfriend, what was that? But

I wanted one, one that I could hold on to and not let go so I could escape from my secret.

Weeks went past and nothing more was thought of that moment. The next thing I knew, one of the friends that had been down in the park with me that day came with a message for me from the guy that I had been talking to. I could not even remember his name.

'He wants your telephone number so he can call you some time.' Well, was she being funny, or had she lost her mind? I could not give him my number; my mum and dad would go ballistic. I could never have a boyfriend and let them find out ever. They would definitely send me away, and at this moment in time I did not want that. Maybe before, but certainly not now.

'The best thing to do is for you to get his number and I will call him one evening when my mum and dad are at work.' My dad was now working in a factory doing shifts, and when he was on nights he would leave about five-thirty in the evening and would not get home until after seven the next morning, and of course my mum was still working nights in the hospital, so this would be the ideal time. She did, eventually, and I phoned him one night when my mum and dad were hard at work. My brother Wayne and I had to put the younger ones to bed, tidied up the kitchen, put the milk

Shoy

bottles out and then we would sit down to watch the TV. I left Wayne in the back sitting room and went into the front one where the phone was, to make my call. I dialled the number (which I had already memorised) and waited. It started to ring. I could hear my heart beating in my ear as I waited for an answer. After three rings, a voice answered. It was a male voice.

'Hello.' It made me jump.

'Hello,' I said quickly. 'Can I speak to Humphrey?' I felt stupid, but that was the name that I was given by my friend.

The voice replied, 'speaking.'

Oh my God, it was him! Well what could I say now? Somehow the conversation started. What we spoke about I could not tell you, but we spoke long into the night, even long after Wayne had told me it was time for bed. We arranged to meet a Tuesday lunchtime, as this was when he could see me. Tuesday lunchtime was going to be tricky as I was always on prefect duty that day, but I arranged to swap it with someone else, so I was free to see him. My excitement grew. He turned up in his yellow Capri and took me out for a ride. We had an hour. Every Tuesday lunchtime, he would pick me up outside the school and we would drive off

Someone to Love Me

somewhere. Sometimes we would just drive up the road from the school and we would sit there talking all lunchtime. I was finally happy. With so many unrequited love attempts, someone was genuinely interested in me and he was mature, in fact he was five years older than me, and all my friends at school, including Alex, hated me. They did not like me going out with someone who was that much older than me, who did not live in our area and did not go to our school. But hey, who were they and who was Alex? After all he had had his chance and blew it, but there was always something there between Alex and me; there was always a look and he always looked so sad whenever I saw him, but I just ignored it. I was never a forgiver and certainly never forgot, but I was tempted with Alex, but never did.

Anyway, Denny and I got closer and closer. I had finally found love: someone who loved me and wanted me. Our relationship went from his picking me up from school and sitting in the car parked up somewhere to going back to his house, which of course led to us having sex in his bed. I was happy, ecstatic and nothing could harm me now. No one could take this happiness away.

Denny and I had been seeing each other secretly now for five months and Christmas was fast approaching. I was still working on the market selling women's clothing on Tuesday after school and all day on a Saturday and had been saving most of my money, which for the two days' work I was earning seventeen pounds. This Christmas I was able to buy what I wanted and for who I wanted. For my mum I had already asked my boss to put aside a dress that I knew she liked. It was cream, the cream being the main colour, with brown, wavy lines on it, but not many. It was fully lined and the outer layer was cream lace; it was a beautiful dress and every time she came to the stall, she commented on how nice this dress was. I had decided to get him a ring; a black onyx set in silver. I bought the ring from the jeweller's and could not wait to give it to him. Christmas came and he bought me a gold signet ring. My first piece of gold jewellery and I could not even wear it; how would I explain where it came from? I hid it in my drawer (which was like an Aladdin's cave) and daily I would look at it. I took it to school and whenever I saw him, I would wear it. The New Year came and went. Our love for each other was growing, but something was wrong. I was missing a vital occurrence to a 'young lady's' existence. I tried not to dwell on it, but it was the strongest thing on my mind. This was one of those occasions where begging for your period to appear seemed the most normal thing to do, and had it arrived, I would have been begging for it to be over. Every time I felt moist, I would rush to the toilets to see if there were any signs, but no. For me, there was no chance of that. YES – I was pregnant. What did this mean now? I told

Denny I was pregnant. What I expected from him did not even enter my mind. He was actually pleased (God knows what would have happened if he were not - I had not thought that far ahead, I just wanted to tell him). His first child; he was going to be a father. After our excitement, reality struck. What were my parents going to say, or worse, do to me, not to mention him? How could this happen? How were we going to explain this to them? Christ, at this point I was contemplating booking my plot, picking the headstone and preparing the order of service. To complicate matters, Denny had never met my parents before and to suddenly say, 'I am pregnant and this is the father,' – well, it did not bear thinking about. I got pregnant in January 1980 on my sixteenth birthday and that summer I was taking my exams at school. I passed most of them, some with half-decent grades surprisingly. The most successful was my dance exam and for this exam we had to choreograph ourselves a piece of work, which had to last a minimum of ten minutes and I gave mine the title, 'Birth, Life and Death'. It was fantastic and I got top marks for it. I worked so hard on it. I would spend all my time in the evening and weekends (once I had finished the housework etc), practising and practising in the front living room, making sure I moved all the furniture out of the way. My dad got me this large sheet of plastic, which was going to be the sack in which the baby would grow and finally escape from. I had chosen three pieces of music: the first

Shoy was the theme music from the South Bank Show, the second was Bohemian Rhapsody by Queen and the third was the continuation of the theme tune from the South bank Show. The first would be slow and mellow, depicting the growth of the child within. We also had to choose what sort of lighting we needed and at this first stage the lights would be low and red. The second stage went on to the baby having grown, needing to escape into the world and the music changed and got faster and faster and the lighting changed to blue and red mixing with the beat of the music, and finally the baby would burst out of its cocoon at the crescendo of the music and would be free, gasping for air as it entered the world alone and helpless, looking to the face of comfort and the supplier of food. The third stage was the growth of the child, which of course depicted being young and dependant, adolescent and getting into trouble, having its own child and finally death. The music slowed right down and the lighting would change to dark blues and purple, which were projected onto the floor in pools of colour that I would enter. The final pool of colour would be bright white. This would be the point of death, the calling of the unknown, and then, finally, the return to darkness from whence it came and the studio would be plunged into darkness for a few seconds. I lay on the floor, my heart racing, but full of excitement because I knew it was good. It was very good and the applause rose from everyone watching. It was fantastic. I was in my element. No one suspected that the inspiration came from what I was experiencing at the time. I exhausted myself performing that piece. I was so stupid and selfish towards an unborn child. I gave myself a terrible backache from prancing around the floor and doing all sorts. By this time I was about four months pregnant. It did not show at all, I did not experience any morning sickness and best of all, I did not grow, but I knew I was pregnant. The only thing that plagued me was fainting, which happened quite a lot, but everyone thought I was not eating properly or stressed about exams. I had no periods, but my mum always bought my sanitary towels and I always hid them in the back of my wardrobe behind an enormous pile of *Jackie Magazine* that I was collecting, so she would not suspect and I would always remind her to buy some more when I knew supplies would be running out. The plan was working, but what was going to happen when this baby needed to come out into the world?

I left school that summer, intending to go back for sixth form, as I did not know what I wanted to do with my life. At sixteen who does? Whilst at home with my mum, we used to go shopping together and do things at home together. It was brilliant to have my mum to myself. We used to look after the vegetables that I grew in the garden, although I must admit it was getting harder to do such strenuous work knowing I was pregnant. It became tricky when I

Shoy

started producing milk, which would leak sometimes. The entire goings on I would follow from a book that I had bought and hid under my mattress from my mum, brothers, sister and friends. No one knew except Denny, the proud father-to-be.

He kept asking, 'When are you going to tell your parents?'

What was the hurry? He began to get suspicious as I did not show and he questioned whether I was actually pregnant, so to prove it I let him feel the baby moving around, as this happened quite often, especially if you prodded the bump in the right place. He was absolutely amazed and totally convinced. He was now planning, planning to be the great father, taking his daughter out to cricket matches and fishing. 'Daughter?' Who said anything about it being a girl? But he was totally convinced that it was going to be. He so wanted a daughter, but he was going to have to wait for the big event and be surprised just like everyone else, and boy, would they be surprised. He was so happy and every time I saw him, he was just filled with excitement and concern as to how I was coping and managing, but most of all he wanted me to tell my parents, but I just could not. I mean, where would you start? How would you start? What would it be? 'Well, Mum and Dad, there is something I have to tell you!' At that point the look and under-the-breath noises would stop you dead in your tracks, but once you had started with that line, there was no return. They would pin you down to the floor, if necessary, until you said what you had to, so you never made the mistake of starting with that line. It was easy for him to say 'tell your parents, they need to know,' but he was not going to be there. He had suggested that we should do it together, but can you imagine? Picture this: I arrange a meeting on a Sunday afternoon, in my head that is, and of course telling Denny what time to arrive. He then arrives on time. Whilst waiting I have kittens by the dozen. If it weren't kittens, then it would be going into premature labour. So, okay, he arrives I anticipate him knocking on the door and I open it before he actually does, thus prolonging the agony of his encountering my parents. I invite him in, quietly, not being able to muster up a smile, as the opening line was being rehearsed ten times to the dozen in my head and had to be right, so no niceties on this occasion. Still parents none-the-wiser to the fact, just having a quiet afternoon sat in front of the TV, not particularly talking to each other. In fact my dad would be sat in his chair with his head slumped against the back of the chair, mouth wide open, and sounds of air gasping and getting no-where, resonating around the room, drowning all possible communications if any were to take place. So then, I open the sitting room door and with a deep intake of breath, say, 'Mum, Dad, this is Denny.' Mum would look at Dad and seeing that he was still resonating in his own world would poke him with

Shoy her knitting needle.

'Marcus, wake up. Shoy is trying to tell us something.' Now that sort of controlled awakening would be good, but oh no - that would never happen. It would be more of a 'Marcus?' And this would be at the highest shriek, decibels enough to break the windowpanes. Mum would now be teetering at the edge of the armchair, knitting flung aside and her eyes would be as wide as the gap in the floor that I would be looking for to disappear into, leaving Denny to explain. Dad, in the meantime would jump out of his skin, taking in the breaths of air that were never allowed to pass through his throat all at once and then, choking, he would bolt upright on to his feet.

'Who the arse is this?' would be the words of welcome. I thought death would be a preferable option, so that picture was well and truly erased, for the time being anyway.

Whilst at home, after doing my exams, which was all a waste of time, my mum had done a big fry-up breakfast which consisted of, for myself, two sunny-side-up eggs, two sausages, about three strips of streaky bacon, a couple of pieces of black pudding, one fried tomato, baked beans and two rounds of toast drenched in butter. No sooner had it been placed on the table in front of me, it disappeared like dust up the Hoover and just as quick; I ate it all. Now bearing in mind that that was about ten in the morning, by about eleven-thirty, I was hungry again, as if I had just woken up and nothing had passed my lips. I started poking around in the kitchen.

'What you up to?'

'I am looking for something to eat, I am starving.' With that my mum peeled some potatoes and made some chips. She had peeled quite a few potatoes and when the chips were thrown on to my plate, it was a mountain. I covered them with loads of salt and vinegar and went into the living room to sit and gorge on the feast. I absolutely adored chips, especially when they were homemade and cut in just the right way, which Mum always made them just so. Chips I could eat it till the cows came home. I sat there very quietly, munching my way through the plate of chips. Unbeknown to me, my mum was watching me with interest, a lot of interest.

'How come you are eating so much and still not full?' How could I answer her? What would I say? I said nothing. I just shied away from the question, knowing my guilt, knowing my burning secret.

Shoy

'When was the last time you had a period?' I swallowed hard. This was my opening. I had to lie, make it up, but she caught me out. I did not lie very well, - well, I was not ready for that was I? She then looked straight at me and that 'million dollar' question came out of her mouth. 'Are you pregnant Shoy?'

I started to cry. I so wanted her to know. I wanted this huge secret to get out so I could get on with my life, be normal again and not be scared any more as I was. There were no more questions. She left me crying over the empty plate that was just sprinkled with grains of salt and little droplets of vinegar. In a moment that seemed like eternity, she returned. 'Get your shoes on, we're going to the Doctor right now.' I did not question. I did not query her reasons. Deep down I knew why the questions stopped and she knew it as well. The walk to the surgery was long and silent. A walk that took about eight minutes tops, just seemed to go on and on. We turned the corner of the road to the surgery. My heart was racing even more now. I was so afraid. What if I was not pregnant and in fact I was dying? What then? The thought of dying brought tears to my eyes, but I dare not let the pools of salty, warm liquid that swelled in the recesses of my eyes roll out and down my cheeks, not now. At the sight of that my mum would just go into one. At the speed at which she was walking, she was a woman on a mission and my tears would only create a panic blow to some part of my body. I wiped the tears. We approached the surgery. She walked in ahead of me. The surgery was actually closed, but the Doctor was a family friend and so made an exception to see me. The receptionist moved aside to let us in. She looked at me with a gentle smile. I smiled back and immediately looked at the floor. As she closed the door behind us, she put a gentle arm around my shoulders and took me in to the examination room. My mum was now in the waiting room talking to the Doctor at some great lengths and crying at what she might have to hear, of what she might have to endure, at the shame, of the disgust and to top it off, how I could have done something like this? This would be the end of her marriage. Now what in heaven's name did my getting pregnant have to do with her marriage? But she was going on and on. The receptionist closed the door to the examination room and waited with me until the Doctor came in, followed by my mum. He sat in his chair across from the desk at which I was sitting.

'So what is going on?' in his deep, African voice. 'Your mother tells me you are pregnant. Is that true?' I just looked at him, dumber than the day I was born.

'Answer the Doctor,' was shouted to me from my mum, followed by a swift prod, which made me jump.

Shoy

'Okay, lets take a good look at you.' The receptionist beckoned for me to come over to the couch. I got on it and lay down, exposed my stomach and waited, once again waited. 'My hands are cold, but it wont take long'. No sooner had he laid his hands on me, he pulled away. 'Oh my God, she is about to have this baby. The head is already engaged. How far gone are you? Do you know?'

I nodded. 'I am just over eight months.'

He took a deep breath, removed his glasses and looked at both of us. 'She is going to have this baby any day.' To the amazement of everyone in the room, my mum fell on the floor on her hands and knees.

'Oh GOD, Oh GOD, how can this happen? My life is over! I can't deal with this.' With every word there was the beating of the floor. I just looked at her. She was hysterical beyond a doubt. She was inconsolable. With her outcry getting louder and louder, the Doctor asked the receptionist to take her out of the room. This she did, helping her to her feet from the floor. Through it all she never once looked at me. She never once asked how I was? She never once asked how the baby was? She left the room and I was

Someone to Love Me

now alone with the Doctor. What was I to say? It was best not to. The receptionist returned.

'When exactly is she due Doctor?'

'In about a week or so. I would be surprised if she made it to the weekend.' They thought it was appalling that I had to go through this by myself, but I was not alone. I had Denny and my book by Miriam Stoppard.

'Right, Shoy, you have a lot of things you have to get done within the next two days. We will start with blood tests, urine tests, ultra-sound.........' His voice disappeared in a muffled fog and returned when he said. 'Okay, you can go to the hospital now. They are waiting for you, after that go home and you must make sure that you get lots of rest. I have telephoned your dad so he knows what is going on and he has come and got your mum, okay?' I looked at him; I was getting quite good at looking at people. I just seemed to be doing it all the time. What had the doctor said to my dad? How angry would he be? Would he beat me? Would I live to see tomorrow? I took the host of forms and letters and printouts and handouts and left the surgery. I walked to the hospital where I was prodded, poked, and bled. Now bleeding me was not the easiest task in the world; my blood just did not want to leave my body. No matter how many times they pushed the needle in, out it came with nothing and just left another hole in my arm that made me look like a junky and bruised just as bad and to top it all, they then stuck a little circular plaster over every wound which made it look like I was a bad shot and missed the veins each time. That was always very painful and would make me feel as though I was going to faint. Most of my results from that day, by the time I left the hospital, had come through. I was healthy as far as it goes, just a bit anaemic, but I was too far along in the pregnancy for them to prescribe iron tablets, so of course the next best thing: injections in my bum and today would be my first. I was given the rest of the ampoules with the instructions that when the midwife visited me at home, - her first visit was going to be in the next couple of days - she would then administer them, one by one every other day until I gave birth. Oh great, so I have an arm that looks as though I am a useless junkie that misses her vein and my bum would look as though I was being beaten and bruised all over. I was given another appointment to go back to the hospital for check-ups the following week (if the baby was still inside). So I left the clinic feeling very relieved that everything was going to be all right. I was now in safe hands and nothing could go wrong from this moment on.

I left the sanctuary. I now had the long walk home. My dad had been to the surgery to get my mum and they had left without me. What does that tell you? Well it did not paint a good picture at all. I should be afraid - very afraid - and I was. I was now standing at the gate to our house, the gate that I wished would keep me out, the gate that would keep me secure, the gate that would keep me safe from what was about to happen, but instead I opened it and it squeaked as it always did, alerting the household to the fact that someone had just walked in the gate and was approaching the front door. The fear of facing my mum and dad now set in and took over and I began to shake violently. What was my dad going to say? You see, when I was younger, my dad had a bad temper. He did not drink, at least I did not think so, but he would always lash out at us, sometimes for very stupid things, simple things such as not putting the milk bottles out on the front doorstep at night for the milkman or even rinsing them clean. He would even wake us up from our beds and not just one of us, all of us, to go and put the bottles out. There was no logic or common sense to this act. Why would it take all of us? But that was just his way. On a few occasions, he even beat my mum when she was pregnant, the younger ones probably didn't remember a lot of this as they were too young, but I did and I hated my dad with a vengeance. I rang the doorbell and my mum opened the door. I walked in. My heart was in my mouth. I was told to go into the front sitting room and wait. A little while later, in came my mum followed by my stone-

Shoy faced dad. Six hundred questions flew at me.

'Who is he?' 'Who are his parents?' 'Where does he live?' 'How long have you been seeing him?' A multitude of questions. Half of which I could not answer, simply because I did not have the answers. I was not computing any of it.

'Stop crying!' my mum shouted, which immediately made me jump and halted my noise to a whimper. 'You are not a child now so you can dry all the tears.' I was trembling, out of fright, but I was also cold, very cold and tired. It had been a long day and I was exhausted and hungry. This my mum could see, despite being angry. She told my dad to leave the room, that I had had enough. My dad left the room in disgust, really worried about who was going to say what to whom. The gossip to follow.

'So who did you say was the father?' My mum asked very softly.

'His name is Denny.' My eyes fixed on the 'lovely' swirls of pattern in the carpet. She paused.

'I don't know that name. Who are his parents?' Well we had been there, asked that one, and once again I told her.

'I don't know because I have never met them.'

She looked at me for a long time. Her eyes were questioning. *'Where has my little girl gone?'* Her voice, now hurt and croaky as she fought back the tears, said, 'I am really hurt. Why could you not tell me before? Why let me find out this way?' I did not answer. 'What did the hospital say?' I showed her the forms they had given me and told her what they did and the date of the follow-up appointment. A feeling of care and concern from my mum came over me at that point. She appeared different towards me. My feelings from the conversations that followed that evening told me that she would have made me have an abortion, but she never actually said as much. I was so relieved that I never told her so this deed could have been carried out. How would I live with myself, knowing I had killed my own baby? Perish the thought. She made me get a cardigan on and by the time I came downstairs she had made me a cup of tea and was making me some dinner. I sat at the dining room table and just watched her, wondering what was going through her mind. What did she really think of me? I felt comfortable with her, but every time I heard my dad, I would go cold and fear would enter my body again. I so hoped that that fear would go away in its own time and we could be as we were before; not that that was any better, but it was sure better than it

Shoy

was now, today. My mum placed the plate of food that she had prepared for me on the table in front of me and told me to eat. Well, she did not have to tell me that again. I was straight in there. I was so hungry. She watched me.

'You know me and your faada have to meet dis boy?' I stopped what I was chewing and looked up at her. Oh my God. Would he come? He would leave me for sure once he had met my dad. That I did not want, but it was what they wanted. So, of course, I had to get on with it. I called Denny that evening. This time I could just dial the number knowing that they knew who I was calling and there was no secrecy. He was so surprised to hear from me and at that time of day, knowing that my parents were both at home.

'Do they know? Did you tell them?' For some reason he knew why I was calling, he knew it would only be a matter of time before they found out. It was a phone call he had been expecting for quite some time now. I told him when he had to come over and he agreed. Usually on a Sunday afternoon, Denny played cricket for the local team, but this Sunday he had cancelled his match and was now standing outside our front door. My stomach had butterflies doing somersaults, or maybe it was the baby, but something was going on in there. I opened the door and let him in. He looked dead nervous, but he managed a smile, but there was no touching or kissing: that would not have been right and we would have been pushing our luck somehow.

I showed him into the front sitting room where my mum and dad had been waiting for his arrival. At this time in the proceedings, my siblings had been packed off to Sunday school, a ritual they hated, and especially today as they knew that Denny was coming over and they did not want to miss all the fun. So we were alone, just me, Denny, my mum and dad. As I walked in, my mum told me to stay out.

'Go into the other room and wait there. We want to talk to Denny. It is Denny?' she said, looking at him. He nodded.

'Yes we want to talk to Denny alone. We will call you when we are ready.' Well that was not fair. He was my boyfriend and they were kicking me out of the room. What were they going to say to him? Why could I not be involved and hear what had to be said or asked of him? Once again, I am the child. They know what's best! Anyway, I left the room, closing the door behind me. I then positioned myself on the step at the bottom of the stairs. There was no way I was going to miss all of this; of course I was going to listen.

Shoy

'So, Denny, this is Shoy's father.' I could not hear what he said, but I assume he answered or made some gesture towards my dad. Oh, if only I were in there.

'So how old are you?' The burning question from my dad!

'Almost, twenty-one.' Came a very quiet reply.

My mum then launched into,

'How could a man of your age take advantage of a schoolgirl, because that's what she is, do you know that?' There was no reply, not that I could hear anyway. 'What were you thinking of? Me and Shoy's father could call the police and have you arrested and put in prison, for having under-aged sex, you know that?' Still I could not hear anything. I was now at the bottom of the door, listening. I had to sit on the floor with my ear pressed at the bottom of the door because it was one of those doors with glass in the middle at the top and if I had stood there, they would have seen me. So here I was scrunched up on the floor trying to hear what was going on. How could they say that to him? What did they know about under-aged sex? Where were they when Roger was having '*under-aged sex*' with me since the age of nine? I was getting really wound up now and just wanted to go in, but I dare not.

Someone to Love Me

It would not be worth my life. So I continued sitting at the bottom of the door. 'Are you going to marry her?' My mouth fell open. We had not even spoken about marriage. I did not want to marry him; I was far too young (bit late on the reality check but I was). I wanted to have my baby, get a career, and then think about getting married. There was plenty of time for marriage. My ear pressed even harder against the door to see if I could hear the answer. It still excited me to see if he would say yes, but of course I heard nothing, nothing at all. The room fell into silence. Nothing was being said. So what was going on now? I needed to know.

'Shoy?' Well, that made me jump. I could have gone into labour right there and then. I jumped back from the door and answered. 'You can come in now.' Finally, I could join in a conversation that was all about me and my unborn child and its father. My dad left the room, still not looking at me, not saying a word. 'Go put a jumper on, it's cold in here. Then you and Denny can sit down and talk. The others should be back from Sunday school soon. You can introduce them to Denny then, okay?' Oh my God, he was sitting in our front living room and they knew he was here and they were allowing this. I ran upstairs (not advisable when you are eight-and-a-half months' pregnant), got a jumper and came down just as quickly. We sat together on the settee, the settee that we had made love on so many nights. We were holding hands. I

Shoy

was so embarrassed I did not know what to say, but eventually we got talking and everything was going to be all right. He was happy and was just concerned that I felt okay. He always loved feeling my stomach. He could not believe how much my stomach had grown in the last week since I had told my parents. It was as if it had been waiting for the secret to be out before revealing itself to the world.

Not too long afterwards, the others came home and they came straight into the front room. They all knew that something was going on and they wanted to know, and they wanted to know now. My mum followed them in, they all sat down, and my mum told them that I was going to have a baby. Stephanie's face lit up and she came over to me and gave me a big hug and a kiss. The others, of course, being boys, showed no emotion at all. They were just concerned with 'when is dinner going to be ready' and 'when can we go out to play'. Stephanie did not want to leave me now. She was always with me. She would always put her head on my stomach so she could feel the baby moving. We would often have baths together, even though she was eight years old.

The next week flew by. My Aunt Shirley and Uncle Michael were the first relatives to be told outside our family. Who knows what was said to them about this whole fiasco, the shame, the embarrassment, but I am sure they were shocked. They were not my real aunt and uncle, but we called them that because my mum and dad had known them forever. When they got married, I had been chosen to be one of their bridesmaids. I had been dressed in a pink (very itchy) lacy long dress with pink gloves to match, white shoes and a pink tiara-looking headset. My hair had been straightened with a hot iron comb, during which process I had got slightly burnt on the back of my neck. This is what happened if you moved suddenly or your mum got distracted. If only I had hair like that all the time, but as soon as it got wet, either by washing or with rain water, then it would return to its old, thick, knotted, tangled self – yuk. My Aunt was tall and very elegant and with it was this very posh accent. She was quite dark in colour, but it was nice and even with her smooth face. Uncle Michael was lighter with this huge moustache and he always smoked a pipe.

My Aunt Shirley still had her cot that she had had when Billy, her youngest, was born, so she offered it to me. Of course, my mum accepted, so that was one item we had and did not need to spend extra money on and it was perfect, not a scratch on it. Of course my mum was not proud of the fact that I was having a baby at the age of sixteen, but she was not ashamed of the fact and did not hide me away, send me away or decide that the baby was going up for adoption. She wanted this grandchild and I could see and feel that. Once she had found out, and of course there was nothing else they could do to stop it happening, she had accepted it wholeheartedly. The town just seem to come alive with gossip of me being pregnant and 'how was that possible when she was never out of her mother's sight?' My friends, of course, were told and they just could not believe that I had not told them all this time. I thought I was going to lose a few of them, if not all of them, but they were great and none of them gave up on me; in fact, it brought us closer. They used to spend all their spare time - of which they had quite a lot since we had finished our exams and had nothing else to do – just being with me. They avoided taking me shopping as I was always fainting and they did not want that to happen when they were around, so I was more or less confined to seeing them at my house, never venturing far. The furthest I would go with them was for a walk around the block and we would talk, mull over baby names and what 'she' was going to look like, the things she was going to wear and how sweet she would be. Of course, they all wanted to be godmothers, but that one I had to avoid. Who would I choose? They were all good friends to me and so I would avoid that one at all costs. For the time being anyway.

My mum had started knitting like mad (as she only had two weeks before the baby was due) and before too long, she had knitted an assortment of cardigans, booties, mittens (all in yellow and white) and now she was crocheting a shawl. It was absolutely beautiful. She was spending lots of money on all sorts for the baby. She had bought me my 'Baby Layette' which consisted of four baby vests that tied on the side with two silk bows, four pairs of booties, four pair of scratch mittens, two pairs of mittens which were knitted, two Babygro outfits, two bonnets which were also knitted, two baby flannels, and a matinee jacket with a hood which was edged with silk. To add to this she had bought a dozen terry nappies and plastic pants along with baby pins, Johnson & Johnson baby powder, baby lotion, cotton buds, cotton wool, petroleum jelly, zinc cream (just in case of nappy rash) and a pack of disposable nappies for use in the hospital. My suitcase was also ready for the hospital with all the things I was going to need during the birth and the short stay afterwards, such as nightdresses, dressing gown (as I never owned one), new underwear, nursing bras with pads and sanitary towels by the packet load. My baby drawer was filling up nicely with all little bits and bobs for the arrival of my brand new baby. I would always be in the drawer smelling everything. It all smelt so clean and baby-like. I loved it. I could not wait for this baby to come out so I could dress her, make her smell all nice, and clean just like the scent from this drawer. Denny would come over nearly every evening when he finished work and we would sit either in the front sitting room or the kitchen, talking. We still could not agree on any names. For a girl we thought of names such as Marcia, I liked Marcia; but he hated it. Apparently he knew someone called Marcia and he did not like her, so that would not be good enough for his little girl. There was Judy Jane: This was my Mum's favourite, but both of us felt that it was too English. For a boy we came up with Anthony, which was not too bad, but Denny wanted his son to have a West Indian name. We could have that as his second name as he was going to choose the boy's name and I the girl's. We left it for a while. We thought we would wait until she/he was born and decide then. He was so good, he would also bring over fifty pounds a week for me so I could help my mum buy the things that were needed and also save because there were going to be some extra expenses such as getting a pram/buggy, baby bath, extra warm-clothes etc. as she was going to be born in October. All these things my mum would buy when I eventually went into hospital, and have them ready and waiting for my return. She felt it was bad luck to buy them before, so we didn't. We had just looked at things in Mothercare and Adams and had decided what I needed and which ones I liked. She made a note of it and that was that. As time went on, I was never left alone. There was always someone with me, whether it was my parents (who just fussed too much about keeping warm, eating enough, sleeping enough, and drinking Mawby. Now Mawby is a West Indian drink and it is made from the bark of some sort of tree – no one seems to know the name of the tree - but you boil it with some water together with some orange peel and few cloves, you then strain it into a large pan and add cold water and sugar to taste. Now my taste is definitely not that of most other people who drink this drink. It is vile, it is bitter and no matter how fast you drink it, the bitter taste just lingers in the back of your throat, but apparently this drink is good for your skin and, of course, 'the skin of your unborn child'. There were also my friends, namely Faye and Brenda, who would always be at my house at some point during the day. They were so supportive and excited. Of course, Denny would come over most evenings once he had finished work, so I had plenty of visitors. Hence my mum's apprehension at my getting over-tired.

STRANGER IN THE NIGHT

I lay in bed awake, so wanting to sleep, but too tired to settle. I sat for a bit watching my sister sleep. She was so funny to look at, because she was always talking in her sleep and every now and again she would sleepwalk. This was always a nightly occurrence when she was younger. Once, when she was a lot younger, she was stopped just in time by my mum, walking out of the front door. So for a while after that I would lock my bedroom door at night so she could not escape. Another curious habit of hers was to play with your ears as she lay there sucking her thumb, half-asleep and as we shared a bed, my ears would always be the ones that she wanted to play with. This would annoy me no end and every time I moved her hand, there it was, back again like a magnet drawn to metal, playing with my earlobes. She was not the sort of child to have a comfort blanket and so I suppose the ears were the next best thing – just not her ears! I got out of bed, as I was uncomfortable and my back was beginning to hurt a bit. I put on the TV, but in those days there was rarely anything on past midnight, so I switched it off again. I could not put on any music as it would probably wake my sister or my dad and we could not have that. So I went back to bed and just lay there in the dark. I hated the dark. As I lay there I would imagine all sorts of creatures and evil beings running around the ceiling and crawling up the curtain. Now the curtains were very bad in that they had these large print flowers in the design, and if you looked at them hard enough they really looked like faces and they would change their expression! Thoughts of this made me go under the blanket and cuddle up to my sister. How she was going to protect me I would never know, and also if there was anything running around the room, what good would it be hurling yourself under the blanket? What protection would that offer? But just knowing you had the weight of the blankets over you made you feel protected and nothing could take them off you. So here I was now, under the blankets breathing in all that carbon dioxide expelled from both of us, and the temperature rising. What was I going to do? Dare

Shoy

I stick my head out of this blanket? Well I had to. It was just too hot. Just as I emerged from the cocoon of heat, there was this sudden, sharp, unexpected pain and to follow I wet the bed. Me, at my age, wetting the bed! For a moment, I could not move and to top it all I could not stop myself. The water was just running and the pain was coming from my stomach. Could this be the beginning? I eventually got out of bed, changed my nightdress and underwear, which were now soaked, and put on a sanitary towel (as told to me by my trusted book – this measure had to be taken just in case anything came out and the hospital wanted evidence). I then pulled back the bed covers. The bed was soaked. I laid some clean towels over the wet patch so Stephanie would not roll into it. I would have to change it later as I did not want to wake her. I quickly returned to my book and this was the moment. My *'waters had broken'* and the baby was going to make an entrance. This was the beginning.

'Ah,' I gasped, and held my stomach again. The pain was really bad. I fell on the bed, lay there, and waited for the pain to stop. With that I quickly left my room and went to wake my dad. 'Dad?' I shook him as hard as I could. He jumped up, and it was as if he knew what I had come in for.

'You sit down. I will phone for the ambulance and call your mother.' Of course on this particular night of all nights, my mum was at work. It was so scary watching my dad go into action, because he really did not know what he was doing. The panic in him seemed to be leading the way, but he was managing. He pulled his trousers on over his pyjama bottoms, pulled off his top, put on a shirt, and then left the room. I followed. He went downstairs and called 999 for an ambulance. They were on their way. He then came rushing back up the stairs. 'Where is your case?' I showed him. It was all packed and ready to go; in fact it had been ready almost a week-and-a-half ago. He grabbed the case and took it downstairs. In the meantime, I had put on my coat. Stephanie was now awake and wondering what was going on, with the lights on and my dad flapping about like a fish out of water.

'The baby is about to come, Stephanie, so I have to go to the hospital.' She was grinning from ear to ear. 'Go back to sleep now and you will see the baby in the morning when you come to see me in the hospital after school, okay?' She nodded and laid her head back on the pillow and just looked at me and smiled. 'Come on, close your eyes otherwise you are going to be tired in the morning for school.'

'Can I come with you now?'

Shoy

'No you can't. You have to wait until the baby is born and then you can come, okay?' She promptly shoved her thumb into her mouth, turned over and off to sleep she went. I left the room, went downstairs, and sat on the bottom step, just waiting. The pains had not returned, so I just sat there. My dad emerged from the front sitting room.

'I don't know where this ambulance is. They'd better get here soon. Me rang your madda and she go meet di ambulance when you get to di hospital, as me ha foo stay here wid di others.'

'Okay, Dad.' He then went back to the living room, picked the phone up again, and dialled 999.

'Armmm, I just called you for an ambulance to come to this address and nattn arrive yet and my daughter is in pain. How long you tink it going to take for the ambulance to come?' All of course said in his best English voice. He replaced the receiver. 'They said it coming soon buddy, me hope so!' About two minutes later there were blue flashing lights outside the house and sure enough it was the ambulance. A man and a woman came out of the ambulance to the house. My dad started trying to fill them in on the events that had taken place, but as he had not asked me what had happened he could not get very far, so I took over.

'What's your name?'

'It's Shoy,' came an answer from my dad as he jumped in to answer for me.

'That's a beautiful name.'

'Okay Shoy, we are going to get a chair to carry you to the ambulance in, so you just sit there and wait for a bit'. One of the crew disappeared out of the door. 'How long has it been since your last contraction?' I knew there was something I should have been doing, according to my book, but I forgot to look at the time when I had the last one.

'I don't know. I forgot to look at the time.'

'Not to worry.'

'My waters have broken though. They went quite a while back and soaked the bed and then I started to get the pains and have only had two sets of pains since then, and I have put a sanitary towel on just in case anything came out and you needed to see it.' Just then, the other crewmember came back and they got me into the chair

Shoy

and lifted me out of the house and into the ambulance, which had to park in the middle of the road because of all the cars that were parked outside the house. My dad always had a thing about cars parking outside our house, especially when they did not live in the road. He would put old oil cans with planks of wood suspended between two of them along the front to stop the cars parking in what should have been our space, even though we did not have a car, but on this night, someone had moved them and had parked there and this sent my dad into a vexed frenzy. Anyway, we got into the ambulance and they shut the door. It was when the ambulance moved off that I realised that my dad was with us.

'How come you are coming, Dad?'

'Oh I told Lesley that I was going to go over with you, make sure you got there all right and see mummy and then I will go back home.' I thought that was just so special. He wanted to see that his little girl was all right.

We arrived at the hospital in no time at all. They did not use the sirens, though! I suppose I was not a medical emergency and because it was the early hours of the morning, there was no traffic about so it was a clear run. I was taken, on a trolley, to a room, which had a big clock on the wall opposite the bed. There was lots

Stranger in the Night

of machinery around the room. My dad stood in a corner whilst they transferred me on to the bed that was in the room and then took off my coat and the nightdress and underwear, along with the sanitary towel, and helped me on with a gown, those lovely gowns with the back missing. They then proceeded to place little rubber discs on my stomach and on my chest. As all this was going on, my mum arrived from the ward where she was working. She and my dad were talking, and I just lay there whilst the nurses hooked these pads up to monitors and everything started beeping and flashing. All this alarmed me and the nurses, seeing this, quickly explained what it all was and why they were doing it.

'The pads on your stomach are to monitor the baby's heartbeat. We want to make sure that its heart is strong and not fading and the other ones are to monitor your heartbeat.' Relieved, I lay back and looked over at my mum.

'Dad is going to go home now, Shoy, and he will come back after he has taken the others to school, okay?' My dad came over and gave me a kiss. For the first time in a long time, my dad had given me a kiss. Did this mean that he had forgiven me? He left, all the frenzied activity had subsided, and I was left with my mum to relax and wait for the events to take place. I was offered a cup of tea, which I accepted, because I loved tea; it was the best drink

Shoy

ever.

My mum came over, sat on the side of the bed, and hugged me. She whispered in my ear, 'Mum is here and everything is going to be all right and soon you will be holding your lovely baby.' I did not answer, but the reality of being sixteen and about to give birth was scary. I drove it out of my mind. I did not have much choice, because just then, pain struck and it was a hard one. The little needles on the monitoring machine starting skipping around from left to right. All this activity and all this pain. I grabbed hold of my stomach and my mum moved my hands.

'Hold on to me, that's what I am here for. You just hold on to me now, come on, breathe.' What the hell did she mean by breathe? What did she think I was doing all this time? The nurse came in just as it was dying down, went over to the monitor and said quite calmly, 'That was a nice one, you're coming along nicely.' Well it might have been nice for her, but it was excruciating for me. Once that episode had totally passed, my mum handed me my cup of tea and I began to sip it, not wanting to be here now, not wanting to have to experience this pain, the pain of giving birth.

'Shoy, when I tell you to breathe you must breathe in, take deep breaths and let out. If you follow me, the pain will become much easier.' Maybe from where she was standing, but that was not convincing. The contractions were well spaced, so I was comfortable for most of the time. Just after one of the contractions, my mum suggested that she went to call Denny, as he wanted to be at the birth. So off she went and then returned, not having been able to get hold of him, as there was no answer.

'Oh, sometimes Mrs Noble unplugs the phone as she does not want to be disturbed in the night.' I suppose I should have told her that in the first place, but it did not cross my mind at the time.

'Well, anyway, I will keep on trying. You never know, she may have left it in knowing you would be having the baby soon.' That I doubted very much. It was a ritual in her house and I could not see her changing that one.

I lay there on the hospital bed, looking at this clock, which never seemed to move, just listening to my baby's heartbeat which was strong and fast, and then there would be weird, bubbly noises as it moved around a bit. Oh it was the best sound ever. I had this living thing inside me, and soon I would be meeting it for the first time since its creation. It was so overwhelming. I so hoped that it would be a little girl, but as long as it was healthy, that was all that would matter. The pains were now getting stronger and stronger and I began to use the 'gas' mask that I had been handed earlier, just in case I needed to. That took me back a bit: back to the time in the dentist's high chair. Dare I use it? The nurses were in and out of the room the whole time. They were really busy, as apparently the whole world seemed to want to give birth that night of all nights, and all the rooms were full and they were short of staff. But they seemed to be handling the situation. I suppose between contractions they had time to see who was at what stage and who was getting closest to delivery. It seemed as if I had been on this bed for ages, with the blip- blips coming from the machine, the tick-tocks coming from the large clock on the wall, the swing door swinging every time someone appeared, my mum stroking my hair when the pains were strong and the smell of that gas, but it seemed to help so I subjected myself to it time and time again. The door swung open again and in came a woman in a white coat.

'Hi there, how are you getting on?' She said smiling, looking at my notes which she unhooked from the bottom of my bed.

'Not too good. It hurts a lot and I don't like the gas. How long is it going to be before my baby is born?'

'Well let's take a look at you. My hands are cold, so I will try to be as quick as I can.' She placed one hand on the bottom of my stomach, and with her stethoscope, she listened. 'That's excellent. Well your baby's head is in the right place and I think we can give you something to get things moving along a little quicker.'

'What do you mean?'

'Well, your baby is very small and her heart is not as strong as it was in the beginning.'
She moved over to the machine that was churning out a long stream of paper with heartbeat lines on it. 'Look, this is the graph earlier when we started to monitor your baby's heartbeat and if you look here,' she pointed to another bit of the chart, 'you can see that the heart rate has changed. There are less squiggles and it could mean that it is getting tired, because when they are small, they use a lot more energy than larger babies, so therefore we may need to get it out a lot more quickly, okay?' I looked at my mum, who looked very concerned. Being a nurse, she probably understood a whole lot more of what was going on than I did, so looking at her would give me comfort if she did not look worried, but she did so there was no comfort at all.

'She' is going to be alright in it?'

'I am sure 'she' will be, but we will induce you now just to be on the safe side.' With that, she instructed the nurse to give me the necessary preparation through the drip that was in my wrist. I lay there waiting. Well, what was supposed to happen? I was expecting this induction to bring on immediate delivery, but there was still the waiting game. My mum left once more to try and phone Denny, during which time I had another contraction and this time it was strong. The nurse that was with me helped me through it, making me mimic her breathing. All through my life I experience pain and this one was the worst. My mum returned. Still no success in getting Denny. He would soon be at work, so she would be able to call him there and hopefully get him here before his baby was born. Contraction mounting, I slapped the mask on to my face and took the deepest breath ever and almost sent myself into a coma. My head was spinning and I felt really stupid, but still the pain persisted. I was screaming and throwing myself around on the bed, so much so that I got my head stuck between the machinery that was monitoring my baby's heartbeat and the bed, and the nurse and my mum were trying to get my head out when the doctor returned. Between the three of them they managed to get me out, but the pain was still there and this time it was not going to stop. It was time. The doctor put on some gloves and proceeded to examine me internally.

'Now, Shoy, I need to place an electrode on the top of your baby's head. It will not harm the baby in any way, but once in place, we can monitor her heart rate much more easily than the machine because there will be a lot of movement and we may lose the heart sounds but with the electrode in place there will be no chance of that, okay? So you may be a little uncomfortable for a while, but I will be as quick as I can.' She was so nice and explained everything so calmly and so gently.

My mum was hugging me and saying all sorts of things such as, 'you are so brave. It will soon be over.' All that sort of stuff, but really paying more attention to what the doctor or nurses was doing.

'There, it's on and it's working.' I was now too drugged up to care. I just wanted this baby out. I was starving and thirsty. I could not eat and I was only allowed sips of water, which did not seem to do a thing.

'Okay, are you ready Shoy. Your next contraction is on its way. Are you ready to push?' How did they know? But they were right. I was pushing as hard as I could.

'Oh no, I am going to do a poo.'

Shoy

'I don't think so. Don't worry, you emptied your bowels before you came down here so you will be all right, but just to make sure we will put some paper towels at the entrance.' The doctor signalled to the nurse for some paper, which she handed to her and she put in place. I continued to push, but I was so tired and just wanted to sleep. I could not do any more. It was all too much.

'I want to sleep. Please leave me alone.'

'Come on Shoy, don't you want to see your baby?'

'No, 'she' is taking too long. It hurts, I am hungry, I am thirsty and I want to sleep.' I tried to roll over in the middle of the contraction, but promptly rolled back again and began to scream.

'Come on Shoy, big push now' came a voice from my mum. 'You just hold on to me, I am here. Come on let's see this baby now. Oh yes, oh yes, the head is here, not too long now, Shoy.' I was trying to look down.

'Okay Shoy, pant really quick.' But I kept on pushing. Now the head was here I just wanted the rest of her out. But that was a big mistake. 'Come on Shoy, you have to pant. We need to slow her down, otherwise she will injure you and we need to find the cord,

Stranger in the Night

so pant NOW.' The calm, gentle doctor was now shouting and she was scary. So of course I panted and panted. 'Okay, that's better. Now when I tell you, push really, really hard down into your bottom and we will have your baby out for you.' Of course, right on cue the pains came and I pushed and pushed. I thought I was going to bust a vessel doing so. My neck was cramping, my brain felt as if it was going to explode, but there she was. I just looked and my mum cried.

'You have a beautiful baby girl.' I laughed.

'Yes, I have my baby girl.' I glanced at the clock. The time was thirteen-thirty exactly and it was the 2nd October 1980. My mum hugged me and she was crying all over me. The baby gave a very little cry and then there were no more cries. No more cries. Why not? She was whisked away. I had not even held her. They took her away to another machine that was at the side of the room and all I could see was a needle going towards her. My mum tried to stop me looking, but I was pushing her out of the way.

'What are you doing? Why is she not crying? Why can't I hold her? Mum, what is going on?'

'Okay Shoy, I am sure the doctors will tell us in a minute.' With that, a few more doctors came into the room and the whole place just seemed to be buzzing. There was I, left with my legs akimbo, the cord still hanging out of me, and all this activity going on around my baby. She was not breathing. That was all I heard. She had stopped breathing. My little fighter was small and she was not breathing. I was now crying and my mum was still crying, although she was trying to be brave for me. What seemed like eternity was only thirty seconds and then there she was. She was crying, albeit softly, but she was crying. She only weighed 3lbs 15ozs and she was 29 cms long. She was now wrapped in what looked like tin foil and then a blanket over that and she was handed to me.

'There you go, Shoy. We lost her for a moment, but she is fine now. A bit cold so you can't hold her for very long. We need to take her on to the ward and put her in an incubator and heat her up, but she is going to be fine and she is beautiful.' She was. I couldn't see her tiny little fingers, and her tiny little feet. She was all wrapped up. All I could see was her petite face and her eyes were open and looking at me. To me they said,

'Hi Mum, I LOVE YOU.' With that she was taken from me. I watched them take her out of the door. The attentions now turned to me. They had to get the after-birth out and tidy me up. Having

Stranger in the Night

been given an injection in my thigh, some time ago, I now had to push, just a little, to get the after-birth out and there it was. The doctor examined it and then showed me.

'This is what your baby has been growing and living in for the past nine months.' It was amazing that such a thing that looked like a lump of liver could sustain life for all that time and now it was being discarded without a second thought, but it was. She then proceeded to look at my vagina. It was a mess.

'Oooo, we are going to have to give you a few stitches.' She looked up at me. 'Do you remember when I told you to stop pushing?' I nodded. 'Well because your baby was coming out too fast, her shoulders came down cross-ways,' she indicated this with her hands, 'instead of sideways and of course, as this is the widest part of her body, you got split in the process.' It sounded nasty and painful, but, surprisingly, it was not hurting at all. With that she instructed the nurse to sew me up and then congratulated me and left. My mum was so relieved that it was all over and that both of us were well.

'Is the baby alright nurse?' she asked.

'Oh yes. She has been taken to SCBU, which is the Special Care

Shoy

Baby Unit, and once Shoy has managed to pass water, then she will be transferred to the ward and she can see her baby. She is apparently feeding well already.' The nurse continued to ready all the equipment that she was going to need for the sewing and then asked me to slide down to the bottom of the bed and place my feet in these stirrups (which of course were on either side of the bed) and just relax. Easy for her to say, she was not the one displaying her fanny to the world. Anyway, I did and she sewed, talking to me as she went. At this point, my mum left to make yet another phone call to try and find Denny, who had missed the whole thing, and also to let my dad know what I had had and that everything was all right. I was so tired that I fell asleep, as the nurse was sewing. Next thing I knew, this lovely West Indian lady came in to wash me.

'What baby have you had?' she asked.

'A little girl,' I replied. I knew her from seeing her around the town in which I lived. She was really nice to me.

'Be proud of what you have given life to and enjoy her. It is not a crime to have a child at sixteen.' She was definitely in the minority with that thought. From most people's reactions you would have thought that I had committed murder and was let off the crime.

Stranger in the Night

She then settled me in the bed. I could now feel a tingling sensation down below. I bet that was going to hurt at some point.

'Have I got to have the stitches removed? How many have I got?'

'You have seventeen stitches and, no, you don't have them removed. They dissolve themselves, you will be glad to hear, so as soon as you have healed, they will disappear.' Oh great, I thought, at least I won't have to go through that again. I lay back on the pillow wondering when I was going to get something to eat. Poor stomach must have thought that my throat had been cut. With that thought, in came another nurse with a tray and on it there was a sandwich and a cup of tea. Well, all I had was the cup of tea, as I did not eat sandwiches; they always made me sick. I could eat the filling separately and the bread separately, but together, that was disgusting. So I left the sandwich even though it looked delicious and just drank the tea, which tasted good. The nurse returned a few minutes later, took the tray away and then turned on the taps in the two sinks that were in the room. I looked at her puzzled.

'Okay Shoy, we need you to pass some urine before we can take you to your baby. The running water will help you.' She was holding a bedpan in her hand. 'Bum in the air for me, that's it,

Shoy

now think of Niagara Falls, and rain drops and listen to the running water; that will help you to go.' So I did. But there was nothing. She returned a little while later, my bum now numb from sitting too long on the bedpan. There was nothing, nothing at all.

'Can't I go to the toilet? I can't do anything on the bedpan, it's not normal'

'Okay, I will get another nurse to help me take you to the toilet. Wait there.' Back they came and off they took me, very slowly, to the toilet, but I still had to pass the urine in the bedpan. The only difference was, I was now sitting on it and not lying. Anyhow, it worked and they were happy and I was now in a wheelchair on my way to the ward to see my beautiful angel. I had my own room and on the other side of the door was a feeding room and beyond that was a room full of babies all wired up to various bits of machinery, wires everywhere and lots of ticks, tocks, blips and blippings going on. Some of these babies were very sick and so, so tiny. There she was, my angel. I could see her. She was in an incubator and there was a tube going down her nose. She had a tiny little hat on, little mittens and little booties and a nappy. On her chest there were tiny little pads, which monitored her breathing and her heart rate. She looked perfect to me, but she was so small. Suddenly I remembered that my mum would be on her way

Stranger in the Night

back to the labour ward and she would not know where I had been taken, but no sooner had I thought that, she appeared. Of course she would know. She worked here and she knew the whole hospital and nearly all the staff. Just about everyone who came into the labour room today she knew, and she would be talking to them. That's nice I supposed. She knew I was in good hands. The nurse in the other room beckoned for me to come in to the little feeding room. In I went.

'Hello, Shoy.' She was a big black lady, I had seen her around town, and I knew her son and her daughter, but could not think why at the time. I knew she did not like me. I could tell from the way she spoke to me, and I knew I did not like her, but I was not rude; after all, I was only sixteen. She gave me a look. 'Whenever you want come in and see your baby. By the way, what's her name?'

'I have not yet chosen one.'

'Well, don't you think you should get a move on?' I looked at her. Now there were a few words I could have told her at this point, but I remained quiet. What was the hurry? What was it to do with her? Cheeky fat bitch! 'Hmm' she continued 'you must put on this mask,' which she removed from a hook, 'and you must put

Shoy

on this apron,' which was blue and was stored in a box on a table by the door. 'When you come back into this room, you must take off the apron, throw it in the bin here and replace the mask on the hook, okay?' Seemed easy enough.

'Why must I wear the mask and the apron?' Well, from the look she gave me, you would have thought I had asked her a rude question.

'Because you don't want to breathe infection all over these babies. Some of them are very, very sick and you don't want to contaminate them in any way, including your baby.'

'Is she very sick as well?'

'No, she is just very tiny and very cold and we need to fatten her up and keep her very warm, but she will soon be with you in your room.' That was the first nice, warm thing she had said since I had entered the room. With that, I put on the necessary gear. I turned and waved to my mum who was looking through the spy window in the door.

'Who is that?' asked the nurse.

Stranger in the Night

'That's my mum.'

'Well if I was your mum, you would be on your own.' What did she mean by that? But I did not question her. I was too focused on getting to see my baby. I walked in. It was so hot in there. I leant over the incubator and just looked. The tears rolled down my face quietly, she was so small. She moved a little and then she waved her arms about.

'Can I touch her or hold her?' Another nurse came over and took her out.

'Only for a little while, then we have to put her back.' I sat down and she handed her to me. I was in awe of her. She was so light and she was perfect. I counted her fingers and her toes and just looked at her, stroking her tiny little forehead. She pinched up her tiny little nose and wriggled.

'Sorry Shoy, we have to put her back now. Don't want her to get cold now, do you?' I handed her back very carefully and went back to the feeding room, took off the blue plastic apron, threw it in the bin and replaced the mask on the hook. With that, in came Madam Miss Hitler to check if I had carried out her instructions. I returned to my room and told my mum what had just happened

Shoy

with my baby. Mum was so happy. She had also finally got through to Denny and he was on his way.

'I am going to go home now, Shoy, and come over later with Dad to see you. I might bring in the others, but I will have to find out if I can as you are over here. I don't know how many visitors you are allowed you get some rest now, okay?' With that, she kissed me on the forehead and I climbed into bed and went to sleep.

I awoke to find Denny standing at the bottom of my bed.

'How long have you been there?'

'Not long. Where is she then?' I pointed at the room.

'She's in there. I will call the nurse and ask her if you can see her.' I pressed the call button and in came a nurse.

'Is everything all right?'

'Yes. Is it okay for Denny to see his daughter?'

'Oh yes, of course.' She took him into the feeding room in which he put on the blue plastic apron and another mask and then he was taken through to the baby room where all the other babies were as well and he was shown her. I stood at the window in my room and just looked at him. He was so happy and he looked so proud that he was the father of such a beautiful thing.

'Baby Deshoy,' as she was called, was so small that she could not always feed properly and I would be left with full boobs. They looked great at last I had big boobs. Mine were never really that big, but these were to die for, but they were only there for one reason and that was to feed 'Baby Deshoy.' I hated breastfeeding. Whenever the nurses helped me latch the baby on, I would squirm. The feeling of the milk being drawn down the tubes and out of the end just made me feel sick and nauseous and I would wriggle on the bed. In fact, it was hurting deep down in my stomach. I told the nurse about this feeling and she said that it was normal. The pain that I was experiencing was the uterus contracting back to its normal size. *Well that made me feel a whole lot better.* (I don't think so, it just made me feel worse and every time she was feeding, I would be half way off the bed). I would insert my little finger into her mouth so as to release her suction and give me a reprieve when no one was looking. I really could not stand it. I would cry and I was really trying to be a good mother and give her the nourishment she needed to grow, but I just could not take it and it depressed me every time I knew she was coming close to feeding. One particular night my boobs were excruciatingly painful. I pressed the call bell and in came one of the night nurses.

'I can't sleep and my arms can't go down. I am in a lot of pain under my arm.' She came over and felt under my arms. I winced as she touched me.

'Oh yes, we will have to get you to express some of your milk. Obviously Baby Deshoy is not taking enough from you, or you are filling up too quickly I will be right back.' She disappeared and returned with this machine. 'Okay, sit yourself on the edge of the bed comfortably and I will show you how to use this. You can use this whenever you want, day or night, to express your milk and store it in labelled bottles for Baby Deshoy when she is ready to feed. That way you don't waste any of it.' She then placed this cup - like device over one boob and turned the machine on. Well, it sucked me in at quite a force, as if it had locked itself in place, and out came the milk and worked its way down the tube into a container. I began to laugh. 'It's like being milked like a cow.'

The nurse laughed.

'Yes most mothers say so. I have not yet experienced it. If you do not get on with this one, or this one is being used, there is also

Stranger in the Night

a hand pump that you can use which is just as effective, okay?' I nodded. 'Right, I will leave you now. Just press the bell when you feel your discomfort has gone completely as that means you have expressed all the excess milk. We will then do the other side.' She left. There was silence except for this milking machine, which was sucking and sucking. I smiled to myself. If only someone could see me now they would fall on the floor laughing. No, that was not such a good idea. I would not want to be seen in this state. Finally, my discomfort on both sides was relieved and I returned to bed and went to sleep. Baby Deshoy did not wake at all for any feeds that night. She was a very content baby.

During our stay in the SCBU, which amounted to nearly six weeks, (because we were not allowed out until baby Deshoy had reached five-and-a-half pounds), we had many visitors, loads of cards and well wishes and bunches of flowers, which my mum had to take home because no flowers were allowed in the unit. My moods went up and down just as much as the many visitors we had. Some days were worse than others, but generally I was not too bad. I was never really alone long enough to dwell too much on my unhappiness. My best friend Ingrid fell pregnant not too long after I did, but she was not having a good time of it. Her mother had thrown her out and she was living in a hostel, which sounded like a prison. She could not have visitors and she

Shoy

had to be out of the room by ten thirty in the morning and was not allowed back until after six in the evening and the doors were locked by ten thirty in the evening, so if you were not back in by then, you were out for the night. Her baby was due in December and she was huge and very uncomfortable. We would sit for hours during the day and we would chat, watch TV, eat, sleep, play board games or card games and she would watch me feed 'Baby Deshoy' and then she would leave and walk back to the hostel and then we would do it all again the next day. Because the nurses could see that she was pregnant and they knew her circumstances, they would feed and look after her as well; it was just that she did not have a bed. It made us both happy and we were strength to each other. She so wanted her baby to be born, just so she could move about more easily and not be so tired all the time. Her baby was going to be huge and she knew it. She had already been told that at her clinic appointments. Unlike me, Ingrid was attending her ante-natal classes and so she was well aware of what was going to happen and at what stages and she was receiving the proper care and attention that a pregnant person needed, which included the scans, the injections, the blood tests, urine tests, examinations, having weight checks and baby heart checks, all of which I missed, simply because I was stupid and scared and could have come to so much harm, not just harming myself, but my unborn child. Looking back now, I would never ever take that line again, but obviously my baby was meant to be and hence the reason she is here today.

It was now approaching five weeks since my baby was born and she was still being called 'Baby Deshoy.' The nurses were always on at me to give her a proper name, but Denny and I could not decide and it was getting desperate as I was going to have to register her real soon and you could not put on the birth certificate 'baby Deshoy.' Faye, who was another friend of mine, brought in a baby name book and it was decided that by the end of that day we would have a name for this child. So between us, that is Denny, Faye and myself and then being joined by my mum, we came up with a short list comprising, firstly, Chenille, Channel, and Mercedes. Well I knew which one I preferred, and as I had the last say of course I chose Mercedes. So there we had it. She was named 'Mercedes Dasilva.' But then came the decisions of second names. Well, I left that to Denny and my mum as they had brought the subject up. It was bad enough finding the first name. The second names were quite easy. Denny chose Monika for the second name and my mum chose Judy for her third, as she always liked Judy Jane for some reason. Finally, we presented to the nurses Mercedes Monika Judy Deshoy. The poor thing did not have a clue what had taken place. I could now register her and make her legal.

Shoy

The day came to leave the hospital and all the good nurses from the Unit. They were excellent and had really prepared me for what was ahead. Whilst under their care, there was none of this, 'you get some sleep and we will look after baby'; oh no, it was all up to me. They were primarily there to make sure that things were coming along in the right direction and that both of us were receiving the care and attention that we needed.

My mum had bought this tiny little wool dress with a drawstring waste. She could not buy regular baby clothes, as Mercedes was so small. Her nappies were 'terry nappies' cut into four squares, one square would be used at a time, and my mum found the smallest plastic pants that would fit over the top. Even these were still too big, but they were better than nothing. There was a store in our town that sold a doll called 'Tiny Tears' and they sold the clothes separately for this doll and the clothes were a perfect fit for her and so her wardrobe was made up of outfits that were made for this doll and the dress that I was going to bring her out of hospital with was one of these such dresses. Actually the sleeve was short on the doll, but on Mercedes, it was long and the dress was well below her feet, but that was fine because it was a cold day and I wanted to keep her warm. She had a pair of 'Tiny Tears' tights on with an all-in-one vest, which did up underneath by poppers, mittens, booties and a little hat, which tied under her neck. Even her pink little jacket with white collar was from the 'Tiny Tears' range. She looked so sweet. Denny left work early that day and picked us up from the hospital. I sat in the back of the car and Mercedes was handed to me by one of the nurses and I cuddled her gently in my arms, all wrapped up in a blanket, and took her to her new home, my parents' house. I took her straight upstairs, took off some of the layers that she had on and placed her in her cot. This was the first time I was seeing the cot, which had been re-painted in pink and cream and had matching quilt with side buffers all around it and a little pillow with matching pillowcase. The room smelt baby-like. I laid her on the bed. Stephanie was sat on the bed just watching.

'Can I hold her?'

'Yes of course you can; come on, sit up here.' I gave her Mercedes to hold. She was so gentle with her. Mercedes started to wriggle and make funny noises. Stephanie's face was a picture.

'Oooo shoosh baby, don't cry.' By this time the others had arrived and they all wanted to hold her and they did, of course arguing who was going first. I quietly told them to be quiet and that I would decide who would hold her when. She was not something they could take possession over, she was mine and I was the only one who could give them permission to do anything with her. They did not want to leave the room, but eventually I took Mercedes away from them, placed her in her cot, and left her to sleep as mum was calling us for our dinner. As I sat around the table, I kept listening for her cry, but she was as good as gold. Not a word. The conversation around the table centred on Mercedes. Even my dad joined in. It was a happy day.

I awoke the next morning, having not had a good night at all. Mercedes had been up most of the night for some reason and I was tired. I left her upstairs with Stephanie after having fed her for the umpteenth time and changing her. I was now just expressing my milk. My mum had bought me my own breast pump as I really could not stand breast-feeding and she felt it really important for Mercedes to get at least three months' worth of breast milk. I stood in the kitchen, just staring out the window at the fence opposite and started to cry. My mum came in, always around at the most in-opportune moments.

'What you crying for?' I shrugged my shoulders, and the question just made my tears worse. 'Look, you have a baby up there and you crying and not eating is not going to help her. You need to pull yourself together and keep up your strength. She will notice if you are tense or upset and this in turn will make her unsettled.' There was no concern; she did not even try to get out of me what was wrong. It was just straight in with what she thought and her solution to the *problem*. I drank my tea amid tears and returned upstairs to Mercedes who was now out of the cot and happily snuggled up in bed with Stephanie. She loved her so much and she was so good and gentle, but she would always get her out of the cot, which I did not like too much as she was not quite big enough to do it without a struggle and I was always frightened that she would drop her. But she never did.

FOOTSTEPS OF FRIENDSHIP

After having Mercedes, the weather was cold and horrid and we were not getting out much, but I would still take her shopping once in a while and, of course, over to the hospital for her check-ups. Whenever I took her out, I would have a hot water bottle wrapped up in a nappy at the bottom of the carrycot to keep her warm and her bottle of milk would be propped up against it, keeping it warm for her. I never liked giving her cold milk, especially as I hated the stuff. She never had the chance to get cold.

Mercedes' first Christmas came and there were loads and loads of presents for her under the tree. She was now just over three months old, and she was still small, but very alert and beautiful with loads of black curly hair and smiles that would melt your heart. My seventeenth birthday came and went with no celebration. 'After all you have a baby now and you can't expect to get anything any more' one of the statements of my loving mother, who had now taken over the care and attention of my child completely, to the point where I was not sure that I was even her mother. This annoyed me on occasions. She would bath her, change her, feed her, wind her, cuddle her, and hold her even whilst she was sleeping. She would not even let me do these things; she would always have something else for me to do and she would be sat down with *my baby* as if she were hers. Denny would visit less and less now. My dad really did not like him and there was always an air of tension whenever he came over, so he stayed away more and more, but we were still speaking regularly on the phone.

Soon after my birthday, I returned to my school to join the sixth form. It was very unusual to rejoin the school you were at when you became pregnant, but I was very lucky and I did, especially as the father did not go to the school, so I had all my friends around me. I had been given strict instructions from the headmistress (the headmaster did not get involved), that under no circumstances was I to get into any explicit conversations to do with getting pregnant

Shoy

with anyone in the school as they would be very interested and the school felt that this would not be appropriate. If this ever happened, then I would be transferred to another school. So I obeyed. But they were right; I was asked so many times:

'What was it like?'

'Where did it happen?'

'How did I do it?'

'Did I like it?' It went on and on, but finally the questions subsided and I was left alone. I was yesterday's news at last and I was fat.

Summer finally came and every opportunity I had I would take Mercedes out shopping. We were always shopping as she always needed so much, but I was so proud to be out with her, until I met someone who would scorn me for having a baby at my age and putting my mother through such anguish; but still they would look at her and goo-goo-gah-gah over her.

It was on one of these shopping days, along with my mum (which was more times than not) that a girl came up to me outside the

Woolworth's store in our town.

'Are you Denny's girlfriend?' I looked at her, having never seen her before, and replied,

'Yes.'

'Can I see your baby?'

'Yes of course.' I looked at her as she looked at my Mercedes. 'What's your name?'

She looked up at me, smiled and said,

'Yvette.' So how did she know whom I was and that I had had a baby for Denny? The thought went out of my head and we started chatting about Mercedes and babies in general. It turned out that she was Denny's younger brother's girlfriend so we had something in common. Yvette was a bit shorter than me, so not very tall by all accounts. Her hair was straightened and every last strand of hair was set in place precisely. She was very pretty and when she smiled, she revealed a gap in-between her incisors. As it was a chilly day, she was dressed in a nice black, warm coat and gloves, but the sun was shining.

Shoy

At this time in my life, a lot of girls wanted to be with Denny. Apparently he was quite a catch and a lot of people, (should I say a lot of girls) wanted him and wondered why he was with me, considering that they had not even heard about me until the announcement of the baby. In particular, there were two, their names would be bandied about, and my mind would work overtime wondering who they were and what they were to him. Their names were Joan Daniel and Mary Paine.

Time went by and somehow Yvette and I became good friends and we began to spend a lot more time with each other. She would come over and visit me at home and I would visit her at hers. We would go shopping together and her friends became my friends and vice versa. Occasionally when I visited Mercedes' grandparents, she would be there as she was with Denny's brother. She was someone I could relate to. It just goes to show that you do not have to grow up with someone to become a pal. She was younger than me, only by four years though, but you would never have known it. Somehow she became very close to my older brother and they started going out with each other, so now she was at our house even more. We really thought that she and my brother Wayne were going to get married at some point; they were really in love with each other. Everyone in the family liked her, she was

Footsteps of Friendship

good fun to be with and we had been raised more or less the same way with parental restrictions on our life (which we never agreed with), but nevertheless they were there (for our own good!!).

A memorable occasion comes to mind and it took place one particular weekend. There was a 'dance', as it was called, arranged to take place in Birmingham somewhere and I so wanted to go. I had asked my parents and, of course, they said no. They did not even think about it, it was just a blunt no. A 'NO' whereby you should have known where you stood. But I was determined to go whatever the cost. I had to find a way because I had already bought my ticket and there was no way I was going to lose my money. As the time got closer to the weekend of the Birmingham event, Yvette, Stephanie and I planned what we were going to do to get me on this trip. We had arranged earlier in the month that I would leave the clothes that I wanted to wear to Birmingham at Yvette's house and then we would arrange to go out on the Saturday night when the event was taking place. For some reason, my parents did not mind if I was out with Yvette and Stephanie, because they saw Yvette as responsible and they liked her, so they encouraged me to see as much of her as I wanted. Lucky for me! Of course, nothing of the sort would take place, we would end up in Birmingham, and no one would know of our cunning plan. It was a plan made in heaven. I then went back to my parents and asked them if I

Shoy

could go out with Yvette and Stephanie to a party which was taking place at Stephanie's relative's house which was local, so this would mean that we would be back home about two o'clock in the morning at the latest. They did not seem to mind this and said yes. Fantastic. I was going to Birmingham. The weekend came, I got dressed up in some outfit at home earlier in the day and left home, kissing Mercedes and Stephanie goodnight and bidding my Mum and Dad goodbye and 'thank you' for letting me go and leaving them looking after Mercedes. I left. I was on my way to Yvette's house. I went down to the bus stop, caught the bus to her house and knocked on her door. Stephanie was already there; she had had to do a similar masquerade, but not half as elaborate as mine. She just had to get out of the house tonight. I had had to plan weeks in advance. I went in, said hello to her parents and then went straight up to Yvette's bedroom. It was some time before we were due to leave, so we just sat around in her room and listened to music and chatted about our plans and how Stephanie had got out of the house. She had actually climbed out of the window as her dad had locked the front door, but for some reason they would never check her bedroom to make sure that she was in. She had arranged with one of her brothers that when she came back she would throw stones up at his window and he would open her window and she would climb in.

As we listened and sung to our favourite songs, we started to get dressed in our outfits. Yvette had this gillet that was made from fox fur (in those days animal furs were accepted) and the fur would get everywhere. It would get up your nose, in your eyes, down your throat and we hated it, so we would not get too close to her and this animal thing, but nonetheless, she wore it. We looked good and we knew it. We set off to get the bus back into town and walked to where the coach was picking us up. I had never been to Birmingham and I was excited. The thought of danger did not even enter my head. What if the coach had an accident? Or, what if I was kidnapped? Even the thought of being found out, because after all it was a trip from our home town and anyone who knew my parents could have been going, and what if they then told them that I was there and with whom? Hey, it was too late to worry now. My bum was on the seat and the coach was moving. Moving on its way to Birmingham. There was laughing, singing, arguing, card playing, smoking and lots going on. Yvette and I just sat quietly in the middle somewhere. We knew a few people, but nearly everyone was quite a bit older than us. Stephanie knew quite a few people and so she went off and was chatting and laughing away and left us most of the time. We always stuck together, Yvette and I. It suddenly struck me that I did not even know what time we were getting back from Birmingham. I asked Yvette, but she did not know either. See, if we were really, really clever we

Shoy

would have arranged for me to stay at her house the night, but we had not thought. The journey to Birmingham seemed to go on forever, but at long last we arrived in Birmingham. I sat looking out of the window and I was sure that I had seen some of the buildings before, but what did I know? It then became apparent that the driver was lost when someone shouted out:

'DRIVER, me see dis building before, about tree times before, is wah you a do?' The driver very sheepishly admitted that he was lost and stopped the coach and shouted down a passing, local male pedestrian who jumped on the coach, smoke bellowing from his nose.

'You aright brudda?' He raised his hands to the whole coach not getting the expected response! He turned back to the driver and patted him on the back, saying, 'Seen,' meaning 'you understand' and started to give directions to the hall. So here we were, getting instructions from some local man because we were lost, and then the bugger tells the driver to stop, bids his farewell in some choice words and leaves the coach and disappears down some road, and of course leaves us even more stranded than before. The uproar from the coach was not good and the driver was now under more pressure. Eventually, after some manoeuvring, we made it to the hall.

Wayne was part of a sound. Now a sound was a group of friends, usually, that had speakers, tweeters, yards, and yards of wiring and plugs and loads and loads of records, both old and up-to-date, in wooden boxes, and then moved around in vans, up and down the country, wherever they got a gig. They would lug all these huge speakers and tweeters and wiring and plugs and records up flights of stairs or down to basements, setting it all up, testing it and then playing their music to the crowds, making them jump and dance, scream and shout into the early hours of the morning. Now, my brothers' sound was called 'Country'. 'Country' because they came from what was considered the countryside and not the big towns like London, Birmingham, Manchester, places like that. In our eyes, they were the best. They had a good following and wherever they performed, there would be a home crowd that would turn up, especially to cheer them on. Sometimes there would be competitions between other sounds all set up in the same hall and battling for various titles such as the best "Toaster." (Now a "Toaster" is someone who rapped in effect, to the sound of any record, making the words up as he went along, but making it flow and be very pertinent to events of that day or week, so people could relate to it and this would make the crowds cheer even more; the lyrics could not be stale, they had to be brand new each time). They also fought for titles of best-sounding sound.

Shoy

This would sometimes mean the speakers of certain sounds being blown because the speakers were not good enough and could not be pushed to the top without a fatal error occurring. This would put a sound system out of action until it was repaired, usually on the spot. Also they would have the newest track out, a track that no one else had. Sometimes this was so, but on occasions one of the other sounds would have it and so that would be shelved.

We entered into the hall, Country was up, and playing; nothing too over-powering as the hairstyle competition was still going on. There were some real funky styles and of course the ones that won were from Birmingham. Everyone booed in the hall. 'Fix,' they were shouting. Hair stylists had come from far and wide to enter this competition, even from our hometown. They had put in so much effort just to be beaten by the home team. Needless to say, a lot of them would not be entering into this competition again in Birmingham. The competition came to an end, with the trophies having been given out and everything was cleared away. The hall lights were then turned off and the real music began. Country was in full swing. They were finding it hard at first to get the 'home side' motivated into dancing and letting loose, but they could not resist the music, along with the toasting that 'Conks' was so good at, and they were cheering and bowing and jumping, they were loving it. Conks, was the sound's best toaster. It came so natural to him and any challenge that was put to him he would rise to and usually come out on top. He was well respected, both by the others in the sounds system and amongst other toasters that he came across. I never found out why he was called Conks, but no doubt it was something to do with the nut. It was a great night, but all through the night Wayne kept teasing and reminding me that I had to go home.

'Hmm does madda and faada know you deh heh?'

I sucked my teeth at him. 'Of course they do, do you think I would be here otherwise?' Some smart aleck remark that was. I wished he would just shut up and let me have a good time for a change. The point was always in the back of my mind, but I was here now and I could not just leave when I wanted to; I had to wait for the coach. A few guys asked Yvette and me to dance, but Yvette would not dance with anyone. She only had eyes for Wayne and no one could get a look in, so I danced with them and she just stood near the sound waiting for my brother to dance with her. She waited for ages, but she finally got her dance and that made her night. The whole evening was just brilliant. I had had a ball, but it was now time to get back on the coach and make the long journey home.

Shoy

We arrived back to where the coach had picked us up. It was now daylight. It was about five in the morning. We were all tired. Most of us had been asleep on the coach all the way home, but now we had to get off and walk home. Some people had cars, but at that time in the morning there were no buses and most people had a long walk. Yvette and Stephanie had quite a walk. Mine was not too far, but I would be all alone. We said our goodbyes and went our separate ways. I looked at my watch. *Well it is almost five-thirty, and Dad should have already left for work as he starts at six and Mum is such a hard sleeper that I will creep back in and she will not know what time I arrived home.* I felt reassured with my thoughts, but I still had a panicky feeling. It would be all right once I was in bed and no one knew. I kept walking. I came to the hill that we usually walked up to go home. There was also the straight road, which was another route, but basically you would just end up walking along a flat road instead of the steep hill and then go up another shorter hill. Either way I would get home. I stood there for a second, looking at both routes. I chose the former, our usual route, simply because I knew it was slightly shorter and I so wanted to go to sleep.

So here I was walking up the hill, dog-tired, humming tunes in my head. I turned the corner at the top and - *'oh my god'* - it was my Dad coming along our road on his bike. In those days there were one or two cars parked along the road, not like now - a bumper-to-bumper row of colour and styles. If that were the case I could have ducked down behind one of them and hid until my Dad rode past, but 'no', there was nothing. I was so shocked that I did not even think to duck into someone's garden, I just kept on walking right towards my Dad. *'Oh my god, I am going to get the beating of my life and it will probably take place here, in the middle of the road. It will wake up the neighbourhood, and they will look on and not even come to my rescue. No one ever gets involved in anything. I can see that gravestone all shiny and engraved.'* So what was he going to do? He was now riding past me. He did not seem to recognise me, but of course I smiled the broadest smile ever and said,

'Hello Dad!' I swallowed hard. The bike came to a screeching halt and he almost fell off as he turned to look, double take. He knew it was me all along but I was in the wrong place, out of place, and so he was not convinced at first and maybe, just maybe, if I had not said anything to him, he would not have noticed me.

'Shy?' as he would call me, never Shoy. 'Is wah you doing out here dis time a maarning?'

I halted and began to walk backwards. 'I am just coming back

Shoy

from my night out with Yvette and Stephanie.' Okay, so was he going to accept this and just tell me to go home and get to bed? Huh? Hell no. At the top of his voice came those familiar words of,

'Get your arse home right now.'

Well, yeah, that's where I was going, had he not noticed that before? This was not the time for my mind to be having clever wordy conversations of its own; I would start laughing and that would really piss him off big time. He would undoubtedly give me something to laugh about and my face would know what it was. I turned and, almost running, made for the house. I kept looking back to see what exactly he was doing. He just stood there next to his bike, watching me in disbelief. I thought I was in the clear, but then he got on his bike, turned it around and started back to the house as well. *Oh my god.* I ran around the back of the house and got in through the door that was always left unlocked (by us) when we wanted to creep in, closed it behind me and made for the stairs. By this time my dad was at the front door, key in the lock, door now flung open, hitting the wall.

'MATILDA?' he hollered, with the front door still wide open. I froze at the stairs. So now my mum was going to get in on the act along with all the others. Bleary eyed and, wrapping the belt of the well-overdue-for-renewal dressing gown around her, appeared my mum.

'What the hell is wrong, Marcus? Close in the door.' I was standing there clinging to the wooden poles of the staircase, wondering what was going to happen next. My mum came down, looked at me, sucked her teeth and said.

'Goan to bed.'

My dad was still ranting and raving, standing sideways on, pointing, blasting, accusing me of sleeping with some man which is why I was out so late and which man was it and where was he.

'Marcus, you go be late for work, just shut up the noise and get out the howse.' She turned and came back up the stairs and my dad left. I fell in to bed and was gone.

I awoke some time past mid-day. The house was quiet and Mercedes was up along with my sister. I looked around the room. The memory of that morning came flooding back all too quickly. What was I going to face? My Dad was not home yet, but my Mum was and she was sure to have a lot to say. I sneaked out of my room and tiptoed down the stairs so as not to be heard. I wanted to be washed and dressed first to face the onslaught.

Whilst in the bathroom, which was past the kitchen, I heard someone come in the kitchen. I held my breath and listened at the door. I was sure it was my Mum. It was too quiet out there to be anyone else. Why was she there so long? I could hear the pot lids opening and closing. Then there was her singing. She started to sing. Was that a good sign? When my Mum sung, it always had two meanings. Sometimes she would sing when she was happy and other times, she would sing to forget what was going on around her. So which one was it? I had to leave the bathroom, besides it was cold in here. I slowly unlocked the door and opened it.

'Morning Mum.' I searched for some sort of clue as to what was coming next.

'Morning.' Came her reply. It was just like normal. I decided not to hang around. I closed the bathroom door behind me and left the kitchen. Up in my bedroom I started to wonder what was going on? Why was she not mad at me? I know, she was going to let me suffer, or even worse, she was going to wait until my Dad got home. Now that would be mean, but it was expected. The whole day, I was walking about on eggshells. I did not like this. If they

Footsteps of Friendship

she was going to punish me, I wanted it over and done with.

It was early evening and as I sat in the living room with Mercedes on my lap, I heard the back gate open and through the window my Dad appeared with his bike. My heart missed a beat. I thought it best if I was not sat cosily in the living room when he came in. So I sat Mercedes on the chair and quietly disappeared up stairs and awaited my fate. I could hear voices in the kitchen, but could not make out what was being said, but there was a hive of vocal interest. It then went quiet and the dining room door opened, then the door to the cupboard under the stairs. It was definitely my dad. He would be hanging his jacket up and taking his shoes off. The door then closed and he went into the living room. I could hear him talking to the others. He sounded normal. Not angry at all. Dare I go downstairs? I could not bring myself to even think too much about it. I stayed where I was, perched on the edge of the bed. I so wanted this moment to be over. I wanted to be punished now, but I think their new tactic was working better; this was punishment of the worst kind. Just not knowing.

The living room door opened and I could hear the bone cracking footsteps of my dad coming up the stairs towards my room that was at the top of the stairs. He walked past my room and on to his own bedroom. What was going on? He must know that I was in my room and that surely I would not be asleep at this time of day. Maybe he was going to wait until we were all sat around the dining room table to start on me. To make an example of me to the others. My mum was now calling us for dinner. Well the moment of truth was fast approaching. I walked down stairs and into the dining room and sat in my place. In came my dad.

'Hello Dad.' I waited for a reply.

'Hello.' Then there was nothing else. I nervously ate my dinner. Watching and waiting, but it was all so normal. Mum was chatting as usual and so was Dad and the others, except for me. I was too wrapped up in my guilty thoughts. Dinner over we left the table as usual and Lewis and I washed up. Our conversation centred on the night before.

To this day, I still could not understand why it was nothing was said or why I was not punished, but believe me, the silence of it all was punishment enough.

Now I can see back then how parents turned you in to liars. You knew if you gave them the truth you would be denied everything and the arguments would not be worth the asking, so you had to invent a story or two just to get a life and on another such occasion a lie would be cooked up.

Yvette, Stephanie and I of course wanted to go to a nightclub in London. I was now eighteen and the other two were just about sixteen, but they always looked older than me, so I was going to have the problem, as always. I got permission from my parents (of course to go out elsewhere) and went through the same routine of leaving clothes at Yvette's earlier in the week and then changing there. We arranged for Wayne to pick us up as he had offered to take us. We were on our way. None of us had ever gone to a nightclub and we were all excited, because this was one of the top nightclubs in Edmonton, London. It was called Palm Trees. We arrived outside the club and decided that we would all go in separately as I would be bound to get them stopped and then they would want ID from all of us. I would of course get in, they would not, and that would be the whole night over. So my brother took Yvette in on his arm, Stephanie linked arms with some bloke that was standing nearby and I just stood near a group of other guys pretending to be with them. Of course all the others got in and I was stopped. The bouncers made a beeline for me wanting ID. I had my birth certificate on me and it showed that I was eighteen. Lucky, so I was in. They could not believe that I was stopped, but they knew it would happen somehow and lucky for them we had the second plan and it worked. We were always good at scheming. Wayne went to the bar to get us some drinks and we just stood there. We could not believe that we were in Palm Trees with grown-ups. Wayne returned with drinks in hand and we disappeared to look around. There were three floors to this club and it played different types of music on each floor. The best floor was at the top where they were playing raga, reggae, soul, studio one, calypso, in fact, all the sounds that we loved. So this was our floor. At some point in the evening, I found myself thinking of the elaborate lie that I had made up in order to escape and be out with friends. I had told my parents that my workplace was having a Christmas do, it was being held in London, and that I could invite a few friends along, hence Yvette and Stephanie coming along. It was not far from the truth as my workplace was having a do, but it was being held that day and there was no evening night out with nightclub jaunt involved. Throwing in the works 'do' being in London meant that, if we were back late, I would not be in trouble like the last time and also if anything went wrong, according to my story we were supposed to be in London, so all eventualities were covered this time. Perfect. I stood there smiling to myself. You see, each time you lied and certain things went wrong, you made sure that they were not going to happen next time and that a better plan would be in place to make sure of it. Simple really.

We had agreed on a story, so if the occasion ever arose, we would all be reading from the same song sheet. Can't forget that angle as well, because my mum was always one for asking loads of questions and then a few weeks later she might go back to it and ask something else that may have just 'popped' into her mind, as things did.

We returned home that night and everything went smoothly. You would think with all this scheming we would never have any time to relax and have a good time, but our philosophy was, *'once out, enjoy to the max and face the music later.'* My brother dropped me off at the top of the road and I walked the rest of the way. He then took the others home and he came home afterwards. Of course, we could not arrive in at the same time now, could we?

As time went by, various conversations were had about different events that I may or may not have been to between the three of us. Sometimes we were in the dining room around the table having a laugh with Mercedes in and out. She was still tiny, but so beautiful. Other times we were in my bedroom that I now shared with Stephanie and all her clutter and Mercedes and all her mounting kid's stuff. Most of the time we could not have a private conversation because there was always someone around: either my mum or Stephanie. So you can imagine, we would be in full swing of conversation, having a laugh about guys we refused dances to and all sorts of things that we got up to and in would walk my mum, take a seat and want to join in the conversation. So we would now improvise. On such an occasion, Stephanie almost let the truth slip about our night out to Palm Trees. It was so close. She had blurted out, 'Remember when we went to Palm Trees?'

Yvette and I just gazed at her, trying to think between the both of us as if linked by telepathy what to say next. What the hell was she thinking about? She knew from the looks on our faces that she had messed up and quickly back-peddled saying, 'Oh no, that was not with you two, that was with my cousin.' We laughed and asked what went on. Well it was a talking point after all and we could have a laugh, as long as she did not say 'do you remember?' Or 'you know that guy?' Or what we were wearing even when she was supposed to have gone out with her cousins. It was too close for comfort and we changed the subject all together. Phew, that was close.

Living at home was no fun at all. I was still the child, even though I had a child of my own. I so wanted to leave home, but I could not afford it. I was working as an audio typist in a typing pool, typing up TV and video rental agreements for customers, earning four thousand pounds a year. It was my first job and I loved it. It gave me an air of independence. I started there as a 'temp' and, within five weeks; they offered me a permanent contract. I was delighted and so proud of myself. I was earning my own money, for me to do exactly what I wanted with it. The thing was, no sooner had I got the job permanently, than my mother made me take out a savings policy which I had to save FIFTY pounds a month in and to and to top it all, I could not touch it for five years. Five whole years, you know, that was an eternity and FIFTY pounds. She was so mean. And if that were not enough, I also had to pay for a third of the bills that came in (i.e., the bills were split three ways between me, Wayne and my parents). We thought this was unfair. We could not argue this point, but even though we paid for a third of the bills, we still could not use anything as we wanted. Arguments with my parents would be plentiful about so-called 'wasting' electricity and 'wasting' the phone bill and 'wasting' water. It would go on and on, month in, month out. So, the two of us came up with another plan, to hopefully halt all the verbal activity that went on. The plan was that Wayne would pay the electricity bill, however much that came to. He felt this would be fairer because he was always practising on his system for up-coming gigs and so used a lot of 'electricity'. I on the other hand, would pay for the telephone bill, because as I spent most of my time actually in the house when not working, I was always on the phone. We put this 'well thought-out' plan to our parents and, much to our amazement, they agreed. It was sorted and it worked

Shoy

well for a time, and then my dad started to bellyache about me using the phone so much. So what was his problem? I was paying for it, wasn't I? But somehow my dad could not understand the concept of *'if the phone rang the other person was paying the* bill' and this was frequently the case; after all, I was not totally stupid. I did not want all my money going out on the telephone bill. But still he belly-ached and the belly-aching got worse, and then it involved my mum and her belly-aches were always worse still and she just burst a blood vessel and that was it, back to square one. But we did not stop paying for the 'bills', oh no. We still had to pay and so of course things got worse, because now we were being out-done and that just would not do.

One night, when I was on the phone in the front living room, my dad burst in, scaring the shit out of me, and pulled the curtain open so hard that the whole lot just fell off the rails and landed in a heap on the floor. Well I laughed; it was like a comedy sketch. He had broken the wooden ball off the end of the rail and with all the commotion, that is, his shouting, my mum came in to see her curtains all over the floor and my dad standing there mouthing off at me. I was still holding the phone, trying to stifle the noise so Denny could not hear what was going on, it was so embarrassing. She went ballistic at him which then sparked off an argument (again). So what was new in our house? I just wanted them to take the shouting out of the living room so that I could continue my conversation in peace and quiet. The phone was still stifled against my chest and there it stayed until they finally left. I lifted the phone to my ear.

'Hi Denny, you still there?'

'Yes, what was going on there? I could hear everything. Has your dad flipped or something?' I embarrassingly laughed it off.

'Look, I will call you tomorrow when things are quiet. It's best that I go now. Anyway, I have to go and put the curtain back up on the rail. I will speak to you tomorrow.' With that we hung up and I left the room to join the two of them, arguing in the back living room. Now you would think that by then I would have learnt that, when parents are having a heated argument, especially when it involved something you did, you should leave them to it, but oh no, Shoy could never do that. Her mouth was too big for that. She would jump in at any point, and make yet another statement of the year.

'If I am paying the bill, then I am going to use the phone as I want, otherwise I am not paying for it.' Well, that was brave. And now I was well and truly up to my neck in the 'heated' discussion and

Shoy

there was no way out.

'So you tink you is woman now eh?' *Well yes I was; after all, I had given birth and I was nearly eighteen; only a few weeks to go.'* I was now silent. There was no way I was saying that. In our house, if we were not arguing, then something was wrong. We were always arguing about the phone, the heating, the water, the lights, friends visiting, noise, mess, food, cooking, the wretched milk bottles, washing-up – actually just about anything. It made you feel worthless. No matter what you did or how well you did it, it was never right and you were reprimanded for it.

Things were now deteriorating between Denny and I. He was not able to see Mercedes and me as much as he wanted and he was not pleased with the situation. A situation we could not put right. I began to hear rumours that he was being seen about town with other girls. My mind would make up all sorts and it would upset me no end. It was getting harder to find him to talk to him. Whenever I called, he was never in and he would not call me back. He now started just to just drop the money in through the front door in an envelope with my name on it, instead of knocking like he used to. What was going on? Did he not love me anymore? Or had he just had enough of what my parents were doing to us? I had no answers and things began to look bleak, very bleak indeed, but

Footsteps of Friendship

I tried not to dwell on it until I got the chance to speak to him. I was so in love with him and I wanted to be his wife, but he would never talk to me about it and would always avoid the subject.

Like the tick tocks of a clock, things ticked on, but at least they were ticking even though not tocking as well. I always wanted to be a dancer and there was a programme on at the time called FAME. It was all about up-and-coming kids in a school in America looking for that 'fame' with their artistic talents. I would never miss this programme. It was always on a Thursday evening and no one would call me during this time, as I would never go to the phone, but one night I broke that rule. The phone rang and it was Denny. I had to speak to him, as it was rare for him to be calling, so I could not miss this call. I was not pleased. He should have known better. As I walked to the front living room, I mumbled all sorts to myself.

'How could he phone me now? It's the last episode of Fame and he calls me now.' I picked up the receiver. 'Hi, how come you're calling me, when you know Fame is on and I always watch it?' There was no real answer to that. I knew something was wrong.

'All right?' came his voice. Well, yeah, I thought. He never started a conversation with *'all right'* so where was this coming

Shoy

from? I sat down and breathed in. This was going to be a long one, I thought.

He started,

'I have been thinking........... Things are not working between us. I do not see you enough and when I am going out with my friends, you are never there. You are always with your mum and never with me. Your parents don't even like me. How are we to build a future together when I don't even see you? My friends think we're a joke. Half of them have not even met you or even seen my child. I am sorry but we're finished. It's over.'

I did not say a word. The tears rolled down my face and the phone went dead. He did not even wait for me to reply to what he had just said. I was still sat there with the receiver to my ear when my mum shouted, 'Shoy?'

It made me jump. I replaced the receiver and tried to wipe away the tears. 'Yes,' I shouted back.

'FAME has started. Are you not coming to watch it?'

'No, I don't want to see it anymore. That's for children.' It was the very last episode and I was going to miss it. It was such a happy programme and I was not in the mood for happy. A thousand thoughts went through my head. I went to the back living room and picked Mercedes up off the floor where she sat with an array of toys around her and took her up to our bedroom. I lay on the bed with her and just hugged her tightly, crying into her shoulders. In her tiny little girly voice, she asked me, 'Why you crying Shoy?' She always called me Shoy. It was what she heard everyone else calling me so it stood to reason, but it only mattered that night when she said it. I wanted her to call me 'Mum'. Just 'Mum,' just once, but it was never going to happen. My mum was Mum and that was all she knew. So even my own daughter was not mine. What good was I to anyone? I was still on my own. I was now alone with an almost-two-year-old child, no father to look after my child and no boyfriend to look after me, cheer me up, and give me an excuse to live for love.

My mum finally came upstairs to see why I was not interested in Fame. I was still crying. I told her what Denny had said on the phone. Her reply was, 'Well it's for the best. Obviously he did not care enough for you, otherwise he would have told you to your face.'

I glared at her, I was now very angry.

'How was he to tell me to my face, when you and dad would not even let him come to the house as he wanted? His seeing his child is just short of making an appointment at the doctor and being told, 'No appointments today, call back tomorrow and see.' I am not surprised he left me. It's all your fault and you have to live with it now'. She left my room. I continued crying. Soon after she left Stephanie came upstairs. What did she want? There was no privacy in that house. There was never anywhere to escape to. There was always someone somewhere. Apparently she came upstairs to be with me just in case I did something stupid. I wondered what would be classed as stupid? After all, I had been stupid all my life and I was too stupid to see it.

That night, I thought of some of the good times we had had, the times I could remember that he made me laugh. I remembered one occasion when we were in his lockup garage near his house and he had driven the car in. He switched off the engine and asked me to close the garage door. I got to the door and I slammed it, and when I say slammed, it was slammed. He jumped out of the car. 'Not that hard!'

I held my mouth. 'Why? What happens if I slam it?'

'Never mind. Get in.' The whole time we were amorous, I kept thinking about the door. When it came to taking me back home, he then revealed to me that, when I slammed it shut, I actually locked the door. Oh shit. We were stuck. How were we going to get out? And how was I going to get home before my parents got back in the morning? This had all gone horribly wrong. He was trying everything to open the door. He was so calm, but I was, - well - words would not describe what I was going through. Finally, he managed to get the door open and take me home. Needless to say, I never slammed the door again.

The next day I called Yvonne and cried to her down the phone relaying the events of the evening. She was very sorry for me and said that she would come to see me later on in the week.

Now Yvonne and I, we were never quite sure about each other when we were at school. She was always the posh black kid who had moved to the area. Her family had loads and loads of money and she would have everything she wanted. There was only her and her sister and they were so lucky. She could choose whoever she wanted to speak to. Everyone wanted to be Yvonne's friend. Once I went to her house after school, can't remember why, but there were all these pictures of her and her sister in different places. In one of the photos, she was holding a baton and dressed up

Shoy

as a soldier in red and white. She was also a brilliant gymnast and could do the splits and back flips and summersaults and all sorts and she had trophies around her room that she had won. She even had her own bedroom. She had been to lots of nice places too and she had so many dolls, which were displayed nicely around her bedroom and all over her bed. It was so 'fairy-taley' but I liked her and I wanted to be with her. She and her sister were always having parties. Most of them fancy dress. I could never go, because I would never have anything to dress up in and furthermore, my parents never let me go to parties for some reason. So even then, they were technically choosing my friends, but against all the odds, Yvonne and I became friends, good friends.

NO ENTIDENO EL ESPAÑOL
(I DON'T UNDERSTAND SPANISH)

At last I was eighteen, but still not an adult in the eyes of my parents. I had my own child who was almost two and I was still the child, even more so. I was still working, just as hard as ever, and still single. Denny was no longer in my life, but he was still dropping the little envelopes in the door monthly with money for his daughter. It was something, I suppose. My mum rated him for that much. Bloody coward!

Yvonne came over one afternoon, as she did often, to see Mer-

Shoy

cedes and myself. We sat out in the front garden chatting away.

'Look Shoy, my reason for coming over today was to ask whether or not you would like to come on holiday with me and Judy and maybe we could ask Faye and share an apartment.' I looked at her.

'What about Mercedes?'

'She could come, too. Children go free on a lot of holidays, especially if they are under two, so you would not have to find extra money to pay for her.' Well it sounded an excellent idea, but there was no way that my mum was going to let me take Mercedes out of the country. She did not even trust me to take her up to her grandparents who just lived a bus ride away. I left her in the garden and went indoors to ask my mum. I always had this very stupid way: whenever I was going to ask something where I expected the outcome to be unfavourable, I would stand at the door, make funny faces at it, and then walk in. So this I did. There she was in the kitchen, cooking.

'Mum?' She turned and peered over the top of her glasses as she did sometimes.

No entiendo el Español (I don't Understand Spanish)

'Yes, what's wrong now?'

'Oh nothing. Is it okay if I take Mercedes away on holiday with Yvonne, Faye and Judy?'

'Who is Judy?' This I was not too sure about, but I knew she had to be someone Yvonne knew, so that's what I told her.

'She's one of Yvonne's friends.' She shrugged her shoulders.

'Well I don't see why not. When are you intending to go and for how long?' Well we had not got that far. First things first: After all. My parents were always the hurdles, and so that had to be cleared first. I was now excited. It was just what I needed to cheer me up especially after that coward dumped me on the phone some time back and there was no sighting of him. I rushed back to Yvonne and gave her the good news. She would sort it all out and let me know the details: how much it was going to cost, when we would be going, where and who was going to take us to the airport – all sorts of details.

'Hey, don't forget to get your passport and you have to have Mercedes on it.' Good job she was on the ball. She left and all I thought about was the holiday. I was going on holiday for lots of sun, sea, sand, and sangria. I went to work the next day and told the girls I worked with of our plans. They thought it was going to be hilarious – four girls and a toddler on holiday alone and where? They were jealous, that's all. Yvonne called that evening and gave me all the details. She had also contacted Faye and she was up for it as well. We were going to Spain on the Costa Brava. We were going to stay in an apartment, ten minutes from a nice sandy beach, situated in an area called Calafell. It was going to cost one hundred and nine pounds return and Mercedes was free, with just insurance to pay. I agreed. I could afford that, no problem. She arranged to pay for the whole holiday, we would write her out cheques for the amounts owed, and all would be squared. The last time I went abroad for a holiday was to the Caribbean when I was twelve years old, and that was with my mum and my sister who was four at the time, but this was now going to be on my own technically with my daughter, out of sight of parents and family. I could not wait.

'We are off in five weeks'. It's all booked. We are in a self-catering apartment and we have it for two weeks.' Oh my god, we were going to Spain. The next few weeks flew by while we sorted out passports. This was quite easy back then. All you had to do was get a couple of passport pictures and go down to your local post office, fill in the necessary form and then they gave you a one-

No entiendo el Español (I don't Understand Spanish) year passport over the counter – simple and sorted and Mercedes included.

I had bought a couple of suitcases. One was a huge grey thing and the other was smaller and burgundy. The smaller one was of course for Mercedes. I began packing. I was throwing all sorts in. Actually it was nearly everything. I hadn't a clue what was needed on this holiday, so I intended to take it all. The evening of our departure eventually came and Judy's parents and a friend of the parents who had kindly offered to take us to Gatwick Airport picked us up. Had never been there either. My sister was so sad to see us leave, but we would be back sooner than she knew it. I would miss her too and she knew this. We said goodbye to all and left. On the way we got badly lost. We were going around in circles. We stopped on numerous occasions and they were having 'confabs', resting on the boot of the car with the map sprawled all over it. We were lost and time was getting on. Yvonne was getting annoyed and Judy started shouting at her mum. Mercedes was asleep and Faye and I, who were in the same car, just sat there and looked at each other. I am sure that we both thought that we were never going to get to go on this holiday at all. We were moving again. Back then, finding Gatwick was very tricky. There was no going down the M25, picking up the M23 and following the signs to the airport. You went for miles before you

Shoy

even saw signs for the airport and that was after getting lost a few times, doubling back on yourself and taking the other exit, hoping this was the one. We finally arrived at the airport with not a lot of time to spare. We boarded the plane and we were off. Here I was in this plane. I watched the safety demonstration. This was the job that I wanted and someday I was going to be doing it, so I paid particular attention to everything the airhostesses were doing. You would have thought that I was a stalker in the air.

We touched down at Genoa Airport in Spain. The doors opened and the smell that we encountered was ghastly. It was like a sewer. If this was the smell of the continent, then this was going to be a one-off holiday. We left the plane to the sound of *'Bye now. Have a good holiday. Mind how you go.'* We got onto some buses and were taken to the terminal to collect our luggage. We then proceeded through immigration and then out to see our 'Holiday Rep.' There she was, holding up a plaque with our holiday destination on it. We all gathered around her. There were quite a few other holidaymakers as well, not just us, surprisingly. She then introduced herself as Rosemarie. Now you would have expected reps to be young, slim, pretty, etc, but not Rosemarie. She was a short, getting-on-a-bit-in-life lady, and her face was not quite what you would expect. She even had grey hair, which was parted on one side and then greased down, sweeping towards the back and

No entiendo el Español (I don't Understand Spanish) over the ears. She wore bright pink lipstick, which definitely was not her colour, but hey! Who was I to judge? She directed us to our coaches that were taking us to our resorts. Our little group got on first and headed for the back of the coach (as you do). As we got closer to the back of the coach, there was a gaping whole in the bottom of the floor and you could see the ground outside. We then did an about turn and sat somewhere in the middle. The back of the coach was abandoned.

It was early morning when we arrived at the resort and it was quiet. We thought we were coming to a resort that was full of life and lots to do, but this was dead, hardly any sound, hardly anyone around. We left the coach and were taken up to our apartment by Rosemarie. She showed us what was what, left her contact numbers and bid us a good first day in the Costa Brava, but before leaving she reminded us about the welcome meeting to be held in the hotel which was next door to our building later on that day. We said our goodbyes and we hugged each other, screaming. We could not believe that we were alone in Spain with no adults. Well we were really, three of us, as we were eighteen, but you would never have thought it. Judy was only fifteen and, of course, Mercedes was approaching two. In fact she was going to be two, a fortnight after we got back from holiday. We looked around the apartment. There were two bedrooms in which one had three beds

Shoy

and the other two. We decided amongst us that Yvonne and Judy would share the two-bedded one and Faye, Mercedes and myself would share the other. Mercedes was already stripping off and standing on the balcony. I grabbed the camera and took a picture of her just standing there. She was all smiles. There was a large living room with a large round dining table and a huge sideboard, which had every item of crockery you would need and more. We could not believe it. We had packed in our cases plates, knives, forks, spoons, cups, and all sorts, not knowing that this was all supplied for you. There were two large settees and two smaller ones and there was another balcony. We opened the doors and looked out. It overlooked the grounds of the hotel next door. Oh how good it would have been to be staying in that hotel, but our apartment was fine. We could make as much noise as we wanted, we had even bought our own little radio cassette and a selection of tapes, and so it was not going to be quiet. The bathroom was small with the usual fixtures and fittings except for one item. We had not got a clue what it was. We had never seen this one before, but it looked similar to a toilet and had two taps placed at the back and what looked like a plughole. The kitchen was well equipped with a fridge, cooker, loads of cupboard space and of course kitchen utensils – unbelievable! There was even a welcome box of shopping for us. In the box there were potatoes, bread, sugar, tins of spaghetti and beans, bottles of water and some juice. In

No entiendo el Español (I don't Understand Spanish) the fridge there was milk (but it was goat's milk), butter and some jam. There were tea bags, coffee and coffee whitener. We had no idea that all this would be supplied. We had even brought in our hand luggage, which was so heavy, food. My mum had baked us some bread, a cake (which she had iced), she had cooked us some rice and we had chicken. We had even bought some salad. It weighed a ton. We quickly unpacked all the food and put it away and then dragged our luggage to our respective rooms and started to unpack. We were all chatting and laughing. We had taken so much clothing, it did not even fit into the wardrobes and drawers that were there, so we left most of it in the suitcases and pushed them under the bed. We put on shorts and T-shirts and went out to take a look around. Yvonne had not been feeling too brilliant; the plane journey had seemed to affect her, and so she and Judy went back to the apartment for a lie down. Faye and I stayed out a while longer with Mercedes. Luckily we had taken a fold-down buggy for Mercedes, because she hated walking, so she would be in and out of the buggy the whole time; it made life so much easier at least I did not have to carry her. This resort that we thought was so quiet was actually full of life. We must have come in the back way. There were large department stores, supermarkets and little souvenir shops all over the place. Fast food places, bag shops, leather shops, shoe shops; you name it, they had it. We had, down our stretch of road, two nightclubs. We were definitely going to one of those that night. We made our way down to the beach, which was right at the end of our stretch of road. The beach was very wide and it was lovely with golden sand. We took our sandals off and Mercedes immediately ran off, down to the water's edge, doing handstands as she went. She was always doing handstands. She came running back and asked for her dress to be taken off. Off she went again in her vest and knickers. She was so happy and squealing with delight. Faye and I carried the buggy and placed it under one of the umbrellas that was already open. We had a blanket with us, so we spread this on the sand and we sat down. Mercedes in the meantime had already found a friend and they were holding hands and walking towards us. They came over and we said hello. The little girl did not speak a word of English. I could not believe it. How did they understand each other? But they seemed to. They played with each other for quite some time, her parents watching on just as we were. It was so nice to see to kids from different backgrounds communicating without words but united in their actions. Faye and I sat there, just silent sometimes, watching the sea, stunned. Stunned that we had made it to Spain.

We eventually went back to the apartment. After all, we had to get something to eat and there were lots there already. Yvonne was really not well. By now, she had lost her voice and she was not

No entiendo el Español (I don't Understand Spanish)

looking good at all. I offered to get Rosemarie, but she declined. She just wanted to be left alone to get some rest. The rest of us got something to eat and we planned our evening. As Judy was too young to go to the nightclubs, she would baby-sit and the rest of us would go to one of the nightclubs down the road. Once we had decided which one, we would let Judy know just in case there was a problem with Mercedes. I was a bit apprehensive about leaving Mercedes with Judy, but as Judy said, she did baby-sitting at home all the time, so that put my mind at rest.

Night time came and the air was full of sounds. Sounds of music. Sounds of laughter. Sounds of shouting. We kept running to the balcony looking out. In the hotel opposite in the grounds, they had a cabaret show on. So, of course, we stood and watched that for a bit. We were in the middle of getting dressed when we heard traditional Spanish clapping. Once again we ran to the balcony. Mouths wide open, we looked on. They had Flamenco dancers all dressed up in their regalia, dancing and clapping. It was so beautiful to see. It did not last very long so we watched the whole thing and then continued getting dressed - again. At last we were ready and left the apartment. Whilst Faye and I were on the beach earlier that day, two Spanish guys came over to us and handed us some cards with the nightclub's name on it and asked us to come along. They also wanted to know how many of us would be com-

Shoy

ing so, in effect, we had free entry to this particular nightclub that was called 'Babylon.' The other nightclub was called 'Eva's', but it did not look as inviting as the Babylon.

So, here we were, the three of us, dressed up and ready to go. I was wearing a dress. It had straps over the shoulders and the top half, which dropped below the waist, was white, and the bottom had two layers, which overlapped in the middle of glittery material in colours of mainly purple and pink. It was my favourite dress and very appropriate for this weather. My hair was braided and long, so I left my braids out to do their own thing, as most of the time I wore them up. Yvonne and Faye both had on dungarees; they lived in dungarees. One had on black and the other a Liz colour and they both had little white T-shirts on underneath. I wore white sandals to finish off my outfit and the others wore mules. Judy thought we looked good and we left kissing Mercedes goodnight. She was already asleep.

We got to Babylon's and sure enough the little card let us in free. It was well air-conditioned and I felt cold, but it was all too late. I suddenly remembered that I had not gone back to let Judy know which club we were at. I told the other two and I went to the doorman and explained. He stamped the back of my hand and I went back to the apartment. Now, before leaving we had told Judy not

No entiendo el Español (I don't Understand Spanish) to open the downstairs door to anyone, so of course she would not and I had not taken the key from Faye. So I had to yell up at her. She finally came to the balcony. I got in and told her. All was well. I took another look in on Mercedes and left once again, heading back for the club.

The club was really smart and had lots of little alcoves where you could sit and talk and just listen to the music, which was good. There was a wooden-floored dancing area and we sat near it. Each time something came on that we liked, we would get up and dance. Halfway through the night, we had quite a few guys looking at us from across the bar, but none of them would come over. Yvonne and I were dancing and we noticed a girl talking to Faye. Who was she? We left the floor and went over to make sure all was okay. Faye introduced us.

'This is Letitia and she was sent by her brother to ask if you,' she was pointing at me, 'could talk to him as he fancies you and has been watching you since we came in.' I was smiling.

'Where is he?' I asked her.

'He is very shy and does not speak English too good, but I can interpret for you until he picks it up again. He learnt it before, but has forgotten most of it as he does not use it.' Well, this was going to be interesting. She pointed him out. Oh my god! He was gorgeous. He was medium/dark tanned with almost black, thick, just-touching-his-shoulder-length hair. He had a to-die-for smile (as he was now looking at me and I at him). He was wearing a black polo-type top with three buttons that were undone and a pair of black trousers. He was slim and he looked magnificent.

'So is he going to come over or does he want me to go over to him?' I asked Letitia. She was beautiful as well. She had mid-length blond hair which was parted in the middle and just like him, she was tanned. She was slim and had lovely dimples, which appeared each time she smiled or said certain words. They were of course Spanish and brother and sister. She went over to the bar where he was seated and spoke to him. We were left chatting about him and looking over and laughing (as girls do), but he was so nice and he was interested in me. He finally came over and squeezed himself in between Faye and I. He was looking straight into my face. What was I going to say? He signalled with his hands whether or not I wanted a drink. I nodded. He then looked at the others and did the same with them. They nodded as well. He disappeared and came back with a waiter carrying on a large tray five huge champagne-type glasses with pink liquid in them and small straws. We each took one and sipped. We hadn't got

No entiendo el Español (I don't Understand Spanish) a clue what it was, but it was tasty. We were only used to drinking Blue Lagoons and Bacardi and Coke, so this was completely different, much nicer. We had no idea how much the drinks were costing, but he just kept on bringing them, as much as we wanted. I looked at Letitia.

'What's his name?' We both laughed.

'His name is Federico.' Finally, we were introduced properly and he held my hand and kissed the back of it. All the senses in my body transferred to the spot where his lips were touching so I could feel every ripple of his mouth. It was breathtaking. He was speaking to me in Spanish. I did not understand a word he was saying, but every now and then his sister would translate. He would say things to her, they seemed to have an exchange of words and then she would tell me what was said. I was sure that she was doing it under duress. I knew I would if it had been my brother. The whole evening was magical and Federico seemed to like me a lot. I could not say much to him because I was too embarrassed to say things to his sister for her to pass on, so for a lot of the time, we just watched each other and smiled. To get away from the embarrassing stares, I would get up and dance with the others and he would sit and watch me intently.

Shoy

Whilst on the dance floor, another guy danced his way over in front of me and Federico got real mad with him and got on to the floor, and they exchanged words in Spanish and then the other guy buggered off. God knows what he said, but it could not have been that nice, cause he left in such a hurry. Who was this guy – Federico? The evening came to an end and we made our way out. I turned to wave goodbye to Federico and his sister. His sister took me by the arm.

'Federico would like to walk you home?'

I shrugged my shoulders and looked at Faye and Yvonne. 'Is it okay if Federico walks me back to the apartment?'

They both answered

'Yeah, sure. We will see you there.' Faye threw the keys at me. 'Here, you can let yourself in, saves you waking us up.'

'I am not going to be that long, it's not that far.' They both laughed and they left. So here I was, going to be walked home (which was literally up the road) by this hunk of a guy who had no idea who I was, or even that I had a child. He did not even know how old I was. Come to think of it, I did not know how old he was. He

No entiendo el Español (I don't Understand Spanish) came over to me, put his arm over my shoulder, and kissed me on the cheek. His lips were so gentle and I so wanted to kiss him, but I had never kissed a 'foreigner' before. I wanted to now. We said goodbye to the bouncers on the door and left. His sister went to their apartment, which apparently was around the next corner, and we headed in the direction of ours. We walked real slow and he was saying all sorts, none of which I understood, but every now and then he would come out with an English word so we were able to make some sort of conversation. We reached the door of the apartment and we turned and looked at each other. I was a bit tipsy. I had not drunk as much as the others, but it had still gone to my head and I had been staggering a bit and laughing on our little walk home. So here we were. His face was very close and I could feel his breath on my face as we stood there just looking at each other. He drew closer and touched my lips with his, ever so gently. I touched him back. We pulled away from each other momentarily and then, like two magnets, our lips drew themselves back to each other and we kissed. It was as if our lips were one. I did not want this kiss to end. We finally came up for air and he looked at the door.

'Can……'

I interrupted him.

Shoy

'You want to come up?' I was trying so hard to make him understand that I wanted him to come up to stay for a while. He understood and nodded. I put the key in the door and pushed the light switch, closed the door behind us and we walked up the stairs, he following me. We got to our apartment door, I unlocked it, and we both walked in. Everyone was in bed already. I looked in on Yvonne, told her that Federico had come up for a while, and hoped she did not mind. She did not. I went in to our room and Faye was up, but in bed reading. I smiled at her.

'Federico is here, do you mind?'

'I knew he would come up with you. His sister has already told me that he really likes you and he wants to spend the night with you. Why do you think I gave you the key?'

'Oh Faye, why did you not tell me?'

'Why should I? It would have spoilt it for you.' I closed the bedroom door and sat on the edge of Faye's bed.

'Oh Debs, he does not know about Mercedes. How will I tell him? I don't even know how old he is, what he does, none of that

No entiendo el Español (I don't Understand Spanish) stuff and he wants me to go to bed with him?' Our conversation was interrupted by a knock on the door. Together we answered.

'Come in.' It was Federico. He came in, went straight over to Mercedes, and sat next to her.

'Ah, bebe.' He stroked her hair, which was braided as well. He looked at me and Faye and shrugged his shoulders as if to say, 'well, who does she belong to?' This was my chance. I could tell him now.

'Erm…She is mine.' He looked back at her.

'She is beautiful,' came a reply in his Spanish accent, which was delicious. Faye and I looked at each other. Well that seemed easy. Maybe because of the language barrier everything seemed easy, or maybe he was just a very easy-going person, but either way he liked my daughter. I got up, called for him to come in to the living room, closed the bedroom door behind me, and left Faye in peace. We sat on the settee and he was really trying to speak English. In fact he knew quite a lot, but said that because of all the noise in the nightclub, he just could not be bothered to speak so much. It would take him ages to try and remember what he was trying to say and the music was putting him off, so it was easier to speak through his sister, which was very difficult because she did not

Shoy

want to translate for him.

Before we knew it we were wrapped up in each other's arms, kissing and touching and kissing, and then we had no clothes on and we were having sex on the settee. Halfway through he stopped, got off me and put his shorts back on.

'What's wrong?' I asked, sitting up and wrapping the sheet around me that was on the sofa. He left the room, went into the kitchen, and just sat in the corner on one of the units. He was not saying a word. I went in to our bedroom and woke Faye. I really did not know what else to do, but something was wrong and it scared me a bit. I explained to her what had happened. She was so good. She got out of bed, went in to the kitchen, and started talking to him. She told me to wait and leave him to her, so I did. A few minutes later she came back.

'He's a virgin and he thought that he was rubbish.' I laughed and she laughed, still sleepy.

'You mean to say he told you that we were having sex?'

'Yep. He said you were very good, but he just felt that he was rubbish (his words) and that he was shy.' We laughed again and

No entiendo el Español (I don't Understand Spanish)

I left the room and went in to the kitchen. I went over to him and put my arm around him.

'Its okay, you were not rubbish.' His head spun round and looked at me. It was a look of *'she told you.'* Well of course she did; she was my friend not his. He came down off the unit and hugged me, we went back to the sofa and lay there together, and he fell asleep. He was so warm, his chest was very hairy, and I fell asleep stroking it.

Morning came and Mercedes, wanting her breakfast, woke us. He put his arms out for her to come to him. She did and they sat there on the sofa and I went to get Mercedes' 'breaky.' I returned with it to find them talking. He had started teaching her Spanish words and she was repeating them. He looked up at me and looked at Mercedes.

'She is beautiful, just like her mother. I wish she was mine.' They looked so good together. I wished he was mine and Mercedes was his, but reality always has a way of returning when you don't want it to. I sat Mercedes at the table and she fed herself, as she did, repeating some of the Spanish words she had been taught.

'Would you like some breakfast Federico?' He shrugged. I went to the kitchen and came back with some toast and he ate some. He was not so keen on tea and asked if we had coffee, so I made him some. We were sitting around the table like a real family when Faye came in still half asleep.

'Morning,' she yawned. 'Any tea made?' Tea made, I thought. She must be joking. It's a matter of get up and get it yourself. Then on reflection I felt it was not fair to be like that towards her. After all, she had helped me out with Federico. Anyway, she made her own breakfast and joined us at the table. I went off, had a shower, and then got Mercedes washed and dressed. I so wanted to get out again. As Federico had stayed the night, he borrowed my toothbrush and had a wash. Was he ever going to go to his apartment? Who cared? Judy and Yvonne were still asleep, so we did not disturb them. The four of us left the apartment, leaving them a note to say we had gone down to the beach and they could join us later. They were really missing the holiday; all they seemed to do was sleep, sleep, and sleep. Mind you, Yvonne was still not too well, so she had an excuse, but I expected Judy to be down on that beach every day getting a tan. The rest of the day was spent down on the beach, eating, drinking, walking about, as the beach got too hot, and just doing nothing. It was glorious. We started wandering back to the apartment and on the way we stopped at a burger bar. The bar was owned, as we found out later,

No entiendo el Español (I don't Understand Spanish) by Federico and his sister. So now we were getting free food as well. Letitia was not pleased with Federico as she had had to open up all by herself and she had not seen him all day. So instead of coming back to the apartment with us, he had to stay and do his share of work. Before leaving, he promised that he would come over that evening. That was fine by me. Back at the apartment Yvonne and Judy had finally gone out. They had left us a note.

Later that evening, everyone was deciding what they were going to do. Yvonne felt she was well enough to go out to the nightclub again and Faye wanted to go out and get her own 'Spaniard.' We felt it unfair for Judy not to go out, so she was going to try to look older and see if she could get in. We had promised her parents that she would not go to any, but as long as she was not going to be getting off with anyone, she would be okay. We told her that, at the first sign of her even kissing someone, she would be back in the apartment. She agreed and they got ready. It was getting late and I had already made my mind up to stay in the apartment that evening. Anyway, Federico had not contacted me yet, so if he wanted to go out, he was on his own. Mercedes went to sleep and the others went out. I sat on the balcony and listened to the renditions of Boney M, which were a blast from the past, and some Spanish songs, which were really nice, even though I could not understand a word they were singing. Although we had only been there a few nights, they seemed to play the same songs at about the same time every evening. It would be interesting to see if we would hear the same things the whole two weeks.

There was a knock at the door. It was Federico. He came in. His English was getting so much better and so quickly. He had bought some food over with him from the burger bar and we sat on the balcony and ate. It was so nice and so romantic. He disappeared in to the living room, leaving me abruptly with my thoughts and came back, calling me. I followed him. He had only changed the sofa into a bed. Well we did not know that all along the sofa was a bed. So now he could stay on the 'sofa bed' and we would not be squashed. Perfect. We went to bed that night, but we did not have sex, we just lay there hugging and kissing each other. He was such a good kisser, so gentle and loving. I could kiss him all night. I heard the others come in. Seeing us in the bed, they crept past, closed the hallway door, and went to their beds. I did not move, so they did not know that I was awake.

The rest of the holiday went uneventfully and sure enough, the hotel across the way played the same tunes every evening at the same time, to the extent where I had even learnt some of the words to the Spanish songs. We had been on various excursions and had the usual tourist pictures taken. Mercedes and I had a photo

No entiendo el Español (I don't Understand Spanish) taken on entering a 'water life' complex that we went to and in the picture there was another little girl. On the way back to the resort, we found out that her birthday was on exactly the same day as Mercedes' and she was the same age. How uncanny. It was a picture to treasure for life. We had a couple of parties in the apartment. At one party, we were the only English-speaking ones there. Some of the others could speak a little English, but it did not seem to matter; we all had a great time. At another party we had, there was a load of English guys (as you could imagine). They were high-spirited and very, very noisy. We had to keep telling them to keep the noise down. They were a nice bunch and one of them fancied me. Federico was not there and I kind of fancied him, but no, I was good. Federico was the man for me now and so I declined his offer of hugs and kisses. To begin with they thought I was Spanish, hence the reason, I suppose, why they were so interested in me. We had gone to Barcelona, which was the most beautiful city in the world (not that I had seen many). I never wanted to leave this beautiful place, but the day was drawing close and now it was here.

We had left all our packing until the morning of the day we were leaving. We were busy and Federico had not come over at all that day. He had already said as much that he would not, because he hated goodbyes and it would make him real sad. He had asked me to stay, but we both knew that I couldn't, not just like that. For me to stay, we would have to plan it. So I packed. We were all so quiet whilst packing. We were being picked up outside the apartment late that evening to be taken to the airport, so we did not have far to go. Our hand luggage was so much lighter now. There was none of the bread, cakes, rice, chicken, and salad that had been weighing us down before. So all in all it was much easier.

The packing was complete; the apartment checked and still there was no sign of Federico. He really meant he was not coming to see us off. I could not believe that he did not want to say goodbye. We had swapped addresses and I had promised to send him some photos when they were developed, but this would break my heart to not have a final hug and kiss before leaving to go home. The tears just rolled down my face and the others tried to console me, but in vain. It was time to go. Rosemarie came up and checked the apartment over and we went down to the coach. He really was not coming. How could he do this to me? Did I not mean anything to him? I could never do this to anyone. Just as the coach was pulling away from the apartment, Yvonne caught a glimpse of him. He was hiding behind a pillar just a couple of steps from our apartment. I ran to the front of the coach and asked the driver to stop. He did and I got off and ran over to him, straight into his arms. We were both crying. I could see that he had been crying

No entiendo el Español (I don't Understand Spanish) a lot too; his eyes were all red, and he looked awful. We kissed each other real hard and promised to write to each other within the week. It felt as though we had been hugging each other for the longest time, but it must have been seconds. Just as I pulled away from him, he handed me a little wrapped-up gift. I had not even got him something. I took it, kissed him again, ran back to the coach, and got on. We all waved at him as the coach went past and he disappeared out of sight. I looked down at the little parcel in my hand and opened it. It was a little silver box and on the top there was a picture of Groucho Marx (I was not sure what the connection was, but that's what was on the top), but it was beautiful.

The flight home was long, sad and quiet. Going home was the worst feeling ever. We landed at Gatwick, cleared customs and were met by Judy's dad and his friend, who assured us this time that we were not going to get lost. Who cared? I just wanted to get back on the plane and go back to Spain. I so wanted Federico. I was missing him so much. Was he missing me? What was he doing now?

I arrived back home and my mum came out of the house to help with the luggage. I think she just couldn't wait to see if Mercedes was all right, but of course she was. Stephanie came charging out of the house and flung her arms around my neck.

Shoy

'I've missed you and I have a surprise for you! Come on, you have to come upstairs.' We dropped everything at the front door and I went upstairs with her. She had made a 'Welcome Home Shoy' banner. It was suspended across the room. It was really good and so sweet of her. She had really missed me. Whilst unpacking, my mum noticed the love-bite that was on my neck.

'So where did you get that from?'

I looked at her. What was she talking about? 'Get what?' She pointed at the mark on my neck. Oh my god, I had forgotten about that. I hesitated. 'Well, I met this Spanish guy. His name is Federico and he really liked me and loved Mercedes. He wanted me to stay with him.' It was all coming out in a breath.

'So are you going to keep in touch with him?'

Well where did that come from? Or was she just trying to catch me out, trying to work out how much went on and then give me a rocketing afterwards? I had to tread carefully.

'Well I would like to, he has given me his address and I said that I would send him some photos when they got developed.'

No entiendo el Español (I don't Understand Spanish)

'Well you had better get them developed quickly then.' Was this my mum talking to me? She seemed so nice. Had she changed since I went away? Maybe I should go away more often.

I wrote to Federico that night, posted the letter the next day, and put the photos in to be processed. I could not wait to hear from him. The photos came back and I sent him copies of the best ones, of which there were quite a few. In no time at all we were corresponding with each other. His letters were full of fun and life just like him. He was getting his sister to help him as some of the words he found difficult, but on the whole he was not doing too badly. I so wanted to see him again, but he was far away. I would think of him when I was awake, when I was at work, when I was out shopping - in fact just about all day. I wanted my Federico.

Denny, in the meantime, had been round to see me and had noticed the love bite on my neck.

'So where did you get that from?' pointing to my neck. I did not answer. Who did he think he was? Asking me questions. Were we a couple? He was now calling me more often and coming round and asking for us to sit outside in his car. What the hell did he want?

Shoy

Christmas came and we got cards and presents from both Letitia and Federico. Both of them had sent Mercedes a large balloon made of plastic which you unfolded and ran along with. One end was open and it would fill up with air and float along behind you and written on it were the Spanish words for Christmas. She loved it. Federico had sent me a little Pierrot doll. Its body was made of material and its face was porcelain. He knew I liked these very much. His card was in the shape of two stars, one pink and one blue with little angels on them and he made up a little poem inside about the two of us. It read: '*I wish you the most beautiful and Merry Christmas and the New Year brings you the best. There are two little twin stars in the sky; they are bright and shinning, clear and sincere. Like you and me they are far away from each other though, they are united by soul and love. I LOVE YOU!*' I read his card over and over again. I so wanted him and it was obvious that he wanted me. But how could I live in another country when I did not know the culture, the language, I would have no friends and where would we live? And where would Mercedes go to school? Too many questions and not enough answers. By now we had exchanged phone numbers and I would call him occasionally; not for long though, just long enough to hear his voice and him mine. That seemed to make things worse as we could not hold or touch each other, as we wanted. Life seemed so unfair and so hard.

No entiendo el Español (I don't Understand Spanish)
Why was I not born in Spain? Why had I not met him sooner? Why did I love him so much? Why? Why? Why?

The following year I returned to Spain again on holiday. This time I went on holiday with my sister. She had missed me so much the last time that I asked my mum if I could take her along and she said yes. There was Mercedes, of course, and there were two other friends who I worked with and their names were Jennifer and Elspeth. Elspeth was white and she was out to get a suntan at any cost. She was ever such a nice person, but did not have a boyfriend and was desperate to get one. No sooner had she got one, she would lose him again. She was always down about it, but we knew that some day she would get someone, because she would. Jennifer and I sat together at work and we would always get in to trouble from our supervisor, who was a right dragon, for talking. We always had so much to say to each other. This particular holiday was in Blanes, which was on the Costa Dorada. I so wanted to go back to Calafell, but the tour operators did not feature it this particular year and if we wanted to go to Calafell, we would have to go to Newcastle and that was definitely not an option so we ended up in Blanes.

Blanes was really nice. Before going, I wrote to Federico to let him know where I was going to be and when we would arrive. I

Shoy

so hoped that he could come to see me, but unfortunately it was not to be. He was far too busy with work, especially as it was the holiday season, and could not get away to see me. I was disappointed, but I did not let it upset my holiday.

During that holiday, we met lots of other guys, but no one compared to Federico. I knew I wanted him, but how much did he want me? And were we ever going to see each other again? There were lots of memories of this holiday as well, such as Stephanie and I breaking the solid marble coffee table that was in the living room of this huge apartment. There were five bedrooms and two bathrooms one of which we left to Jennifer because she always took so long in the bathroom. This marble table we had tried to move so we could clean the floor, but we did not realise that it was not attached to the base and so when we pushed it, the top slid off and cracked in half. We dragged the pieces into one of the rooms that we were not using and hid it in the bottom of the built-in wardrobe and did not tell the others for the whole holiday. I seriously thought that we were going to lose our deposit of fifty pounds, which was my money to buy my bus pass for getting to work when we returned home. But no one noticed and we did not get penalised for breaking it. There was another memory of Stephanie and Mercedes sitting on the main balcony at midnight eating spaghetti with their fingers and then taking their sticky

No entiendo el Español (I don't Understand Spanish) fingers and placing it against the patio doors and leaving big handprints everywhere. They laughed so much, those two. They loved it.

I met so many different guys on this holiday. They were Italian, French, English, Spanish and even Germans. They were all so nice and when we returned and developed the photos, all there seemed to be was pictures of me with all these different men, but I did not look happy. My mum could see that. It was fun, but they were not happy times. Jennifer and Elspeth had found themselves some guys, but there were tears for them when we left. That I could relate to. Whilst we were there we had met our first, live transvestite. Shim (She/he) was scary. We had spotted 'Shim' in one of the nightclubs that we went to and the whole holiday was spent trying to work out whether this person was a he or a she. On the last night we found out that he was a transvestite and Shim was dressed up in Spanish flamenco dress and was putting on a show. Shim looked quite good and we took a photo with Shim. Close up, Shim was even more scary with the make-up caked on, but Shim was pleasant enough.

Federico was becoming a distant holiday romance in my mind. Although we were writing to each other regularly, it was all becoming so unclear and there were no plans for us to be together.

Shoy

I wanted him to make a positive move, but he was as unsure as I was. Or was it that we were both too young and inexperienced to know what we wanted? Maybe if we had met with the minds that we have now, all that heartache would never have taken place. We would have made a decision and gone with it. We would be living together and learning about one another. Maybe.

Denny was now hanging around me even more. He wanted to know more about me. He wanted to see me more often. He was once again interested because someone else had paid some attention; he was now back sniffing around. I, of course, being too stupid and gullible, took him back. So now I was justifying why I should take him back. Well, he was the father of my child and she loved her dad, so why should I not take him back? He said that he wanted me back, so why should I not give him a chance? My mum was not happy with me at all. She still hated him and would rather that I became a nun and left the country than get back with him, but she could not stop me although she would try.

Almost a year on from our holiday in Blanes and I was pregnant again. Yes, it was Denny's. The only person I told to begin with was Wayne. He did not have a lot to say on the matter except that I had better tell Mum sharpish, as he was sure that I was not going to stay small this time around. He kept on at me, 'tell Mum'

No entiendo el Español (I don't Understand Spanish)

'tell Mum;' I then wished I had not told him, but it was too late for that now. I finally plucked up the courage when I was about three months gone and told her. She was not at all pleased. She wanted me to have an abortion. She never said as much but she would say things such as: 'You are still young and have a full life ahead of you.' 'It will spoil your chances in life if you go ahead with this pregnancy'. She had even gone as far as involving a friend of hers who was actually Mercedes' godmother. She had phoned me up to try and convince me to have an abortion. Apparently she had had one soon after her first child so she knew what she was talking about. I ignored them all. This time around I was not going to be stupid with this pregnancy, I had been checked out in the early stages and I had been signed up for antenatal classes. Everything was in place and it was all going well, but at home I was under so much pressure. My dad was not even aware of what was going on.

One night, quite suddenly, I had this strong pain low down in my stomach. It was excruciating and unbearable. I was threw myself about on the bed uncontrollably, holding my stomach and trying so hard not to scream with the pain. What was happening? I got up to go to the toilet and all I saw was blood. What did that mean? I was scared, but I did not tell anyone. It just so happened that the next day I was going to the hospital for a check-up. So I cleaned myself up and put a pad on (as the good old book told me to). The next day I went for my appointment as usual, but I felt that I had lost the baby. I felt empty as if there was nothing inside. I was worried. That morning, before going to the hospital, I passed a huge blood clot, which I collected and put in a specimen bottle and took along with me. When I got to the clinic, I explained to the nurse the events that had taken place the previous night and morning through all the crying. She was very sympathetic, but said that I should still see the doctor as maybe the baby was still present. I waited my turn. The pains in my stomach were getting worse. I finally got in to see the Consultant. I was all alone and quite scared, because I knew that I had lost the baby really. He examined me and basically told me that I was wasting his time and he sent me off to have another pregnancy test. He disappeared out of the examination room and I sat there and cried. I had never been treated that way before and I felt so small and insignificant. The nurse looked embarrassed. She sent me off for the pregnancy test and told me that once I had had it done to come back to the clinic, as they would tell me the result straight away. There was no waiting for the result. The test result came back and it was negative. I was devastated. I could not think, I could not see for all the tears that filled my eyes. There was no comforting me. I wanted my baby back. I went through a few formalities with the nurse and left the clinic. I made my way back to work. How I

No entiendo el Español (I don't Understand Spanish) got there I just don't know. I did not see anyone. I did not speak to anyone. I don't even remember paying to get on the bus. But somehow I made it to work. I walked into the office and everyone started asking questions, as they knew why I had gone to the hospital. I sat down and just started to cry all over again. I could not even get the words out properly, but they caught the gist of what had happened and they called Denny to take me home. He arrived and not a word was said between us all the way.

I was sixteen weeks pregnant and I had lost my baby in the night. The remains had been caught in the blood clot that I took to the hospital. Apparently it was a clean miscarriage and there was nothing left, but the injection that the nurse had given me was just to make sure.

We sat outside my house in his car for a bit before my mum appeared. It was as if she would be looking out of the window the whole time and knew exactly when I arrived. She just infuriated me all the time. She approached the car and enquired as to why I was not at work. I just blurted it out at her. 'I have been to the hospital for a check-up and I have lost the baby. Happy now? It's just what you and that friend of yours wanted.' With that, she turned and walked back into the house. She had wished this curse on me and now she had got what she wanted. I hoped it made her happy.

Shoy

Not a word was said between my mother and I about the miscarriage, not a word. It lay dead between us. Her so-called friend, on the other hand, made it her business to call me with words of comfort. 'It was for the best. Obviously it was not meant to be.' What did she know? She never knew who I was really. She never knew what went on in my head. What I wanted. What my dreams were. What I wanted out of life. What I was searching for. How could she know, when no one bothered to ask?

Nearly a year later, I became pregnant again, and this time I decided not to tell anyone because of what I went through the last time. The pregnancy was going well and I reached the three-month mark and thought once again that everything was going to be all right. Once again, my mum found out. It was as if she was always looking at me, waiting to see if I was going to get pregnant again. Well anyway, she was right. One day, I stayed at home from work because I was not feeling well enough to go in. I had a bad stomach all night and it was no better the next day. I had diarrhoea and vomiting. I thought I must have caught a bug or something. Every now and then she would check on me. Why? I don't know because she would not help me. I lay there on my bed, clutching a hot water bottle; the pains were getting worse and more intense. I cried out for my mum, she came running up the stairs and into my room. I started to explain to her what was going

No entiendo el Español (I don't Understand Spanish) on. At this point my sister arrived home from school and she was very worried about me. I was rolling around on the bed, the pain was so unbearable, but my mum was nowhere to be seen. I could not believe that she would not help me. I asked my sister to get a basin for me from the bathroom. In my heart and in my head, I knew what was going on. I was losing my baby again. I went over the basin and I passed lots of clots and lots of blood. Once again I collected the contents in a specimen bottle and the larger clot, which was quite large, I wrapped up in a towel and placed in a carrier bag and I went straight to the doctor. I did not even book an appointment. He sent me straight to the hospital in an ambulance. When I got there they took the specimen bottle and the towel that I had wrapped the larger clot in. I had been examined and made comfortable. Two doctors and a nurse came in and gave me the worst. There was no beating about the bush. I had lost the baby and this time it was a boy. I had lost my baby boy. The completion of my family and he was gone. Would I ever get pregnant again? And would I ever give birth normally, hold my baby, take him home, and love him as I loved Mercedes? This time I had gone nearly twenty weeks, but things were wrong, probably from the start and so the baby just would never have survived. 'It was for the best.' This time I had gone through proper contractions, hence the pains and the rolling about on the bed. And the large clot was actually the placenta and inside would have been my baby. Thank god I did not go poking about. I might have seen more than I bargained for.

The nurse called a taxi and I arrived home, home to where you should be safe and happy. Home that should make you feel happy and wanted. I told my mum what had gone on. From her reactions, she knew exactly what was going on and to think she just left me there. I could have died. How would she have begun to tell me what was going on when she could not even tell me, when I needed to be told, what would happen to my body as I got older and began to have sex. The so called 'Sex Education' talk, the one I was not allowed to attend at school, because it was her job to inform me, but never did. I was so ignorant and stupid and only had my one book.

My mind was made up after that harrowing experience. I was not going to have any more children. Mercedes would be an only child and my dream of wanting two children (a girl and a boy), were now dashed and I was looking forward to my life and building a better one for me and my daughter, who I loved so much. Having been to college and gained results in English and Maths O Level, a BEC General Diploma in Business Studies and a few other qualifications, I was in good stead to move on up. Quite where up was, I had not figured out yet. I was still working in the

No entiendo el Español (I don't Understand Spanish) typing pool churning out the rental agreements, but had moved from copy typing to audio typing. I had always thought that audio typing was hard in that once the tape started, you kept on typing until it stopped. But of course this was not so and I increased my typing speed enormously so much so that I was the fastest audio-typist they had and I did not even touch-type. So to me that was an achievement. Whilst working there I had met some really nice people. There were three of us in the audio-typing pool: myself, Trudy and Jennifer.

Trudy was a white girl, originally from up North somewhere, and her parents had returned to where she was born and she was left alone at the age of eighteen to fend for herself and a great job she was doing. She was tall with natural blonde shoulder length hair, very slim and beautiful. When she first started working with us, she had had braces on her teeth and as a result her speech was funny, but in a cute sort of way. She was very shy and unsure of herself, but she was so funny with it. She was dating someone of her own age for quite some time and he was an up-and-coming footballer, played for a top team, and was just waiting for his break. He was very handsome and they were so in love with each other, although Trudy always got a bit jealous of other girls wanting him. We always told her that she would have to put up with it, especially when he made the big time and was in the limelight

Shoy
all the time.

Jennifer was black with a figure to die for. She had a mass of hair, which she had no idea what to do with it. She was beautiful with the whitest, perfect teeth you had ever seen. She lived at home with her parents (as most of us still did), along with her sister and brother. Considering we had lived in the same town all our lives, we had never met. We had become great friends and would get in to trouble at work for laughing and talking and then have to work extra hard the next day to catch up on the work which should have been completed the day before. We would have races to see who could type the most tapes in a day with the fewest mistakes. Someone in another department always checked our work. Once corrections were made, if any, they were then posted. The tapes would come up to us fast and furious which meant, to keep up, we typed faster and faster, but somehow, the quality of our work got better and better.

We would talk about all sorts of things during work. Our office was open plan, so nothing was ever kept secret for long. Jennifer and I had decided that we were going to do some exercise classes at the local sports centre. Denny offered to help us with a workout plan, which meant we did not have to spend any money. He had bought us some leotards, which did not leave much to the imagi-

No entiendo el Español (I don't Understand Spanish) nation. Needless to say, we did not wear them. We started on our plan. A few weeks into it, Denny asked me if I would mind leaving him and Jennifer alone, as she needed extra help with some of the exercises that he had put together. I thought this odd, as she seemed to be doing better than me. She later told me that he wanted her to go to bed with him, but of course, being a true friend she declined. After that the exercises were disbanded.

BATTLES OF DEGRADATION

Denny was always messing my life up. Just as it got good, something (or should I say, someone) would come along and just hit me square on and I would loose my sense of direction, dignity, pride and worth. I was now at ease with my life and one such someone came along by the name of Mandy. Mandy was what I would call 'a child.' She was tall, skinny, and as black as the ace of spades, but in a pretty sort of way. She had a multitude of sisters of varying sizes. They were depicted as the mafia mob of our town.

Christmas was approaching and I was doing overtime whenever I could to get a bit of extra money. This particular night a few of us, namely myself, Elspeth, Jennifer and Trudy, had worked until eight o'clock. After the overtime, we caught the bus home, getting off at various points, except for Trudy who was always picked up my her boyfriend. Jennifer and I were the last to get off as our journey terminated at the bus station. We parted and went our separate ways home. Just as I turned the corner out of the shopping centre, I spotted Mandy outside the Wimpy bar across the road. I was going to have to walk past her to continue my journey home. As I crossed the pelican crossing, she started towards me. What the hell did she want now? As I got across to the other side, there she was, in front of me.

'Hi, Shoy.' She grinned at me with her chalky white, spaced - out teeth that shone like a beacon against her dark skin.

'Hi. What do you want?' I replied very cautiously. Mandy and I had been on semi-talking level. We had met each other a few times on the bus on our way to work, but she always got off at the next stop after ours. She also knew Jane and Claire as they all lived in the same area at one time and went to the same school. She was now fidgeting. I knew there was something agitating her and immediately Denny came to mind. She started to talk.

Shoy

'Well, I wondered if you could give this necklace back to Denny as I will not be seeing him for some time and I want him to have it back?' I stood back and looked at the necklace. It was the silver one I had bought him the previous Christmas and he had given it to her! I was shocked so shocked in fact that my mind went blank. I knew long before this meeting with Mandy that he was taking her and a couple of her sisters to the Reggae Awards which was being held in London the coming weekend. If I had been on form, I could have replied to her that she could give it back to him herself on that day, but it passed. I took the chain out of her hands and walked off. My mind was full of what I was going to say to Denny when I saw him and handed the necklace back to him. I walked faster and faster as my mind raced with what I was planning to say. I wanted to see him that night, but there was no chance of that.

The next day dawned as usual. Jennifer and I met at the bus station and the others got on at their usual stops. I was full of chat that morning, all about what went on with Mandy and the chain. I was upset really, but now that I was talking to the others, I was getting more and more annoyed, especially as Jane and Claire revealed to me that they had seen Mandy at their stop after work the previous evening and she had told them that she was going

Battles of Degradation

into town to wait for me as she had something to tell me. Mandy had planned this all along. Well, had I got plans for her! All day at work, my mind was elsewhere and I hardly did any work. I came up with a plan. I had to get this bad feeling off my chest and Mandy had to be taught a lesson, especially as she had messed with me knowingly and cunningly. I planned with Claire and Jane to arrange with Mandy to meet her on the bus in the morning. The bus we caught every morning. Mandy did not always get on the same bus, so they would have to encourage her to get on it and I would be waiting.

The next morning, no one wanted to miss that bus. Jennifer, Elspeth and myself were already on and as we approached their stop, I could see that Mandy was there. Yes. My plan was coming together. We had planned previously as well that we would sit in certain places, which would force Mandy to sit next to me. As we always got on the bus first, we always sat at the back, so Mandy was going to have pride of place, in the corner on the very back seat next to me. That way, I would have her undivided attention. As everyone got on and took their places, Mandy came bounding down the bus, shouting morning to everyone. She squeezed passed me and sat in her 'reserved' seat. No sooner did she sit down than I started to question her.

'Mandy, why were you waiting for me the other evening?' I planned to keep calm, but already my voice was raised. She turned to look at me.

'What do you mean?'

'You know exactly what I mean. You waited from around five o'clock to eight thirty to get to see me, just so you could hand me a chain that you knew you could return yourself to Denny when you go to the Reggae Awards on Saturday. So what was that all about?' I was right up against her face and I wanted an answer now. She glanced over at Jane and Claire. Jane looked at her and replied to her glance.

'Don't look at me. You did say that you had something to tell her.' I looked at her, still waiting for an answer. I took the chain from my pocket and threw it at her. With that I slapped her in the face. It was never planned, but I was so worked up that it came from nowhere.

'Don't you ever mess with me again, do you understand?' She nodded with tears rolling down her face. Oblivious to us, the rest of the passengers on the bus were listening in on our disagreement. We came to our stop and we got off leaving her on the bus to continue on to the next stop. I felt so much better. The whole situation was pathetic, but if you are thrown in to a pathetic situation, then your response will be pathetic. Denny was never told what went on, but he was always the cause of my 'falling from grace.'

True to form, I had made myself a target to the 'mafia' sisters. They had questioned Jane about which bus I caught, where I got off, where I lived, etc, in order to track me down away from work and have words with me. Jane, being a friend, did not divulge any of the information requested and they were left to find me themselves. They were apparently angry at the fact that I slapped their sister. In the meantime, Claire had also been approached and she told them the real truth about what went on. They were not at all pleased with Mandy and the fact that she had been trying to get in between me, and the father of my child. They were not having any of that and were now not looking for me. So I was saved. Wow!! As if I was scared. Mandy was told, in no uncertain terms, that she was to keep away from Denny and away from me. I never set eyes on her again and she never caught the same bus as us. The last I heard, she had moved to London with one of her sisters to keep her out of trouble.

A MASKED ESCAPE

The time came when my parents decided that the house needed renovating and extending, as the family was getting 'larger,' and that meant that we would have to move out until it was completed. Oh yes, this meant freedom, because I knew once I moved out I was not moving back in. I had to plan this carefully. Anyway, as I had Mercedes I had to get somewhere decent. There was a friend of the family who had a room I could rent for both Mercedes and me. She lived with her husband in a very large house, which was split on three floors. It was a really nice house and she and her husband said that I could come and go as I pleased

A Masked Escape

and use everything in the house as if it were my own home. Perfect. The bedroom itself was small, but we were only sleeping in it. The house was clean, large, happy and comfortable. It felt like home in the short space of time that I had been there. After about three days all hell broke loose.

Denny used to pick up Mercedes and I had given him a copy of the front door key so he was able to wait in my bedroom until I got home from work (of course, I got permission from Ivy and Norman before doing this and they were happy with that). Ivy was a very petite Jamaican lady full of enormous energy. She walked everywhere and had this very high-pitched voice, but she had a heart of gold. Nothing was ever too much for her to help you with. Norman was her husband and he was white. When he was a bit younger, he had had a throat operation, during the operation his voice box was damaged, and he had lost his voice. He had a permanent hole in his throat through which he could breathe. You had to listen very, very carefully to what he was saying to understand him, but he, too, had a heart of gold and he was very loving towards both Mercedes and myself. Well, anyway, my mum got to hear about this arrangement, she went mental, and that was no exaggeration. She rang up when I got home and she called me all the names under the sun. I could not even get a word in edgeways. She had told Ivy and Norman that whilst I was at home, they would never allow Mercedes' father in the house (which was a lie if ever I heard one; okay, he was not as welcome as I would have liked but he was once again coming over to see Mercedes). She also went on to 'lay down' some home rules, in their house no less. She told them that I was not to go out once I was in from work, or receive any phone calls, and if I did they were not to let me have any. Who did she think she was? I was over eighteen now and technically an adult and no longer under her roof, so how could she lay down laws and rules when I was not in her sight? She carried on ranting and raving on the phone. Ivy and Norman were in the room whilst I held the phone about two feet from my ears. They could hear everything. Norman could not believe what he was hearing and left the room wiping his face and shaking his head. Ivy just stood there and watched me and we both watched the phone. What could I do? When she finally hung up on me, I replaced the receiver real slow and turned to Ivy and shrugged my shoulders. Norman returned and started on at Ivy for telling my mum our arrangement.

'How dare you tell her parents what we had arranged! It has got nothing to do with them what we do in our home. This girl is an adult. She has her own child for god's sake and she takes care of her in the best way possible, and you had the nerve to tell her mother. I am so disappointed in you, Ivy.' Now look what she

A Masked Escape

had caused. He was now coughing because he was so upset and worked up. Ivy was crying. What could I do to put this mess right that my mother had caused? If only she would leave me to live my own life and stop interfering.

That evening I telephone Denny and told him what had happened and asked him to wait outside in the car with Mercedes until I got home from work, and then we could either sit in the car and chat, go to his mum's house or he could go, whatever was best. He was fine with this, but could not believe what my mum had done. At least I was not in range for a good slap! That day at work was so hard, I just kept on thinking of the 'conversation' with my mum and I would start to cry all over again. I worked with someone called Sally and she could obviously see that something was wrong. I went through the whole saga with her.

'Well, no problem, you can have a room in my flat until you get something sorted. Give me a day to clear out the room and then you can move in, how does that sound?' It sounded too good to be true, but she meant it. As I had paid my rent at Ivy and Norman's for the week, I decided that I would stay there for that time and then move on the Friday. She agreed. Denny picked Mercedes up as usual and waited outside. Whilst out in the car explaining to him the new plan, Norman came out of the house and signalled for us to come in. He was not pleased with me for thinking that he would make us sit in the car. He was not part of that nonsense and made it quite clear that Denny could come in any time he wanted. I thanked him for being so kind and then told him of my next plan. I had to make him understand that I had caused problems between him and his wife and that was not my intention. He was fine about it and understood completely. He did not want me to go, but he knew I had to. The bed they had in my room was brand new and he gave it to me as a present. I was so grateful because I needed one to move into Sally's flat, as the bed that she had was her daughter's which was a child's bed anyway.

Friday came and after work Denny turned up as usual, but this time with a small van to help me move the bed and our few belongings as he said he would. We drove to Sally's, her boyfriend helped Denny move the bed in, and I was settled. The room was small, but big enough for the two of us. I was in a warm, cosy flat far away from the clutches of my parents and their influences and they, not knowing Sally, could not get to me. Sally lived over a small shopping complex, which consisted of a mini-supermarket, dry cleaners, a Chinese takeaway and a betting shop. Her flat was above the Chinese takeaway, so you can imagine the lovely smells that made their way up in to the flat. She was also in Denny's neighbourhood, so now he would not have far at all to come to see

A Masked Escape

us. He had friends in the block of flats across from Sally's where he would go every Friday night to play cards and there were other friends dotted about around the flat that I was now living in. Yvette was just down the road within walking distance and this meant I could see her more often, not having to catch a bus and even then walk a bit to get to her. It was all falling into place nicely. Life got better and I was happier than I had ever been. Yvette would come round and spend evenings with us or I would go around to her house and spend evenings there. Sally and her family were so easy to live with. She was mostly out, and on the evenings that she wanted to entertain her friends I would make myself scarce by staying in my room with Mercedes, watching TV, reading to Mercedes or playing games. My family was the furthest thing from my mind. I did not go to see them for quite some time and they had no idea where I was living. I suppose they were concerned, especially about Mercedes, but I did not care. They had made my life a misery, now they could suffer a little, and when I was ready, I would take Mercedes to see them. After all, I knew they loved her and she adored them and I would never keep them apart, not for long anyway.

Yvette and I had lots of secrets that we told each other. She had even told me that when she was younger, she had had a crush on Denny. He would be down at the garages fixing cars with his friend and she would hang around trying to catch his eye, but once her brother found out what she was up to, she was told in no uncertain terms to stay away from him, mainly because he was too old for her and also that he was not good enough for her, but she would still try and try.

Life went on, I finally got back in with my parents, and we were all on talking terms again. It was always me who had to give in and break the silence, but I just could not be doing with bad feelings, hang-ups and holding grudges. Sally now wanted her second bedroom back. She was not nasty about it, but felt that, given the situation, there were too many of us living in the flat, which I agreed with because there were three adults and two children in a two - bed roomed flat. She suggested that I went back to the council to request housing. By this time, I had been on the council housing list for nearly four years, but still nothing was available. Things were getting desperate. As Sally wanted her room back, I felt under pressure to vacate it as soon as I could. She did not mean for me to do this, but it was just the way I was. I did not want to over-stay my welcome. My last resort was to go to Yvonne's dad, who was in charge of the Ethnic Minority Community Relations Office. So I made an appointment to see him to talk through my housing problem. Telling my mum about the possibility of moving to a hostel until I was re-housed sent her demented once again.

'So you think you can look after your child all by yourself in a hostel?' I dare not answer. What was her problem? 'You're not that child's mother you know. It's me. I am the one who brought her up. I am the one who she calls Mum all the time. Does she ever call you Mum?' Well of course she didn't, she grew up in a house where everyone called me Shoy and everyone called her Mum. So what was she getting at? 'You see, Shoy, I know exactly how many hours I have been a mother to that child and you cannot compare with that'. So this was her plan. She had made me go back to school, then go to college and then find a job, just so at the moment when I wanted to give us a home of our own and assume my responsibilities, she would step in and do this. Why? Why would anyone do this, especially a mother to her child? 'Well, if you take her to any sort of a hostel, or if you think you are going to move out of this town, I am going to take you to court and see where you get to then.'

I was shocked and frightened (again). I felt so sure that she could do this. I knew that I had not been with Mercedes all of her life since she was born. I was out there trying to better myself to prove that I could be someone and to give her a home, somewhere safe, but I was now losing. My mother was expecting me

Shoy

to return home once all the renovations had been completed. She did not expect me to find a place of my own in the meantime and never come back. I had escaped and I was going to have to take a chance and move on, but it was in my mind that she could do it and I would lose. After all, I had no idea what the law was capable of and she made it sound so conclusive.

By the end of that week, I was sent to a hostel. This hostel was located about ten miles out of my hometown in the middle of nowhere. It was a huge stately home that was converted into flat-lets and single rooms for single mothers waiting to be housed wherever. It looked so beautiful from the outside. It just sat there in the middle of fields with its little tree-lined dirt-track road winding up to it. It then ended in a huge, gravel-lined circular courtyard. Once again, I packed all my belongings together and arranged for Denny to help us move again. It seemed such a good idea at the time, but when I arrived it was far from it. They were not really ready for us. The warden had no room as one of the girls who was supposed to move out that day had some problem and was still there, so in effect my room was not available. Her suggestion was that she put a bed up in the hallway, albeit a big hallway, and Mercedes and I sleep there for the night and then in the morning she would sort us out. I started to cry and declined. What sort of set-up was that? In a hallway where everyone would walk up and

A Masked Escape

down at night because the toilets were shared and so you would have to come out of your room, walk down this so-called hallway, to go to whichever one you were assigned to. This was not good. Whilst standing there arguing the point, one of the girls who was pregnant offered us a bed in her room. She had three beds in her room and a separate kitchen/sitting room and she would be glad of the company, as she did not have any friends or relatives that would visit her. I agreed to this and off we went to her room. We settled down for the night. I hardly said a word that evening. Denny left us as men were not supposed to be there after eleven at night. I already hated it. That night I heard the warden doing her security checks. She came walking down the corridor, jangling her big bunch of keys as if in a prison and her footsteps would disappear and the noises of this huge house would become very apparent with the crying of children, mothers voices, the heating pipes hissing and creaking as they shut down for the night. The cold air would penetrate the skin of your face as if a mask was placed over it and the heat was being drawn from it. I huddled up to Mercedes, who was fast asleep, and finally fell asleep myself.

Early the next morning I awoke to the sound of shouting from one of the other girls (you almost wanted to call them in-mates). I lay there, hoping it was all a dream and I would wake soon, but it was not and I was already awake.

Shoy

Mercedes eventually woke up and off we went to the bathroom that we shared with the girl whose room we were in and one other person in a single room, which was next door to the bathroom. Well, it was gopping. It was cold and I did not even want the air in it to touch me. I went straight back to our kitchen and got the bottle of bleach and bathroom cleaner that I had brought with me and began to clean it. It looked so much better when I had finished, but I was still not satisfied. It would do for now. We were in and out of it in no time at all. We had breakfast and then went to see the warden, as I was keen to find out when I was going to get my own room. She had bad news. Apparently, the girl who was supposed to leave the day before was now not leaving and so there was no place available. I returned to Liz with the warden and the warden explained to her what was going on. Liz did not mind sharing with us. So that was settled. Mercedes and I would share with Liz until something came up. Liz was paying seventeen pounds a month for the flat-let, but as we were sharing they wavered that cost until they could give us separate accommodation. We still had to punch for our own electricity and gas.

Over the next couple of weeks I got to know Liz very well. She was pregnant and looked ill all the time. She had straw-blonde hair down to the nape of her neck. She looked skinny by all accounts

A Masked Escape

and her voice was very soft and full of sadness and rejection. I felt so sorry for her; she had no one to care for her. She never had any visitors and she barely left the place to visit anyone. She hardly had any money, even to buy food and nourish herself or her unborn baby. As we were sharing with her, I would buy food for all of us and I told her to eat properly. To begin with, she would not touch any of it, but I had a chat with her, quite strongly, and she began to feel all right about it. She really perked up and we would have a laugh. She told me stories about her life and it seemed so sad and how she came to be there. There is always someone worse off than you who makes you see your life as simple.

Within three or four weeks, a single bed-sit became free, Liz moved out of the double room, and kitchenette that we shared and into the single bed-sit as it was smaller and she preferred that. I now had a so-called 'place of my own.' It was in a dismal location, but it was mine and I had a key to the front door, and I was paying seventeen pounds a month and punching for my own gas and electricity. As we were not going to be there more than three months since this was short-stay accommodation only, I felt I could cope with the damp, the mice, the noises, the lack of hot water and heating when the system broke down, and the fact that I worked and had to be up early in the morning. There would never be any water or heating on and it was freezing, but this would all be just for a short time and we were already into our second month, so technically there was only a month and a half left. I asked the warden if the extra beds, the cot and other items of furniture that I felt I did not need could be removed to give it more room and also so I could make it much better for us. She agreed and removed all the items. I had a big tidy-out and cleaned everywhere. It was spotless and I felt so much better. As for the toilet and the bathroom, well that remained a sore point with me. I am too scornful for my own good. We were now sharing these with Liz, which made me feel much better, but still not happy. I would use Mercedes' old baby bath to wash her and myself and then empty the water into the bathroom that I never used.

My first weekend in our own little place and we were all alone. Denny did not come to see us and he did not even phone. I rang him a couple of times, but he was never there. As planned on the Monday morning, he arrived at seven o'clock to pick us up and drop us off at my mum's house (which was still being renovated). My parents and I were back on speaking terms again and I would wait there until it was time for Mercedes to go to school, drop her off and then I would hare down to the bus station to get my bus and get to work. I was always rushing about and relying on other people to help me. I was always exhausted, but just kept going. My mum would pick Mercedes up from school and I would then

A Masked Escape

go to my parents' house and wait there for Denny to pick us up and take us back to the hostel. I would finish work at five o'clock and we would be hanging around my parents' house until about seven to seven-thirty. I would hate this, but there was nothing I could do. It was the only way that I could get back to the hostel. The last bus that would run past the hostel was at two o'clock in the afternoon and that would be it until eight twenty-five the next morning. There were four buses going in to town from that direction in the morning and only three returning and none of them was any good to me. So once again, I was wholly reliant on Denny. So much time was spent just travelling back and forth to the hostel. There was no way that I could afford to drive and get myself a car and, anyway, I would not be here for long.

Sometimes in the evening when Denny dropped me 'home,' he would stay and I would have to okay it with the warden, just in case he wanted to stay over, but that rarely happened. He would, most of the time, be clock-watching and itching to go. He always had somewhere better to go. I would never question him or push him on anything. I never wanted to upset him, as he would stop picking us up and then where would I be? I was so lonely. Mercedes liked this god-awful place. She had a little mouse as her friend that she would feed from a little hole in the kitchen near the sink. The mouse would actually poke its nose out of the hole and

Shoy

sit there as if waiting for her to feed him. She would go over to the hole, place a bit of cheese or bread down, he would nibble it, and she would sit and watch, talking away to it. She was such a gentle child and I loved watching her, but with the mouse – well what could I do? I did not have the heart to stop her. Mercedes was also friends with the warden's daughter and she would spend most weekends with her in their house, which was across the way from where we were. They would have baths together and sleep together and they became really good friends, for which I was grateful. There was no chance of Mercedes getting bored. The warden was motherly and very understanding. She had looked after so many other girls in my position before and would do the same for me.

There was a farm just down the lane from the hostel and in the field there was a lovely white horse, and at weekends we used to walk down (if the weather was fine) and feed it. Mercedes loved animals. It was as if she talked to them. She would also collect packages and wrappers (especially shiny ones) and we would make things with them. We had 'rubbish' all over the place in bags, under the bed wherever, but it made her happy. I was happy seeing her happy, but it did not take a lot to make her content and as long as she was loved she was happy. I loved her so much; no one was ever going to take her away from me.

A Masked Escape

The three months at the hostel turned into eight long, hard and depressing months and I was there for Christmas. I bought a small silver Christmas tree that stood on a tabletop and we decorated it and put some lights on it. It looked good, but I was so alone. I asked Denny if he would come and spend Christmas day with us. He would see and let us know! But we did not see him until Boxing Day and then that was only for a few hours. I did a lot of crying during this time, because I wanted him so much and my daughter wanted him as well, but he always had somewhere to go or someone to see - why?

Finally one day the warden came to see me and said that I was going to be interviewed for a flat – oh my god, a flat! I was so excited I could not contain myself. The day came, I took the day off work, and Mercedes did not go to school, as I would not be able to get back for the appointment. They arrived. I say 'they' because there were two ladies and a man. They looked so official. I was very nervous. They asked a lot of questions about Mercedes and me. They wanted me to go to live in another town in the opposite direction, but Mercedes was already settled in a very good school and there was no way I was going to move her now. Anyway, I wanted to move back to my old town to be near my friends and family and as I did not drive, I would, once again, be isolated. I

Shoy

declined the offer. A few days later I got a letter to say that I was being offered another flat and they gave me the address. Well, I did not know where it was. The letter explained that as the council did not have any accommodation to offer me within the location of my daughter's school, they had turned me over to a Housing Association and they were offering me this flat. I just had to find out where it was. I rang Wayne, giving him the address, and he found out for me. I could not believe my luck. It was five minutes' walk from Mercedes' school and about ten minutes' walk from my mum's. My parents' house was now complete and Clarence, John and Stephanie had long since moved back. Wayne had no plans for moving back and neither did I.

I went to see the flat within the week and accepted it. All the paperwork had been completed and I was given a date to pick up the keys and move in. The flat was better than I had expected. It had two large bedrooms with a separate bathroom and toilet and a big enough kitchen. The flat itself was on a split-level as it was built on a hill. Up four steps took you to the living/dining room, which was a large room, the full length of the flat from front to back. At the point where the stairs went up, there was living space to the left and living space to the right. So I had decided that the living room would be on the left and the dining room would be on the right, as that was the back of the flat which looked over the communal car park. I was ecstatic. I now had my own home and it was amazing.

Now, the money that my mum made me save when I first started working came due that very year and I was to get two thousand pounds. With that two thousand pounds, I bought all my furniture and paid for the carpets and any electrical equipment that I needed – which was everything. (In my heart and my mind, I thanked my mum very much for making me save wisely, but I never told her). Before moving in, everyone came to see the flat and they were so happy for me, even my parents, mostly because I was so near and they could come over whenever they wanted.

Saturday arrived, the day I was actually moving in, and Mercedes stayed with my parents, so she would not be in the way. During the week, I had been on a 'cheap' spending spree, buying all the items of furniture and electrical equipment that I was going to need. Denny had chosen the carpets for the living room and the bedrooms; I had given him the money so I had no idea what they would be like or whether I would even like them. He had arranged to pick up a van on the Friday evening to collect all the items of furniture that I had bought over the week. Prior to that, he arranged for the carpets to be delivered and fitted on the Saturday morning before bringing all the furniture in which was standing outside in the van. It all went very smoothly. I was so happy that day. He had some of his friends come over to help with the lifting and shifting, and by the evening everything was in. The only thing that needed to be done was some decorating. The wallpaper was not my style, but that could wait. The main thing was getting in and settling down. My parents came over that evening with Mercedes and my brothers and sister. They all liked it and the things that I had bought (some of them second hand, but decent). I had bought a glass-top dining table and six chairs that was second-hand, a mahogany-look double wardrobe with a dressing table in the middle for my bedroom and a white double wardrobe for Mercedes' bedroom. I had to get another double bed, which I did, and this was new (of course). The settee was also bought by Denny, but with my money. That was an olive green colour with stripes of gold in it. It was okay, but not a colour I would have chosen myself. The carpets were a mix of blues and subtle reds. It was nice, but just did not go with the rest of the furniture. I had also bought a bookcase unit with a matching television cupboard, which was also second-hand. I had to buy a fridge-freezer and an electric cooker, which I got brand new, and the washing machine I hired. Denny had also arranged for someone he knew who was a qualified electrician to come and put the cooker in on the Saturday evening. There were various other bits and pieces I bought to make my flat look like a home. By the end of the evening it

A Masked Escape

looked really good, and it was warm and inviting. I had no curtains though - completely forgot about them - but in the true style of having family and good friends, I had curtains. My mum gave me enough nets to put up at all the windows in the flat. She would always change her nets every Christmas and keep the old ones, never throwing them away, so somewhere in the attic there were bags and bags of nets just waiting for me to have. Denny's sister, Yvonne, gave me some thick curtains, which were, of course, olive green and matched the settee perfectly and also some very dark green ones, just in case I preferred them to the olive ones. For Mercedes' bedroom, she gave me a pink pair that Tanya, her daughter, had had in her room and she no longer needed. They were all very long and I had to take them up, as the windows in her house were huge. Yvette gave me thick, brown, velvet-looking pair for my bedroom. So there it was, my flat all kitted out with curtains, curtains from all over and nothing looked good. At least, I did not think so. In my mind, they were the first things I was going to change when I got the chance. I did not like them at all, all this green everywhere. But for now, it would do.

Everyone who had been helping was now going home, back to their lives. Denny had to get the van back, and he left, offering to take Yvette home. My dad left with my brothers and my sister and my mum wanted to hang on just a bit longer. Of course,

Shoy

once everyone had gone and Mercedes was now tucked up in bed having had a story read to her, the real reason for staying became apparent.

'So now you have this flat, who is going to live here?'

Well, what sort of question was that? Who did she think was going to live there? 'What do you mean?' I knew exactly what she was banging on about, but I would not give her the satisfaction of cutting short what she wanted to say. If she had something to say, she was going to have to say it and I would never make it easy for her. She glared at me.

'I suppose Denny is going to move in now?'

'Well, yes, if he wants to. It's up to him.'

'So you think that is going to look good?'

'Look good to who? Look mum, he is the father of my child and I don't care what people want to say. Quite honestly, they should all mind their own business. They all have enough scandal of their own without worrying about ours, if that's what you want to call it.' She was not at all pleased. But now I did not care. I was

A Masked Escape

in my own home and this she could not mess up in any way. She was not paying my bills and she had not bought anything that she was looking at that very moment. She left it at that. The conversation on that subject was well and truly over.

The flat was now quiet. Everyone had gone and Mercedes was asleep. I stood in her bedroom just looking at her, lost in the big bed, but so beautiful and peaceful. I kissed her on the forehead and left the room, leaving the door slightly open so that the light from the hallway streamed into a corner of her room and if she woke she would not be scared of the dark, like I was. I made myself a cup of tea, the first one of the day, went and sat down in my new olive green settee and switched on the TV. The TV was on, but my mind was pondering on the events of the day. I looked around the room. Now I could sit on the phone for as long as I wanted. I could have my friends over whenever they wanted to come over. I could put the heating on whenever I was cold. I could run the hot water as much as I wanted to and fill the bath as high as I could, but most of all, Denny could come and see me and we could make love as much as we wanted to and not have one ear open the whole time or go off to awkward, uncomfortable places just to be close. My mind drifted to Denny. Why was he not here? He left hours ago and I really thought he would be back in a flash to be with me. I wished Denny would come back and stay the night. Now he had the chance to, was he going to take it? I did not think he would for a minute. He had already had sex with me earlier that day. When we first arrived at the flat with no one else there, the only place that had carpet on the floor was the cupboard, which was big enough for a small office. We had made love on the floor and christened the flat then. So why would he come back tonight?

A few hours went past. I somehow could not get to sleep. Maybe I was over-excited, or maybe over-tired, but it was not happening and the TV was boring. Unexpectedly, the buzzer for the door went. It made me jump a mile. This was a sound I was going to have to get used to. I rushed to the door and picked up the intercom.

'Hello?'

'Well open the door then,' came a voice. It was Denny. He had come back and it was late. I opened the door and unlocked my front door. He came up and came in. As soon as he entered the front door he kissed me, long and hard. I was in heaven. He did love me. There were no words between us to speak of. That night we just made love over and over again. I so loved him and for the first time in our relationship, I felt warm.

A Masked Escape

Morning came and I was up early. Mercedes and Denny were still fast asleep. I looked out of the window in the kitchen. I was within walking distance of so many things. The train station I could see from the window and through the night the goods trains had thundered past, sometimes shaking everything in the flat. To begin with, I had thought it was an earthquake, but it's a sound you soon become familiar with. Further down the road was the town centre with the library. Mercedes and I belonged to the library. She loved books and we could spend more time there, as we were so much closer. About fifteen minutes' walk away was the hospital the fire station and the college, and in the opposite direction was the huge park with the dyke and the waterfall. I was going to love living here. I would not have to spend any money to get to anything, except to work, but that was now only one bus ride away. Mercedes' school was literally around the corner. It was all perfect, slotting into place nicely.

I made breakfast for the three of us. We sat at the glass-top table and had our first meal together as a family. I sat there watching them as they spoke and he helped Mercedes cut up her sausages. 'A father and his daughter. Together.' Now he could see his child whenever he wanted to and be a real, proper father to her, instead of a part-time one. It was magic.

Shoy

'So what's happening today then?' he asked me.

I shrugged. 'Why, what have you got planned?' This was a road I was not used to at all. We never planned anything together, so which angle he was coming from, I was not sure. I waited until it became clear what he was on about.

'Well, I thought we could go to my house and you could help me pack?'

'Pack what?' My heart was racing. I knew exactly where he was coming from, but I wanted to play the fool just a bit longer.

'Well, don't you want me to move in with you and Mercedes and be a real family?'

I could not hold back any longer, I flung my arms around him and tears came to my eyes. I could not say a word. My actions spoke volumes.

Getting used to living in the flat was quite difficult. I had always had so many people around me, day and night, and now most of the time it was just Mercedes and I. I was so lonely in the eve-

A Masked Escape

nings. Friends would come over, especially Yvette, but once they had gone home, I was all alone. Again. At the weekends, Denny would disappear from Friday evening, after coming home, having a bath and then getting dressed and going out, and I would not see him again until sometimes Monday evening after work. I would not know where he was at all and he would not tell me even on the odd occasion that I asked. I never liked asking him too much as he had said in the past that what he got up to was none of my business. He was providing me with money and food. What more did I want? At least he came home to me even if it was not at the weekends.

Even though I was where I wanted to be, there were still moments of sadness, but all I was waiting for was the day when he would ask me to marry him. He was difficult to live with, with all his friends that would call him at all hours of the evening and night and then he would go. He was always at their beck and call, always doing things for them. What about me? The few Fridays that he did not go out in the evening, come the Saturday morning he would be up and out, off to his mother because she would have already phoned, letting him know that his dinner was ready whenever he wanted to come and get it. What the hell was wrong with my food? It was good enough to eat during the week, but on a Saturday, he had to have his mum's food. This used to nark

Shoy

me something chronic, but I never said a word, until one Saturday when I had had enough.

'If you go off to your mum for food today, you can get all your meals from her from now on.' He knew I meant it.

'So what am I to say to her?' I stood in front of him with my arms folded.

'Say what you want, but I have said what I want.' He called her back and told her that I had planned a special meal of some sort and that he could not have any food that day. So that took care of that particular Saturday, but we would see what would take place the next Saturday. From that day on, he stopped going to his mum. Of course she called me, demanding to know why I had stopped her son from having her dinner. Well, at some point her little boy had to grow up, leave home, and take his chances with his girlfriend's food. This was a fight I was not going to embark on. She so wanted to make a big issue of it, but I would not rise to the challenge. She left it.

Our life together was not really romantic; in fact, it was far from it. I would watch other relationships and wish that ours could be like theirs. We would never go out together, and I hardly knew

A Masked Escape

his friends, only the really close ones that came to the flat. There were so many that called and I never got to meet them. We would never, ever hold hands, or kiss in public, not even in front of Mercedes, let alone anyone else. He was not one for showing his emotions and he would never tell me that he loved me. I would always say it to him, but all he would say, is 'Hmm' never returning the words that I longed for. I began to think that maybe he did not love me, but he must have done. Why else was he living with me?

On many occasions, Mercedes would stay with my parents as my sister always wanted her over and I would suggest to Denny that I cook us a nice romantic dinner with things that he liked. His favourite food was lobsters and any kind of shellfish. I knew how to cook paella and so I would suggest to him that I did this, with starters and pudding of his choice. The difficulty was tying him down to one of the Fridays so he would not go out. One particular weekend, I wanted us to be alone and have a nice meal together. At the beginning of the week, he agreed, but as the week went on I knew he was not going to be around, so I did not plan anything and never mentioned it either. Mercedes stayed with my parents as planned and I was alone. In a way I was glad that I had not planned anything too extravagant, as I had not been feeling well since the Thursday. I lay on the settee, very uncomfortable and irritated. I kept getting this dull ache in my stomach. Maybe it was something I had eaten, or not as the case was. The whole day I had not been able to eat properly as I kept on being sick and waves of heat would consume me, and as quickly as it came it went again. I knew something was wrong, but I thought I was going down with the flu or something similar. As the evening went by, I began to get worse, to the point where I could not stand up properly without experiencing excruciating pains radiating out from my stomach in all directions. I was now getting quite worried. I knew something was seriously wrong. I called the hospital and explained my symptoms over the phone. Without hesitation, they told me to get off the phone and get over to the casualty unit immediately. The only problem was, I did not drive and Denny was not at home. The hospital was only about fifteen minutes' walk away, but the amount of pain I was in meant I could not chance it. It happened that a friend of my sister's, Sunil, ran his own taxi company and I knew that he could be at my flat in no time at all, so I called him and, just as I thought, he was there and helping me into the car. The journey to the hospital seemed to take forever. Once there, I asked him to go and get my mum and bring her over, as I had not thought of calling her and she would want to be with me. Of course, I could not get hold of Denny because I did not know where he was. Sunil left and brought mum back as he said he would. The hospital casualty doctor examined

A Masked Escape

me and diagnosed a ruptured appendix, which needed to come out immediately. Without delay and because I had not eaten all day, I was prepared for theatre and by the time my mum arrived, I was almost on my way down. She only had enough time to tell me that she would be there when I came back.

'Shoy, you're all right. Try not to move.' Too late, the pain struck me and I turned back trying not to scream. What had gone on? My side felt as though I had walked into a sledgehammer and it had won. Of course, I had my appendix removed and it was my mum's voice I woke up to. I turned and looked at her, trying to force a smile, but the tears were greater. She wiped my face. 'It's all right, Shoy, they caught the appendix just in time, so you'll be fine. By the way, where is Denny? I have tried ringing and ringing the flat, but there is no answer.'

I did not really want to answer, but why should I stick up for him again and again? 'He went out with his friends.'

'Well okay, I will keep trying the flat. Actually, I need to go and get you some clothes, so when I go up there, I will leave him a note so he knows where you are. I will not come back tonight, as it is late. You get some rest and I will see you in the morning, okay?' I just lay there knowing that he would not get that note,

Shoy

probably until Monday evening when he came in from work expecting his dinner to be ready and his daughter to be smiling and ready to play with him.

My mum returned the next morning with my clean clothes and of course she brought the family with her, including Mercedes. Still there was no sign of Denny. She did not mention it, but I knew it was on her mind and she was aching to ask me again, but it would be of no use, because the answer would still be the same.

Sunday night came and visiting time was over, but he was nowhere to be seen. I knew he was not going to get home until Monday evening. It was one of those weekends where we were left alone to our own devices. My mum was not at all pleased.

'So where is he? He has not been home all weekend, because the note I have left has not been touched. What if I was not here to look after Mercedes, hmm? Who would have made arrangements to look after her?' Asking me all these questions was not going to give her any answers, simply because once again, I did not have the answers. I wished I did. Mum took Mercedes home and collected her school uniform, lunchbox and all the other bits and pieces that she needed and took her back to her house. That was one less thing to worry about. I knew she was in the best place ever and I could concentrate on getting better and out of this hospital bed.

Monday morning came and Mum came over to see how I was after she had dropped Mercedes off at school. Still there was no sign of him. She had passed by the flat on her way over and he was not there. She was now livid.

'So this is the man you let move in with you and he does not give a dam about you? Is that the kind of relationship you want? You'd better wise up my girl and tell him where to get off.'

I had no energy to argue. I wanted her to go and never come back. I knew she would find a way of dogging our relationship. We never had a chance. Late that evening, long after visiting time was over, one of the nurses came to see me.

'I have a visitor for you. It's a bit late, but he says that he is your fiancé and that he has been away and so was not able to see you earlier. Is it okay for me to bring him over?' Of course it was. An instant smile appeared on my face. I had known he would come, but it was a matter of when. He came over and there was no kiss, no flowers, just a,

'You all right?' Well of course I was not all right, but I said, I was. He looked so uncomfortable sitting there. There was no explanation of where he had been or an apology for not getting home sooner. It was as if he had really been away and he was now home. I told him to go, as his uneasiness upset me. He left with no hesitation, no kiss, just a goodbye and 'I will see you tomorrow'. I sank heavy into the hard hospital bed. I was losing him.

As my mum was a nurse, I was allowed out of hospital sooner than I should have been. The day they let me out, of course, we had to get a taxi home, because Mr Denny was busy and could not fetch me for some reason. I insisted on staying at my flat, which my mum actually agreed to, but of course, she would come over every morning once she had taken Mercedes to school or if she had to work that night. Stephanie would get Mercedes ready for school, walk over to my flat and then she would meet them there and take Mercedes to school, once she had prepared me something to eat. When she had had enough sleep, she would come back and stay with me until it was time to get Mercedes from school. She had it all planned. That was fine by me. I was in no fit state to move about anyway. During all of this, Denny played no active part whatsoever. The only thing that my mum insisted that he did was the shopping, as she did not drive and was not going to pay for a taxi when he had a car. What would I have done without

A Masked Escape

my mum? She was the best thing even though she moaned about everything. I knew she loved me, as only a loving mother would help in this way, unconditionally. Both she and my dad had shown a different side, a side I had not really seen before. Lying there in all that pain, I could see what they were trying to do for me. I knew in the bottom of my heart that Denny did not want me. There were plenty more fish in the sea and he was tired of me, but I had to get back to full health to deal with him. For the time being, he came and went.

Yvette, Yvonne and most of my friends would visit me regularly. Yvette came over every day and stayed with me until it was real late. We would sit and talk and she would prepare me things to eat, saving my mum the time and bother. She would even cook dinner for Denny and have it ready for him when he came home. She was so good. I was getting better now and could move about a bit more.

Whilst all this was going on, Yvette told me that she was pregnant and that Wayne was the father. I was so pleased for her. Finally, she and Wayne might get married. They so suited each other. Their relationship was not all there, but now that Yvette was pregnant, maybe they would get things back on track and settle down together. She was like a sister to me and marrying Wayne would

Shoy

make her my sister. She was never happy, though. We would spend hours and hours talking things through. She did not want the baby. She wanted to get rid of it, but did not have the guts to go through with it. I was never sure if my brother wanted the child as well. Once she had even told me that she had deliberately thrown herself down the stairs in her parents house to try to have a miscarriage, but this child was here to stay and there was no going back. The only way out now was to give birth and then put the child up for adoption, but I was sure that she would love the child once it had arrived and she had seen its little face. I was right. That November she gave birth to a lovely little boy and they named him Mike. He was a big baby, not like my little Mercedes. She absolutely loved him and she was a perfect mother. Later on they got a council flat and my brother moved in with her. They were so happy. They would spend so much time together, they would visit me, and things were just fantastic. I wished they would not end. I was not happy with my relationship, but I was happy for them and seeing them together made me happy. There was nothing I would not do for Yvette and she for me.

That year, I had lost a lot of weight with the appendicitis and all the worry of losing Denny. Even though he did not move out, I knew he did not really want me. I never felt wanted. Even though our sex life was still strong, that was the only thing I had to keep

A Masked Escape

him with me. Once again, sex came in to play. That was the only thing that men wanted me for. Was this how my future was going to be mapped out? Me losing all that weight was short-lived, though. I knew I wanted two children and I wanted both of them to have the same father. I did not want them to have to go off at weekends to different locations, having different surnames and different identities. I deliberately started to mess up on taking my pills. I would go for days without taking one and then just as I knew that I would get a period, I would take a few more. The whole thing was a mess and I finally got pregnant.

Once again, my planning was so bad. I knew I wanted to get pregnant, but nothing was happening. So, forgetting the idea, I had booked a holiday to Spain for the summer. On this holiday I was taking my youngest brother, John, (Clarence did not want to go as he was afraid of flying), Stephanie, Jennifer, who had been with us before, my mum as she had never been to Spain before and really wanted to go, and of course, Mercedes. I had asked my dad, but there was no way he was going to cross the water to the continent as he was convinced that everyone abroad were against black people, but nonetheless, he had been asked. I had booked an apartment in Blanes where we had gone a couple of years previously and knew that it would be good there. As my mum had never gone to Europe before, this would be a good place to take

Shoy

her.

So here I was with two exciting moments in my life. I was going to have a baby and I had a holiday booked. I broke the news to my mum about being pregnant.

'So what does that mean? You are going to cancel the holiday?' That was all she could think about, the holiday. She had even asked me if I was going to get rid of it, because I did not need to have another child. She even went as far to say that 'in this day and age, you no longer need to have more than one child. It is too expensive and you can make something of yourself and have better things for the one you have got.' But why should I have an only child? I never wanted just one child. I had always wanted two, I had always wanted them to be with the same father, this was happening, and there was nothing she could do about it. Mind you, I had lost two before, so anything was possible.

I checked with the doctor and the airline and I was okay to fly with my dates to go on holiday and would be back well before the last travel date was due. So my mum would still get to go on her holiday and have a ball at my expense! In the back of my mind I was still worried though. What if I miscarried whilst on holiday? I took out the necessary insurance, but still I worried. I had so much hassle with this holiday, especially as I did not want to go now. It was all getting too much.

The day arrived for us to leave for our holiday and various people took us to Luton Airport. We arrived in Blanes. It was glorious and I so loved Spain. My mum thought it was fantastic and could not stop talking and her voice just got louder and louder with her excitement.

We arrived at the apartment and unpacked our things. Mum, Stephanie, Mercedes and Jennifer went out to get some food as it was self-catering and John and I stayed in, as it was very hot. That evening Mum cooked us all a meal and the others planned to go out to the disco. There was a knock at the door. Jennifer went to answer it, but we all stood in the hallway to see who it would be as we were not expecting anyone. The door opened and there standing in the doorway was a pair of legs with a huge basket of red roses, no head to be seen behind the screen of roses. We all stood there, just looking.

'Hello.' My mum finally said and broke the amazed silence. The basket lowered and it was Federico. I ran to the door and flung my arms around him. I could not believe that he had come. I never expected him to, as I had not heard from him. We had still been in contact with one another and I had written to him and told him when I would be in Blanes. He was here and I was so glad. I pulled him into the apartment and closed the door behind him. The basket of roses was just out of this world. He must have paid so much for them and they were real. I took the basket and proceeded to introduce him to everyone. From day one, he was with us and my mum loved him. He could do no wrong in her eyes. We talked and talked. His English was so much better. He had been practising, just waiting for this day when we would see each other again. The only thing was, I was pregnant and it was not his child. Seeing him made me feel so guilty. I felt as though I had betrayed him. He was okay with the whole thing. He asked me loads of questions. He knew I was not happy with Denny. He even proposed that I stay with him, and have the baby in Spain. Even after all this time and then returning to Spain pregnant with another man's child, he still wanted me. He wanted to marry me and never let me go home, back to England. He promised that he would look after us and that we would not want for anything. I believed him, but stupidly I declined, simply because I was in love with Denny and it would be unfair to Federico. The holiday turned out fine and I did not have a miscarriage whilst there. I waved goodbye to Federico, once again breaking his heart and returned back to my dull, wanting life.

A Masked Escape

Within a few weeks I had my baby boy. He was small, only weighing 4lbs 7ozs. He had not got into trouble like Mercedes but he was cold. This time I was able to hold him a lot longer before they whisked him off to the incubator and we were on a normal ward and not in the SCBU. He was perfect and very greedy. In no time at all we were out of hospital and home. Home to our flat. Denny was so happy. He had always wanted a son and now I had given him one. The family was complete. Denny chose his name. He was called Ezra. His second name I chose: Anthony followed by Leroy. Mercedes and Ezra were so similar. In fact, Ezra was a smaller version of Mercedes. Together my children were gorgeous and I loved them so much. I was now satisfied and did not want any more children.

Denny was more of a father this time around. In all fairness, with Mercedes all of that had been robbed from him, as we were not together. He would change him (but only when he was wet; if he pooed himself, there was no way he was going to even attempt that). When I stopped breastfeeding (as I hated it so much), he would feed him with the bottle, but never in the night. That was my job. I can't ever remember him bathing him, so it probably never happened. Mercedes and I would bath Ezra together. I would let her hold him (as best she could with her little hands) and she would wash his hair ever so gently. Sometimes he would

Shoy

wriggle so much that I would have to hold him so she could wash him, but she really wanted to do it all herself. She loved him so much. She was like a proper little mother to him. She would sing to him and play with him for hours and hours until he either fell asleep (which was never for long) or scream and scream, and then she knew that he was not having any of it. Sometimes, I would think, what a horrid child; his poor sister is trying to make him happy and all he does is scream and scream.

The family was 'happy,' but still I yearned for Denny to tell me that he loved me, that he wanted me, just for him to acknowledge his feelings for me. It was a wait in vain. I decided that I would ask him to marry me. I could not decide which day and how I was going to put it, but I had to, I needed to know. One evening, with the kids safely tucked up in bed, I took a deep breath. I was so nervous. I breathed out and carried on watching the TV. I took another deep breath and watched him as I did. He did not even notice that I was twitchy. I breathed out again. This was all well and good and, yes, I could breathe, but I was now getting light-headed and even more nervous. I rehearsed in my head how I was going to say the all-important words. I decided that I would count to three and then I would let it out.

'Denny, will you marry me? After all, we have our two children

A Masked Escape

that we wanted and we are now living together and we are happy and I love you, so what do you think?' That was definitely desperate. I said it all too fast and it did not come out the way I had planned it at all. I said far too much. I showed my weakness and the fact that I had been thinking about it too long. He did not even look at me when he replied.

'I don't think that now is the time. We have only just started living with each other and have to get used to things, but when we get a house with a nice garden, then we can get married.'

'Hmm,' was all I could say. Well, what sort of answer was that? But it was as good as I was going to get. So now we had to get a house. When the hell was that going to be? I had only just managed to get this flat, I was not made of money, and my job did not pay me enough to get a mortgage. So it looked as though it was never going to happen. I wiped my mind clear and left it at that.

Life went on and Yvette and I would spend lots and lots of time together as our boys were within a year of each other. They would run under the glass top table in my dinning room without touching it as they were that short. But soon they would bang their heads on it as they tried to get under it, not realising that they had grown. We watched them grown up together. By this time, Wayne and

Shoy

Yvette had separated and she was on her own, but happy enough. Even though she did not work, she would still be flushed with money and have all the best things in her home. I could never understand this and envied her for this reason and this reason alone. I worked so hard and would be away from my children for hours and still not manage to have the things she had or even get close to having them.

I had been made redundant from my job whilst on maternity leave and now I was working as a secretary in the local hospital. I was getting into this job, but it was hard work. I remember during the first week of their taking me on, I rubbed off the audiotape of one of the Consultants before typing it. I thought I was going to be fired for sure, but she understood. She said, 'It was one of those things. You did it once, but you would never do it again,' and she was right. I would work very hard in this job. It was a very busy department and I would sometimes work weekends as well. I made lots of friends. Of course a lot of people heard about me through my mum and my Aunt Opal as they both worked there. Mum worked nights and my Aunt Opal days and she was on the same floor, although in a different department. There was one guy in particular who had caught my attention. His name was Derek and he was one of the porters. He was a lot shorter than me, and was thinning on top, but had this long ponytail that he sometimes tucked in the back of his shirt. He was quite a drinker, but I think he was really sad and that was just his way of covering things up. He had lost his mother the year before and never really recovered. He had three sisters, but only saw one of them as she lived near him. He was the sort of person who would be joking around, making everyone laugh, and would do anything to help if he could. I would talk to him whenever I saw him and his mate. Whenever he was near the floor that I worked on, he would pop his head around the door, just to say hello and have a quick chat if I was not too busy. He knew nearly everyone in the hospital as he had worked there for some time. He also knew my mum and my Aunt Opal. My Aunt Opal would tease me about him, saying that he fancied me really badly. Apparently he had told her this, but I just ignored it. We were good friends and that was that. He would always invite me out for a drink, but I was never a pub girl and would decline. As my Aunt Opal had told me of his affections for me, I tried not to encourage him, because I never felt the same way about him. He was never my type, and anyway, I was in love with Denny.

When Ezra was a couple of months away from his first birthday, my mum and I had a barney. God knows what it was about. Did it ever have to be about something important to have a barney with my mother? She used to look after Ezra, and Mercedes would go

Shoy

to her house after school as usual. I realise that she was getting tired of breaking her sleep to look after Ezra during the day as no sooner was she asleep, she would have to get up and collect Mercedes from school, but she had offered to do this. So, okay, we had this barney and she told me to take my children and not bring them back because she was fed up with looking after them and getting no thanks for it. So I did. I had to take a few days off work, as I had to sort something out. The people at work were very understanding and I was under no pressure as to when I was going to return. As it was, it only took three days to sort things out. Yvonne, (Denny's sister) would look after Ezra during the day and she would collect Mercedes from school as she had to collect Tanya (her own daughter) from nursery, and then she would drop all of them (including Tanya) at my flat when I got home and I would look after Tanya until she finished her evening job, as she was also having problems with babysitters in the evening. It was a great plan. Of course, the whole thing upset my mum. You see, she would say things to shock me and try to reduce me to tears or a bumbling wreck, which most of the time it did out of her sight, but it was always done thinking that I would not be able to sort my life out and would have to go running back to her and beg. But I would never do that. I would get home, have a rant and a rave to Yvette on the phone or she would come over, and then I would think about it logically and sort it. Like they say, 'Where there's a will, there's a way'. So in the long run, she had to talk to me again; otherwise she would not see the kids and that she could not stand.

During this time, Yvette met someone else once she was sure that her relationship with Wayne was well and truly over. His name was Lloyd. I was never sure how they met. She was always telling me about him and how gorgeous he was and that he had blue eyes. He was light skinned, from the West Indies and she was so lucky to have found him, or he her. She was really happy again. I was so glad for her. It took some time before I actually met him as he was a shy sort of person and did not want to meet too many people. My relationship was not so good, but was it ever? And I suppose that deep down inside I envied her again, but never told her and never gave her any reason to know it either. I was really happy for her, but so wanted that happiness for myself as well. Finally, I got to meet this man that she would go on about and yes he was nice. Soon the two of them would spend a lot of time at my flat, simply because they drove and I did not and I was always on my own at weekends, and so I would cook and get some drink in and we would have a laugh. Yvette was never one for playing games, whether board games or any other type of games. So Lloyd, sometimes my sister, Denny (if he happened to be in) and I would play board games until the early hours of the morning.

Shoy

The kids, of course, would fall asleep and we would put them to bed. Ezra was still in his cot as he was far too fidgety to sleep in a bed and Mike and Mercedes would sleep in Mercedes' bed. There were many evenings like this and we were all good mates. We would talk about anything, and nothing we had was ever too good for the other.

AGAIN

The following year, Denny went to the West Indies on holiday. Since arriving in this country when he was about twelve or thirteen, he had never gone back, so it was a holiday well overdue. He had arranged to stay with some family members of his that lived in the village where he was born. I missed him to bits and could not wait for him to return. I did not go to the airport to see him off as I did not drive and there was not enough room for us in his friends' car. So we had to say our goodbyes at home. It was very tearful and I missed him already. He promised to write and phone as soon as he got there.

Shoy

Very late that night, he called. He had arrived safely. I could relax now for the next six weeks, knowing that he was there. The six weeks went by with Yvette and some of my other friends all visiting at different times, family included. I was kept so busy that the time went by really quickly. There was only one phone call and only one postcard. There was nothing else from him. I was so surprised. The thoughts in my head were of him having a good time and catching up with all those girls over there. There were so many rumours of these girls that would go after the English guys that came over, purely because they wanted their ticket off the island. They would do almost anything to get it and this worried me no end.

The day came for him to return and Winston went to fetch him from the airport. Winston was one of his old school friends and they would go everywhere together. He was a mechanic, but worked in a paper mill as it paid more money. I got up early in the morning and cleaned the whole place, not that it needed cleaning. My kids were not mess-makers, so it was just something to do. I cooked his favourite meal and waited. The car arrived back and we ran down to the car park to greet him. He hugged the kids and then hugged me real tight. Tighter than he had ever done before. I knew that he had missed me. Winston helped him with his cases

Again

and we went up to the flat. He began to unpack in the middle of the living room floor. So much for tidying up! He handed a bottle of rum to Winston, which immediately brought a smile to his face. The video camera came out. He had borrowed his brothers' camera and had shot a lot of footage. I was so looking forward to watching it as I had been there before, but I was twelve and I was sure that a lot of things were different and also it was another part of the island, so that would be interesting as well. We had planned to live there one day and so I was going to take it all in. It was his dream to have his home there. The tape began to play and he was showing me all his cousins. There seemed to be so many girls in the video, most of them large and big-butted, baring their arses in front of the camera. They were so slack, but I guess they were like that with all that free and easy living. I went down to the kitchen and when I came back I knew they were whispering about something, but I did not hear, so I dismissed it, but it made me uneasy. I never trusted him and it was always burning away at me. That evening he watched the video over and over again. There were so many visitors. I never had a moment alone with him. Finally, they left and we were alone, but of course, now he was tired and went to sleep.

That holiday bugged the hell out of me, but being 'subservient' I dare not ask him about it. I really wanted to know if he had got off with anyone. But never asked. Time ticked on and sure enough he booked another holiday to the West Indies the very next year, and without us again. He had promised to take us the next time he was going, but his excuse was that there was not enough room at his cousins house and we could not afford to stay in a hotel'. Not that there were any hotels in the village where he wanted to stay. So he was going alone again.

The day came when he was off. I thought I would miss him again when he left, but it surprised me that I really did not. In fact, I was free to do what I wanted, to buy what I wanted, to feed the kids what I wanted. It was so good. The only thing that held me back was the fact that I did not drive. Whilst he was away, there was a certain up-and-coming young doctor (although older than me by one year), who had taken a shine to me over the year. He would flirt with me at every opportunity that he got and there were many. I was always declining his offers. He was tall, dark and very, very handsome. He was astounding, but he was not single. He was married, albeit just, but he was not as committed to his marriage as he should have been. Whenever he went past the floor that I worked on, he would pop his head around the door. He would have little messages written that he would just come into our office with (the door was always open), thrust into my hands and then disappear again. The other girls that I worked with thought he was so romantic. They knew nothing about him and the fact that he was married and they both lived in the doctors' quarters which was just up the hill from the hospital. He was always hanging around. So needless to say, whilst the cat was away, the mouse played. Eventually, I gave him my telephone number and sure enough, the very same evening he called. We arranged for him to come over the next evening after work. That day, he was in and out. He sent me a bunch of roses, for no reason at all. He was so excited. I could not believe that he really, really wanted me and tonight was going to be the night.

I left work that evening and quickly went over to the supermarket and bought some mince and kidney beans, as his favourite meal was chilli con carne. I got home, after collecting Ezra from the nursery and Mercedes from my mum, (who was once again looking after her after school) sorted the children out with their tea and baths and left them to their own devices in the bedroom whilst I got this special meal sorted. I packed the children off to bed and he arrived at about eight-thirty. My heart was racing. I could not believe that I was inviting someone over to my flat in the absence of Denny. Had I stopped loving him so soon? He had only been gone about two days. So what!

The buzzer went and I stood at the door and counted to ten before answering it. Well, I did not want to appear too keen now, did I? He came up, handed me a bottle of wine, and then planted a kiss right on my lips. We stood there with the flat door open, kissing and kissing and kissing. Finally, we parted and I shut the door. Well, what could be said after that? He was definitely pleased to see me! I turned away from him, showing him the way to the living room, but he hesitated.

'Where are your children?' What a strange thing to ask. I showed him Mercedes' room door, which was slightly open. He walked over to the door, pushed it gently, and looked in. He walked over to her bed and stood over her, just looking at her. He kissed his hand, placed it on her forehead, and then backed out of the room. 'Where is the little boy?' Ezra was in his cot, which was in my room. He was too much of a rebel to have his cot in his sister's room as he would always wake up and wake her up as well. I showed him to my room, in which he performed the same ritual. He followed me in to the kitchen where everything was ready to go. 'Wow, something smells really good. Are we eating now?' Thank God he said that, because I was starving as well. I dished up and we ate, sitting opposite each other at my glass-top dining table, as if the couple of the house, and it felt so good. Not sitting in front of the TV with the plates balanced on our laps and the glasses of drink placed on the floor besides us, and no conversation as the TV was the centre of attraction. This was what couples did and we were doing it. Whilst eating, I asked him.

'Why did you do what you did when you came in?'

'What?'

'You know, with the children.'

'Oh that. I so wish that I had children and I always imagine that I would come home, just like tonight and the first thing I would do would be to kiss my wife, and then kiss my children without waking them.' That was the most sensitive thing I had ever heard. I did not reply. I could not reply. He was not mine to comment on.

The weeks that led up to this occasion were so insignificant. My mind flashed back to some of the moments we had spoken to each other in the hospital. How he looked into my eyes and told me how beautiful I was and that he so admired me for what I had done, what I was doing (meaning running Ezra up to the nursery, working full-time, looking after both of them and looking after myself). What was left to achieve?

Shoy

We moved from the table and ended up on the floor of the living room. It felt so right and I loved it. He was so gentle and loving and I wanted him more and more. Over the six weeks that Denny was gone, we stole every moment that was possible. One evening, I knew he would be studying in the Post-Graduate Centre (as he did this most evenings) as he had exams coming up. I thought I would visit him up there before going home, as this was one of the evenings he was not coming over. I stood at the door. There was no one else around. He sat there with a pile of books opened at different pages. His head was resting on one hand and he had a pen in the other. He looked so intelligent. Sometimes I felt that we were worlds apart, but he was what I wanted. The kind of man I should have had in his white shirt and tie and his suit with the creases down the front of the trousers just so. I looked on for a while, not wanting to disturb him, but I wanted to say goodnight to him. I wanted to feel him and kiss him. I walked in, trying to be quiet. He lifted his head and the broadest smile spread across his face.

'Oh Shoy. You are a welcome break. I have been sat here with my head buried in these books and nothing is going in now.' I walked over and sat on the table alongside him. He looked at me and started to run his hand up my legs. I loved every moment of it. I did not want him to stop. His hand went higher and higher

Again

until eventually he was touching my fanny through my underwear. I slid along the table so I was directly in front of him and parted my legs. He pulled himself closer to me and buried his head between my legs, moving my pants to one side to reveal my moist fanny that was in need of some attention, and attention it got. I lay back on the table and engulfed myself in the emotion of the moment and the feel of his warm wet tongue. He stood up, his lips glistening. I came up towards him and we kissed. I could taste my juices on his tongue. As we kissed, he unzipped his trousers and released his stiff, shining cock. He sunk it into my juices and then fully into my vault. He was large and filled every inch of me. He was gentle and pushed himself into me. As he did I looked at his face. His eyes were closed and his head was leaning back as far as he could possibly lean it. He was breathing in and out quite noisily, but in a rhythmic way. He occasionally opened his eyes to look at me and we smiled together. I was sweating through my clothes. I could see beads of sweat forming on his forehead and running down his cheeks. His pace quickened and he thrusted himself into me harder and harder. I moved towards him in movement to his. He was obviously full to the tip of his penis and now it needed to escape. He was moaning and I was groaning and…and…and…there it was. We came in unison, panting and swallowing hard, but sealing the event with a long kiss. I stood up and tidied myself. He did the same. The thought of someone

Shoy

interrupting us did not enter into our minds. We were caught up in the moment and it was sensational.

After that epic moment, he packed up his books and promised to come and see me later that evening. He wanted more of the same, but under less stressful conditions. Anyone could have walked in at any moment, but it had not been a deterrent. Of course there was a juggling act, because he had to make some excuse to his wife and I had to put friends off from coming over, but somehow we managed to see each other almost every night. It was heaven.

In between all these rendezvous, I was busy making a dress to wear to Wayne's wedding as he was getting married a week after Denny got back off holiday. It turned out that I had only chosen the same style dress as the bridesmaids were wearing, (which pissed my sister-in-law-to-be off), but there was no way that I was going to change mine, because it was all cut-out and practically sewn up. Mine was in a blue taffeta material with a white lace petticoat that was attached to the underside of the skirt and a fitted top to the dress with herringbone running through it to keep it up, and over the top was a top with long sleeves made of the same lace that was used under the skirt. It was quite perfect and beautiful – if I might say so myself?

Again

The phone was ringing early on the Friday morning. It was my day off. Who in the world would be calling me so early? I rushed up to the living room and answered it, eyes still closed and slamming the door against the wall as I went.

'Hello.'

'Hello.' Came a voice. It was Winston. He was going to pick Denny up from the airport and he wanted to know if I was going. Now before Denny went he had already told me not to come to the airport, just to be ready and waiting for his return. If possible, to get rid of the children for the day and we could make up for all the time we had been apart.

'Sorry, Winston, Denny wanted me to stay here and have something ready for him to eat.'

'Oh okay. I did not realise.'

'Well thanks for calling and thinking of me.' He hung up and I was now wide awake, not wanting him to come back, but he was and he was on his way – well in a few hours he would be taking off, anyway. Besides, I had to finish my dress, as before he left I had told him that I would have a surprise for him when he got

Shoy

back and it was to have the dress finished. He bet me that I would never complete it, but I was going to prove him wrong and he would love me in it.

That night, I did not see my doctor. We spoke on the phone and kept it brief. He was sad and so was I, but we both knew that it would end: we just never expected it this way. The next morning, I was up early. There was no way that I was getting rid of the children, because what Denny had in mind, I did not want. Anyway, I had this gut feeling that he had not been going without, and let's face it, neither had I. Whilst he was away, he had written to us once and that was in the form of a crummy post-card (again) - a post-card that you would send to your friends, not to your girlfriend, the mother of your children who you loved and adored. And as for calling, that was once and only once right at the beginning of his holiday, just to say that he had arrived safely and that it was sunny and hot and the sea was calling. Huh. Who was I kidding?

Winston's voice was at the door. 'Open the door.' He was shouting it in a funny voice. I was not expecting it, but someone had left the security door downstairs open and so he came right up. I opened the door and let him in.

Again

Denny followed, struggling with his case up the stairs. He came in and his first words were. 'Aalrait dready?' He pecked me on the cheek. No embrace. No kiss that would take my breath away. No kiss that meant he had missed me and he loved me. He walked up to the living room and started to unpack right in the middle of the living room floor again. Of course, by now he had seen the kids, looking at me with surprise. 'So what are you all doing here? I thought you lot would be with your grandmother or your Aunty Yvonne?' No one answered. He handed a bottle of rum to Winston and he left, content with his gift, leaving with the words, 'see you tonight.' So there you are, he was off out that evening. I pretended not to have heard. He had brought the kids some gifts and they disappeared off to their bedrooms. I followed them to see what they had got and when I returned to the living room, he had a video on. It was a video he had made in the West Indies of his holiday and so far all I could see was girls, girls everywhere, all over the beach again. Jokingly, I asked him, 'so which one was running you down?'

He pressed the freeze frame, right at that moment and there she was on the screen. 'That one there!' What did he mean 'that one there?' Was he joking? I looked at him and he could see that I was worried. 'I am only joking. She was after me, but I was good.' I smiled. He beckoned for me to go to bed with him. We went

Shoy

to bed, having locked the bedroom door from the kids, and we made love. It was surreal. I wanted to be with him, but I was not thinking of him. I was thinking of my doctor. It seemed to go on forever. We lay there sweaty and out of breathe. I turned to him. I just had to ask him another question. I could not leave it alone. My mouth and my brain could not lie dormant and dead; they just churned and churned. Why was it so important for me to know?

'So, really, did you get off with any of them in the video?'

'Of course. The one I showed you. *I am going to marry her.*' There was silence. I sat upright in the bed and just looked ahead at the mirror in the dressing table. I did not like what I saw. I was fat and ugly and he could see this. 'It's funny', he continued, 'but I have finally fallen in love.'

'*I HAVE FINALLY FALLEN IN LOVE.*' The words ripped through me like a guillotine on execution day. I suppose this was my punishment for betraying him whilst he was away. I could not cry, but I was angry. I did not want him anymore.

'How could you make love to me and then tell me that you 'have fallen in love' and not with me? Did you ever love me?'

He did not answer. That was my answer enough. He got out of bed and vanished to the bathroom. I just sat there numb, but shaking, shaking with anger. He had to go. No sooner had he walked back into the bedroom than I was hurling abuse at him. 'I want you out of my flat, yes MY FLAT and I want you out now. Pack your things, because if you leave them I will rip every last one to shreds and fling them in the bin downstairs.' I was now standing in my dressing gown at the window. He attempted to touch me. 'Don't even think about touching me, otherwise I will not be responsible for my actions.' I repeated myself. 'Do I make myself clear?'

'Well if that's what you want. Where am I to go?'

'Well I am sure that your precious mother will have you. After all, your bed is still there.'

'Look, Shoy.'

'Don't you look Shoy me! When was the last time you called me Shoy? You can't even say it properly.'

'Look, we have to talk about this. What about the children?'

Shoy

'What about them? They are mine and this is where they belong - with their mother. For all you know, they may not even be yours.' He knew I was lying there and did not bat an eyelid to that one.

'Okay. Can I borrow a case to pack?'

'No. Go get one from wherever and you have until Monday to clear all your stuff out of here before I get home from work. I don't want to see you when I get home and make sure that you leave the keys. You no longer live here.' He left quietly. I could not believe how easy it was. He was leaving me. But then, if you don't love someone it must be easy just to walk away. Just like he did.

An hour must have gone past and the phone rang. It was his wonderful mother.

'So what is going on?' No hello. No how are you. Just straight in with the questions, questions defending her precious son who could do no wrong.

'Look, no disrespect to you, but it is none of your business. If you want to know what is going on, ask your precious son.' With that I hung up and took the phone off the hook. I did not want any calls.

Again

I took the kids over to my mum. I just wanted to be on my own to deal with him if he came back. I did not want the children to hear all the horrid things that might be said. Mum did not ask any questions, but she knew something was wrong. A little later on, Yvette and Lloyd arrived. They knew that Denny was due back and Lloyd wanted to see him to talk about 'yard.' Yard, being the West Indies. They were at the door for ages, just buzzing and buzzing. Finally, I opened the door. Immediately, Yvette knew something was up. I half told her and Lloyd. Lloyd's words were, 'how could he leave someone as nice as you for one of them down there? They are only after one thing and that's their passport off the island. Denny better watch himself.' I showed them the video and pointed out the girl to them. She looked so young. I had no idea of her age, but she was young. At this point, there were still no tears. In my head, I was consumed with guilt. The guilt of having slept with another man behind his back and now I was lording it over him. But this was for all the other times that he had cheated on me with Joan. She was large, apparently they had been lovers since school, and she was hanging around waiting for him to come back to her. Mandy, the dark one with the chalky-white-spaced-out teeth. Mary, who was another large behind, spoilt brat if ever I met someone spoilt and who had even tried to commit suicide if Denny did not return to her. Then there was Val, who had a child with someone else, but wanted Denny to be a father to him. She

Shoy was actually skinny, but nothing special to look at. But then I would say that wouldn't I? And of course, countless others that I am sure I never found out about.

Lloyd and Yvette offered to stay with me, but I declined. I was not in the least worried. I could deal with this. It was my flat and this was my chance to get rid of the bad.

Monday evening came and I returned home from work with the children as usual, but this time I hoped that he would have left the keys and would be out of our lives. I walked in, only to find his cases packed at the front door and him sitting on the settee, waiting for us.

'So why are you still here?'

'I wanted to see the children before I left.'

'Okay, so here they are. Say what you have to say and leave.' The kids ran over to him and hugged him. They had no idea what was about to take place and they did not need to know. I would never stop him seeing his children, I just did not want him living with us. If he had fallen in love with someone else, then I was setting him free to love her and not feel guilty in any way. Huh. Who was I kidding? I did not want him to go, but I had to be strong. This was my way of making him make his choice without actually telling him to make a choice. I was trying to be clever. Would it work? The kids kissed him and left for the bedroom. I stood near the bookcase and just watched him.

'Well, have you changed your mind?' What did he expect? Did he think that I would? Obviously he did. I looked him straight in the eyes.

'I want you out. I have not changed my mind and I will not, so don't waste your time asking me again and again.' He stood up and walked towards me. I backed away. There was no way I was going to let him kiss me. He carried on down the stairs, picked up his cases saying, good bye to the kids and that he would come and see them the next day, turning and looking at me to make sure that that would be okay. I did not acknowledge the statement.

'I will be back to collect the rest of my things at some point. Do you want to know where I will be staying?' I did not particularly. If he wanted to tell me, he should just say, not get all arsy and ask me nonsensical questions.

'Look, if you want me to know where you are staying, then say. If not keep it to yourself. Either way it is of no bother to me.'

'Well, I will be staying at my mum's for the time being.' With that he left. I felt nothing. I thought I would be empty and low, but I was overjoyed. The phone rang and it was Lloyd.

'How are you?'

'Oh, hanging in there. He has gone.'

'What do you mean gone?'

'Well, I have thrown him out and he is not coming back. He came home today and packed all his clothes and is coming back at some point to collect his stupid weight bench and all the other crap he has cluttering up my flat with, and if he does not come and collect them soon, then I will sell them or throw them away, whichever is easiest'.

'Well, obviously you are all right.' It was so nice to have someone who cared enough to pick up the phone and make sure that I was. My mum knew what was going on, but I would never expect her to call. After all she would be jumping for joy and singing from every rooftop in the town.

Time went by, and of course, we got back together. Stupid, brainless, and totally pathetic, I fell for his charm and he wormed his way back into my life and back into my flat. Of course, he pulled the 'I miss the kids' routine and his feet were back under the table. So many of my friends said it was the worst decision I had ever made, but if the truth be told, I was lonely and I did miss him. My affair with my doctor had ended no sooner had it begun and quite honestly, it was never going to go any further. We both knew it was a short fling and he was being moved from our hospital to another one to continue his training, so he was gone and there was no-one. It was okay for them. They had their 'fit into a box' routine lives with their 'fit into a box' lovers and relationships and what did I have? Nothing. It was just myself, and my beautiful children. I loved my children and would do anything for them, but when they were asleep and the world was all tucked up in their beds with their husbands, wives, partners, lovers, I would be watching the late night rubbish on the TV and getting brainless, useless information and then be so tired the next day I would swear to be in bed early, but the routine would never change.

So he was back and for a while things were really good. I say things were 'good.' They were as good as I pretended they were. There were times when he would be away from the house for the evening and he would return. I knew instinctively that he had been out with another woman, to the point where I was convinced that he had had sex with her, but I would block the whole thing and I would force him to have sex with me. He would be knackered sometimes and not even able to get an erection; that was my proof. But what could I do with that? I would still have sex with him, if he was able to have sex with me and if he was not, I would make him give me oral. After all, I needed to be satisfied. I would do all the work sexually and he would just lie there and then fall asleep, sometimes not even ejaculating. I knew what was going on really, but I chose to ignore it. How low can you sink? I hated myself for what I was doing. No woman should ever want a man that much that she would do anything like that. He was my dream. He was the one who saved me from the living hell that I had endured all those years and now I was in a worse predicament. I was begging for love and affection and I was not getting any of it – again.

Sometimes when he was away from the flat, or no sooner had he left the flat, I would receive phone calls and no one would answer. They would just sit on the line. On other occasions the person would talk to me. I could never understand the voice and it was hard to tell whether it was male or female. They seemed to know when he was out or would time it impeccably. I felt I was being stalked and they wanted to make me as unhappy as they possibly could. I was sure that they were watching the flat and I became obsessed with drawing the curtains as soon as there were signs of darkness. I would say this to Denny and he just dismissed it. He dismissed it to the point where he called me a liar and that I was making it all up. I went out and bought an answering machine and on one occasion, I actually managed to tape the person. I played it to him when he came home, but neither of us could work out who it was. He even played it to some of his friends when they came over, to see if they knew who the voice belonged to, but there was no luck. He now believed me, but he did not change or try to make me feel more secure. He would still go out, stay out, and just leave me in alone with the kids. I was paranoid. Soon after getting the answering machine though, the phone calls stopped and I was left in peace. I stopped using the machine for a while and sure enough, the calls started again. Who would be so cruel? Why would they do this? If they wanted him so much, all they had to do was let him know and he would oblige. There was no need to torment me. They were so nasty on the phone. They would make comments about the way I dressed and combed my hair. I was not fashionable enough for him and I was too skinny. They even commented on the fact that he was only with me because he loved the kids and if it weren't for them, he would leave me. They divulged to me the fact that he had another son who lived near us. This I knew nothing about. For a time I did not mention this to

Shoy

Denny. I just thought about it and thought about it. I would search through his things looking for clues and finally I asked his mother. If anyone knew, she would know, sure enough she knew, and she told me everything. She did not even hold back. His name was Nigel and he was two years older than Ezra. Denny, after some time of denying the child, was sending his mother money to look after him regularly. The mother had even gone up to his mother's house begging for money and so that was how it all started. I had no idea this had happened. I now had to confront him. How was I going to do that?

One Saturday, he was getting ready for cricket and just before he left, I asked him, 'who is Nigel?'

He looked shocked and sat down.

'Who told you?' What sort of question was that? I was expecting him, still, to deny it and not have any knowledge of what I was talking about. It was true, very true. He told me the whole thing and how for years he knew nothing about Nigel and then suddenly he had this son. They had blood tests to prove it and Nigel was his. My heart sunk, the lowest it had ever sunk. Ezra was not his first son. Ezra was second and now he meant nothing to him. All this time, I thought I had given him his first two children and his only two children, but there was another one in between and he was a boy. The tears rolled down my face. I did not know what to think. He tried to comfort me, but I was cold, angry, and scared. Did he love my son?

'So where do we go from here?' he asked. I shrugged my shoulders. At this moment in time I did not care. He could go to hell. Everything was happening too fast and there was too much to deal with. Firstly, the 'finally fallen in love' saga and now this. Where did I fit into all of this? He left for cricket, as I was not talking. Whilst he was away, I had time to think rationally. I sat there looking at Ezra as he played on the floor with Mercedes. The tears welled up in my eyes at the thought of Denny having another son older than mine. Well there was nothing else, the children had to meet. When he returned home and the kids were in bed, we made arrangements for Nigel to come over and stay a weekend, if he wanted to. Apparently, his mother had already told him about Mercedes and Ezra, so it would not be new to him, I just had to break the news to my two. They took the news quite well, as children do. The weekend came and he was here. Here in my home. The eldest son of Denny! He was a lot lighter in colour than Ezra, but he was just an older version of Ezra and a younger version of Mercedes. The resemblance was amazing. I could have given birth to him myself. Yvette came over. I had already told her

Shoy

about the whole thing and she could not believe it when she saw him. It was yet another 'thing' to get used to in my life. Just one of the many, many presents from Denny. Only they were never gift-wrapped and sent with love.

I never mentioned that god-awful female 'the love of his life' and he was decent enough not to mention her either. I had come to the conclusion that she was there and I was here. So we ticked along. That was until an airmail letter arrived for him. I had to open it. I steamed it open over the kettle one morning when he had gone to work and I read the contents. I went straight to the signature to see who it was from. It was signed 'Teresa.' That was the name he had mentioned before. The name I had forgotten, but it was there, written in blue ink and a lipstick print of her lips along side it. The bitch. They must have been talking to each other since he was back as she had made reference to it. They were so much in love. This was your regular love letter and there was no way he was going to get it or any others. I went over to the warden of the flats as she would deliver our post and I asked her to hold onto any airmail letters that came to him and hand them only to me. She knew our problems and tried to get me to fling him out for good on numerous occasions, but I did not listen. She could see that he was a bad sort and wanted something better for me. She was like a mother. She had two daughters of her own and no husband.

The letters started to come in thick and fast, almost one every other day. I never gave him any of them. I stopped opening them as I was only upsetting myself, especially when I knew that he was calling her. He came home from work one day and asked if he had had any mail from yard. Well, I was really going to tell him that! Of course I lied and denied having seen anything. Besides, the mail came before he left for work and he would always look through it. He did not seem bothered, but I knew what he was expecting. No sooner had he enquired about his mail from yard, they all stopped. So what had happened? I perked up, thinking they must have broken things off, but how wrong I was. His sister called one day when I was off work.

'I have something to tell you.' Well what could this be. For Yvonne to call me it had to be serious, as she hardly ever called to speak to me. 'Denny has had his mail from that girl re-directed to my address and he has about three letters waiting here for him. Can you tell him to come and collect them?' Why, oh why would she call and tell me that? Did she not know what he meant to me and how it would upset me? I thought it was planned. Surely it had to be. Why else would she do that? I had never done her any harm and now she had destroyed my world. The world that had long been destroyed, but I did not want to believe it.

Shoy

'So what do you want me to do about it?' My voice was shaky and I sat down.

'Well, look, Shoy. I did not want to tell you, but I don't like what he is doing to you and the kids and you have to wake up. You don't need him. When you threw him out, I thought it was the best thing you had ever done, but then you took him back. I knew that that would happen, but if I'd had my way, I would have prevented you from taking him back. He is no good for you. Come on, wake up!' Her words rang through my head, over and over again. I knew what she was saying was true, but how would I survive without him? I was useless and I had two children who needed him. I had to resolve this. There was no easy way. Things got worse and worse, even though he was no longer living with me now. He had borrowed a substantial amount of money from his boss to make his account look good, because he was now going to have to prove to the authorities that she was not coming over just to get married, that he could keep her and that she was really his lover, girlfriend, whatever to avoid her being deported. He had secured another flat for them both and he was going to enrol her in college (the dunce bitch at her age). Yet another angle to make it look as though she was coming across for educational purposes. All this information various sources gave me voluntarily. Why

Again

did they feel the need to tell me? I did not ask them to spy on him and report back. I just wanted to be left alone. But it was gathering moss now and I could not leave it alone. I wanted to hurt him. I had given him so many years of my life and he just threw me aside like a used rag, and to top it all, he did not even love me. I was like a woman possessed. I called the immigration authorities and made some discreet enquiries, not mentioning any names, just giving an account of the situation and how it would pan out should I divulge the names and incidences. They told me what I wanted to hear. She would be deported like a criminal, never to return. She would be out of our lives and he would have to come back to me. He would have to beg my forgiveness and come back to me. It seemed a good idea at the time. I held off from informing the authorities as some further information had come to light. Now, his so-called 'friends' were donating all this information. With friends like them, he would never want for enemies. It turned out that his boss had not lent him the money that he had asked for and so he was now in financial difficulties and could not afford the flat and other bits and pieces. Oh dear, what a shame! A little while passed and I was consumed with this whole event. I wanted to know all the time what he was up to. I was not making a nuisance of myself, but like I said, some of his friends made it their business to tell me his business and so I was getting my fill and it was making me feel good. He was miserable as hell and was losing

Shoy

weight. The bastard. In my heart though, I knew I wanted him back and I was going to get him back. He would come over to see the kids and I would be cold and hard towards him. He would try endlessly to make conversation with me, but I would keep it to a minimum, deliberately. He knew what I was like and I knew that my lack of conversation with would make him think: think about what he was doing and what effect it was having. I also wanted him to feel that I was all right without him. Which I was. Really. If only my head and heart would think the same way. When you have loved someone since your school days, it is hard to suddenly drop all those years of commitment and devotion and walk away.

So here we were, he had put the kids to sleep and now we were alone in the living room. I just wanted him to go. I felt different tonight. I knew something was going to happen, but I did not want to face it. He looked nervous, which made me nervous. What did he want to say? I wished he would just come out with it. We sat there in total silence watching the TV. I could hear my heart thumping. I did not say a word, not even to ask him if he wanted a drink. After all, he knew where the kitchen was. He finally came out with it as he was getting up to leave.

'Shoy, I miss you so much. I want to come home. I am not happy. I am so miserable. Do you think we can give it another go?' I should have given him some ultimatums, like we get married, or at least engaged, but no, I just said, 'Yeah.' The all-important 'yeah,' to him. The only single word that he wanted to hear. Who was stupid now?

I was still very uneasy with all of this. I felt worse letting him back than when we were apart. I did not really want him to touch me anymore. I would not melt in his arms when he touched me. Everything had changed and I knew I did not want him, but there was nothing better out there. So I put all those feelings behind me and got back on track, but to the way Shoy was – loving and caring.

As if I had not got enough problems to deal with in my head, I had developed a funny discharge, which was not usual for me. Embarrassingly, after some time of not being able to get rid of it and forget it, I finally went to my doctor. He was gorgeous and I could never look him in the eye. He had lovely silky dark hair and his voice was smooth and caressing. It's a shame he was a doctor, my doctor. I would get off with him any day. Anyway, back to my problems. He asked a few questions and from the questioning I could tell that this discharge was not a 'normal' discharge developed naturally by the body. He took a smear and asked if I had been with anyone else. My mind wandered. Now how long a time span were we talking? But the affair with the doctor had long since been over and there was no one else. So I declined to give him that information. I knew whatever it was I had, it had to have come from that bastard. The doctor told me that I was going to have to get my partner to have some treatment as well if the smear showed anything untoward. Well, how the hell was I going to get him to a doctor? He never went to a doctor and then he would blame it on me. I was told to make an appointment for a couple of days' time and he would have the results. They were the longest two days of my life. I returned to the doctor with my heart heavy, knowing that it was not going to be good news. What was it? Did I have AIDS? That was always on my mind. Did I have cancer? That too was always on my mind. What the hell was it? Was I going to die? Who would look after my children? I was finally called and I knocked on the surgery door and waited for the.

'Come in.'

I walked in and turned to close the door. (Now in interviews you never ever turn your back on the interviewer to close the door. I knew I was not being interviewed, but this went through my mind at that precise moment). I sat across from the big oak desk and watched in anticipation. His gorgeous smile greeted me.

'How are you feeling?' Well how did he think?

'Not good. What is the result?' I was impatient. He looked down at the piece of paper.

'Well, it's not good, but it's not bad. The results have shown Chlamydia.' Okay, so that made me feel a whole lot better. I really knew what that was. The tears welled up in my eyes. I did not want them to roll out.

'So, am I going to die from this?' What a question. He must have died in his seat.

'No, of course not. You have to have some medication and also your partner has to have some medication to clear it up once and for all.'

My partner. But he never goes to a doctor. How am I going to get him to go? He does not even know that I have something wrong with me. I can't tell him.'

'Well, you will have to somehow.'

'How did I get this, this thing?'

Shoy

'Well you would have got it sexually. It's sexually transmitted.' He went into detail about this, that and the other. I knew it had to have come from him. The bastard. That was all I could think of. How could he bring something home to me? I knew he did not love me, but this? The doctor was bombarded with thousands of questions and he answered all of them. He had so much time and patience. He made me feel better about things, but I still had to go home and tell the bastard what he had done and I just felt that he was going to blame me for all of this. In some ways I wished that his dick would fall off, but no chance. Unless I cut it off myself, it was there to stay and there to cause havoc. He handed me a prescription for antibiotics, explaining how I had to take them. I left the surgery, my legs heavy as lead, my eyes red and stinging from the tears, my heart thumping like two kettle drums in competition and my head banging like a woodpecker against the trunk of a tree. I walked home. How was I going to get rid of the infection from him? How was I going to tell him? I turned the questions went over and over in my mind. I finally got home and started the dinner. Whilst dishing up the dinner, I had an idea. I could crush up the tablets and put them in his food. He always ate everything. This way he would get the medication and we would both be rid of it together. It was a plan made in heaven. The next day I got the prescription and set about my plan. When he came home that evening, as usual, I dished up the dinner and sprinkled the crushed tablets into the rice. I knew this would be okay, because the kids never ate with him and if for some reason they attempted to, I would have to come clean and stop them. There was no way I would put them at risk of his infection. One particular day, I was in the kitchen making him one of his drink concoctions. He would never drink any drinks without them being mixed with about three other drinks. They were never alcoholic, but they would be things like orange juice, mango juice and blackcurrant juice all mixed together. They were always disgusting, but it was what he wanted. The kids never liked them. This was another way of getting the tablets into his system. So here I was crushing the tablets for the drink when Yvette walked in. She was over this day.

'What you doing?' She made me jump. I tried to hide the tablets, but was not making a good job of doing so. I did not want to tell her. The less people knowing about my little escapade, the better. But there was no way of keeping her from knowing. She was too nosey and too persistent. She wanted to know everything and to be honest, we told each other everything. Well, I had to tell her now. I explained the whole thing to her in a whisper whilst stirring the crushed bits into a little warm water and then adding it to the drink. Very smooth, no detection at all. She was so concerned about the infection, asking me lots of questions, questions I had

Shoy

no answers to. All I knew was that I was going to get rid of it, whatever it took. She thought I was so clever for thinking the way I did. She would never have thought of that. But there again, she was not as devious as I was. She never had to be. Our whispering was broken by Denny calling for his drink. I gave him his special drink and he drank the whole lot, as usual.

The medication for both of us came to an end and the discharge cleared up. The only thing that worried me was the fact that I had not told him about it. Would he re-infect me again by sleeping with the person who had given it to him in the first place? I hoped not. My life was always based on hopes, dreams, and prayers to the 'Almighty God,' but still I would be unhappy, without money and lonely.

LOOKING FOR WHAT?

Life was so boring for me and all I wanted was commitment - commitment from Denny - but there was no way of getting that. I started to look at other men and wondered what they would be like to be with and how would they treat me in a relationship. Would I be happy? The only people that I really used to look at were the friends of his that I came in contact with. Yvette was having problems with Lloyd, who was now her fiancée. By this time she had two children, Mike and Marcia and she was expecting another. She was not getting on with Lloyd at all. She used to spend a lot of time with us and he used to as well. I would have

Shoy

both of them talking to me about their problems with each other. I really felt sorry for Lloyd because he was a good guy who loved her so much, but she did not want to know. All she wanted was to have her light-skinned kids (in her words). I really wanted to tell him this. Although she was my friend I thought what she was doing so wrong and she did not keep it a secret that she felt this way about their relationship (if you could call it that).

One day at my mum's house and in front of other people, she said that she wished he would leave her alone with her children and go and find someone else to love. I could not believe what I heard. I wanted him, because he was everything that Denny was not. He cared so much for her. He would stay at home with the children whilst she went out clubbing and partying, he would help her with the shopping and even go shopping with her whether it was for the children, herself, or the household. He would take them on trips and on family days out and she would be telling me all of this. He would plan surprises for them, especially for her. They never had much money - who did? But he always seemed to be trying to make good of a bad situation, and time and time again, she would mess him up and he would just bounce back and they would be happy again. All for what? To be kicked in the teeth again and again by her. To my mind, she and Denny would have been ideal partners because they played around with people's feelings and walked all over them and could not give a damn about anyone or anything, just themselves.

I started to see Lloyd in a different light. He would call me sometimes when he knew I was alone and we would talk for hours or sometimes until Denny came home. He lived with a friend of his and they both used to come round to our flat on a Friday evening and sometimes Saturday to play board games. I was getting more and more used to these evenings. Unhealthily so. If I were honest.

Life for me was now beginning to look up. I had been made an offer from the housing association that I was renting the flat from. I was given (not in my hand), thirteen-and-a-half thousand pounds to use as a down payment on a house of my own. I could not believe it. They were giving me the chance to own my very own home. There were lots of terms and conditions and I had a limited time in which to complete the buying of a house, otherwise the money would not become available to me. Decisions had to be made quickly. Of course I accepted the offer and Denny and I set about going through the motions of buying a house. It was so exciting. Finally we were going to own a house and we could get married. Every opportunity was spent in estate agents and at weekends we had almost set up camp in them. They were all within walking distance of the flat, so it was easy to fill our arms with all the pamphlets of houses on sale and just dump them off in the flat and go back for more. It was brilliant. We were being inundated with mail from the estate agents as they were sending us all sorts of property information, not to our specification. That got a bit much; it became junk mail. The ones we felt we could afford, and which met our specification of at least three bedrooms with a garden, we viewed. We were viewing at least three houses a week. I loved viewing other people's property. It was being really nosey. You would look at the décor and the furniture and get ideas of how you could arrange your own home. Some of them were really beautiful and others, well, what can you say?

Once we had found the house of our choice, we went through the various procedures that were now going to take over our life for some time. The first hurdle was getting the mortgage. This took an awful long time, because I had been diagnosed with SLE (Systemic Lupus Erythematosis). No one wanted to give me an endowment mortgage (as far as they were concerned, I was on the scrap heap, on my way out, about to kick the bucket in the not too distant future); they had written me off. I wrote to various doctors whose care I was under and got them to write to the mortgage company explaining this condition, and finally after some time of anxiety and depression we got the mortgage.

Back in 1992, I was still working in the hospital, but by this time I was an office manager, in charge of the computer system within the department amongst other things. The consultant in charge had seen the potential in me and nurtured me to this point. He was such a good man and would help me enormously from being a timid little thing to someone with a voice and afraid of no one. I would attend meetings – and present figures and reports generated from the computer systems. I would interview new staff and train them. I was now somebody and I was liked as well. I always felt that to get the most out of your workers, you had to treat them the way you would like to be treated - with respect and understanding. After all, we are individuals created from different genes and no two people are ever the same, not even twins. I loved my job enormously. I was still typing clinical letters as one of my many roles, but this I did not want to give up, as it was the best aspect, being involved in other people's lives.

I had not been well for some time. I was still walking the kids to school. Ezra was now at school and no longer at nursery, but to top it all they were both at different buildings; still the same school, but the school was split on two sites about twenty minutes' walk away from each other. I would drop Mercedes off first as she could stay in the playground with her friends and Ezra I would drop off later, as he was not allowed to be left alone in the playground before a certain time and also because his building was nearer the hospital and made more sense. I would be absolutely exhausted when I arrived at work, but I plodded on. I would get the odd comment that I looked tired, and that was never an understatement, but I never told anyone how I really felt. Whatever it was, it would pass. I began to take vitamin supplements and cod liver oil - anything I thought might boost my energy levels - but nothing seemed to work.

One particular day, I was typing away when my left arm went completely numb. I could not feel a thing.

'Oh my God, I am having a stroke!' Everyone in the office, of which there were four of us, looked at me. They immediately called Dr Smith, the head consultant, who was in his office next door. He came over to me and asked me what was going on. I could not explain, other than my arm had lost all sense of feeling and movement. He prodded and moved my arm up and down and around. He took me into the examination room near our office and began to do some prick tests with a sharp instrument on my arm and surrounding areas. I could not feel a thing. I really thought it was all in my head. It was all a bad dream. I was sure to be dying now.

'What is wrong with me?' I asked, wiping the tears away.

'I am not sure. It's best if a neurologist checks you out. Now don't worry; I will make a phone call. You wait here.'

Carmel came in to wait with me. She looked at me and we both smiled. Carmel had not been working in the department very long. In fact she was the first person I had taken on in my role as Office Manager. She was black and fast becoming someone I liked a lot. She was fun to be around, but had had a lot of ups and downs in her life, so we were on the same wavelength.

'So is wah? You want all di attention?' She would always make me laugh. In no time at all, Dr Smith returned and I had an appointment with a Consultant Neurologist. He examined me. I was so apprehensive. What if I had a tumour and only had months to live? Who would look after my babies? My thoughts were broken.

'Okay, you basically had a migraine attack.'

I looked at him puzzled.

Shoy

'What in my arm? I didn't have a headache.'

He continued.

'No, migraines can occur in different ways and in this case it transcribed itself into your arm.' He handed me a prescription and I was on my way. So there you have it. Simple. A migraine attack! So now I joined in the fun with my mum, who was always getting migraines. I returned to work.

For a few days nothing happened and I thought maybe it was a one off, but how wrong I was. The same thing happened again. This time, Dr Smith took a record of the symptoms himself along with his wife, who was also a doctor in the department and had studied neurology. They did a lot of different things; things that the other neurologist did not do. He then made a phone call to one of the teaching hospitals in London and spoke to another consultant there. By the end of the week, I was on my way to London to see a doctor who was the world leader in his field. He was a Consultant Rheumatologist. All these 'ologists' just lost me and I did not have a clue what they did as they were in another field and even though I worked in a hospital, I did not have any contact with any of the 'ologists' I was seeing now.

Looking for What?

I walked into the hospital and up to the floor where the clinic was located. I walked through the big double door and went over to the desk. My mum had come with me for support, but she was just as worried as I was. We took a seat in the waiting room, which was dismal and grey. There were a lot of sick people around. They looked dreadful. I really did not want to be there. I was never that sick. Finally I was called and I walked into the room with a lot of other doctors. Twelve to be precise. I was asked for permission for them to stay. It did not bother me in the slightest, as long as they made me better. That was all I was concerned about. They all introduced themselves, most of them being from some other country, and the Consultant proceeded with his questions.

'Okay, what can we do for you today?'

I explained the sequence of events that had taken place over the week. He also referred to the letter from Dr Smith. His questioning changed to my health in childhood. Why did that matter? He asked about my hair (which incidentally had a patch in the centre of my head at the back, which never grew as well or as long as the rest of my hair; that was the result of a slip and banging my head in that spot on the ice one cold morning, going to school). Generally my hair was brittle, but manageable. He looked at my nails (which I used to bite until there was hardly anything there.

Shoy

When I started secondary school, my Home Economics teacher was appalled at the number of us that bit our nails, so she offered ten merit marks to any of us that had nails on every finger by the end of that school year. I won the ten merit marks and never bit my nails again). He looked in my mouth. In my eyes. He took my blood pressure and temperature, height and weight. He poked and prodded. The examination seemed to go on forever and ever. Finally I got dressed and sat across the desk from him.

'So what's wrong with her?' My mum asked, hesitantly.

'Well its difficult to say precisely at this moment. We need to conduct a few blood tests and the picture will become clearer, but for the time being we are working with a diagnosis of Lupus.'

Well what was 'Lupus?' I had never heard of it. Could I die from it? He continued with the explanation, trying to make me feel better. It was not working, not in the least. I left the room with a handful of blood forms. Now, giving blood was always a pig of an experience. My body just would not give it up. I sat there waiting for my turn, after having pulled my number. I was called. The phlebotomist was trying to be calming and nice, but my mum had already put her arms around me, knowing that I was going to cry and make a fuss. I hated blood tests. She had to fill so many bottles. She had them lined up on the little table beside me. She tightened the strap around my arm and positioned my arm.

'Here goes, just a little scratch.' Why do they say that? It is never 'a little scratch'; it's an intrusion with a sharp implement. She drew the needle back out. Nothing was happening. The vein was non-existent. She prodded about with her finger for a better spot.

'Okay, let's try here.' So in it went again and once again there was nothing. This went on a further two times. She then called for another phlebotomist to try, as by now I was so much in tears, I was ready to walk out and forget the blood tests. The other 'vampire' handed me a bunch of tissues and chatted to me for a little while (not that she had the time to, with a waiting room full of people). She then suggested that I put both my hands in hot water in the sink: as hot as I could bear it. So I did and then returned for her to try again. This time it worked. But not for long. No sooner had she got a good flow going and the bottles were filling, than the vein gave up and so she had to find yet another place. That day I ended up with about ten holes divided between both arms. They went from the usual place in the crease of the elbow to the wrist and on the back of one hand. Blood had been taken from wherever it would give itself up. I had to lie down before leaving: I felt so weak and nauseated.

Shoy

My return appointment was in a week. Before I knew it, we were on the train again on our way back to the hospital. All the results were back from the lab. There were quite a few things wrong and I was started on Prednisolone tablets (steroids). These proved nasty. They would upset my stomach all day, every day and they increased my eating two fold, which meant I put on weight very quickly and my face just ballooned out and I began to look hideous. I was also given Hydroxychloroquine. These were big orange tablets and I could never swallow them in one go. I don't rightly remember what these were for, but they upset me as well. So with that I was also given some little white tablets to take. These were to counteract the upset that the Hydroxychloroquine was causing. In all, it was too much. Too many tablets displayed in my hand every morning, mid-day and in the evening. I would always have tears in my eyes, just getting them down, but I also lost all self-esteem. I put on so much weight and hated the way I looked. My clothes got far too tight and I had no money to buy new clothes, so I would go to the second-hand shops and buy them there. This was quite good, because I could get quite nice things that had hardly been worn real cheap, but still, it was embarrassing to do. However needs must. There was no end in sight to all this taking of medication. They would cut down the dosage and the problems would all return more or less immediately and so the dose was put back, and so it went on and on. I sank deep into depression and did not want to leave the flat, even to take the kids to school. I was off work for some time, but knew I had to go back sooner or later when things settled. My employees were so understanding and gave me all the time I needed. My mum was very concerned and supportive. She would help me whenever she could and would have the kids so I could rest, even though she was working herself. Yvette would help out as well. All said, my true friends were there for me, but I just wanted them to leave me alone. I wanted to do this alone. I wanted to get better. I wanted my energy back. I wanted my smile back. I wanted my mind back. I wanted my life back.

A year went by and finally I was weaned off all the medication. I quickly lost the weight and more that I had piled on due to the steroid to a certain extent, and due to the enormous appetite that had taken a hold of me that I could not control. I was back to normal.

Of course, when it came to buying a house, this Lupus thing the invasion of my life, was now invading my life again, but this time externally. This infuriated me. The fact that the adviser at the estate agents did not know what Lupus was or had even heard of it prompted me to ask the question. Who exactly was looking at my case and decided that I was not worth the risk? I had been told that the medical adviser had looked in all the textbooks. Well, with that I knew that the black and white textbooks were written depicting even more doom and gloom. I had read them myself and this was not the way my consultants had explained the 'whole' picture to me. I appealed against their decision, insisting that they wrote to my consultant in London to get a report purely about me, not about the worst-case scenarios they had read about.

This they did and reviewed my case, but still not entirely satisfied they agreed to let me have a mortgage, but only on a repayment mortgage: not an endowment mortgage as they still believed that I would not be around for the next twenty-five years. This was to make me happy! Anyway, wanting our own home, we accepted the terms and signed on the dotted line.

Then came the next hurdle. We viewed lots and lots of houses, as we were not sure what we were really looking for. We knew we wanted three bedrooms, but that was about it. So the more we saw, the more we began to define what we wanted based on what we had been exposed to. One thing was sure: we knew what we did not want. We saw some really awful houses. One in particular needed to be dragged from the sixties. It still had all its original fittings and fixtures, some of which would have been a fire hazard, maybe even a health risk. The furniture was very, very sixties and you just could not see beyond what you were faced with. Needless to say, we declined that one. Finally, we found a house that we both liked for different reasons. This house had a huge garden. It was set on three levels and on the second level there were mature fruit trees and a pond. The bushes and shrubs were mature and so beautiful. The house itself had great features with its parquet flooring throughout the downstairs and a fitted kitchen. It had a real fire which would be a great feature in the winter months. It needed a bit of work to the outside, as it was somewhat shabby. The windows would need changing as some of them, the wood especially, were in need of attention and a patio door would be a great addition, so you could access that beautiful garden from the house rather than just through the kitchen.

We put an offer in and to our amazement, they accepted. We thought that that would be it. We pay the money, they moved out and we moved in. We were in for the surprise of our lives. We had to order land searches and surveys of the house – all of which had to be paid for out of our own pockets. This was all so unexpected, but we managed. We waited for the report back on the house to see if it was sound and safe to go ahead with the purchase.

The long-awaited report came back and there were endless things wrong with the house. It needed the pointing done, the roof needed to be replaced, the flue had to be changed behind the fire, there were floorboards in desperate need of repair (some of which were actually on the stairway), a couple of the windows definitely had to be changed as they were rotting, the whole house needed to be re-wired and the drainage needed to be sorted, just to name a few things that needed attention. We looked at the whole report. Taking advice and weighing up all the pros and cons, we offered them another price for the house, cutting it by ten thousand pounds as this amount would cover the cost of the work that needed to be carried out, some of it before moving in.

We waited for two weeks, not hearing a thing from the owners of the property. In the meantime, the Housing Association was getting anxious as they had tenants to move in and obviously wanted us out. We were under the impression that we were not in a chain, whether from our end (as we had nothing to sell) and from the other side (as they were moving into parents' accommodation until they sorted themselves out), but this was all taking too long. Finally, they responded after solicitors got involved. The events that next took place were unbelievable. The vendors actually pulled out. They had got a copy of the report (that we had paid for) and had decided that it was cheaper to put things right themselves and then sell the house for the original asking price. There was nothing we could do. All that money that we had spent doing the land searches and having the house surveyed (and we had chosen the most comprehensive type of survey), had gone to waste - a waste that we could not afford - and now we were over our budget. We had no savings left and were forced to find another house and do all the searches and surveys again and use our wages, which meant that it was going to be tight for a while.

We found another house, which was in fact a few houses up the road where the first house was situated. Originally, we did not look at this one as it was overpriced but the estate agents persuaded us to look at it and maybe if it had been on the market for quite some time, the sellers would be prepared to drop their asking price.

This house was gorgeous. The kitchen had marble-tiled flooring. It had beautiful-wood-fitted units with a split-level cooker and extractor fan which had all been imported from Germany, and loads of room for a washing machine and drier, fridge-freezer, and even a space for the bin. The ceiling comprised of wooden slats that matched the units and individual lights which were set back into the ceiling giving a spotlight effect which could be angled to whichever part of the kitchen you wanted light on. It had a through sitting and dining area with patio doors that led out on to a patio with sweeping staircase up to the middle garden which was mainly grass, fringed with a couple of apple trees and a plum tree and mature bushes and shrubs. The third part of the garden was hidden by a wall of fir trees and had the potential to become whatever you desired. Denny had decided that it would be the vegetable garden and he would take great delight in digging it over and planting his first crop. Alongside the patio was the wall of the garage with a side door. Upstairs, the bathroom had an enormous corner bath (you could fit the four of us in it and still have room for a few more). I was sure that that was going to take some filling, but it was amazing. There was an over-sized washbasin and the usual toilet, which had a half-sized wall alongside it hiding it from the bath. It was all in grey, which matched the grey carpets, which were laid throughout with walls of magnolia (not my favourite colour: in fact, I absolutely hated magnolia. I grew up with it and wanted it eradicated). There were two very good-sized bedrooms and the usual box room, which was bigger than normal, but still a box compared with the other two. In the master bedroom, along two walls were floor-to-ceiling wardrobes with one side having complete glass sliding doors from ceiling to floor and just normal sliding doors on the other side, and on the end near the window there was a built-in dressing table. The windows were wide and let in vast amounts of light. It had a front lawn and off-road parking alongside it, which led to the garage.

Looking for What?

The entrance hall was quite spacious, big enough to have a standing coat hanger and a broad corner table.

We had landed on our feet and, to top it all, they agreed to our offer. The usual time frame followed, basically waiting for solicitors to finalise details and get the keys sorted for us. Finally that day came and we were on the move. The children were so excited. At last, they were going to have their own bedrooms and me, my very own home. The news to various people elicited various reactions. Most of them could not believe that I was going to buy a home with Denny, especially as we were not married and there was no mention of marriage. At the end of the day, it was none of their business, although of course people were full of advice. But I did not need to be married to him. He would marry me once we were settled in our house. This was what he had promised all along. 'As soon as we got our own home.' This was what he wanted, I was able to give it to him, and now nothing would stop us getting married and me having his name and being a proper wife in the eyes of the law and in the eyes of my parents. Everyone would be happy, but most of all me.

At long last, we were handed the keys to our very own home. We had an army of friends to help us clean the new house and the old flat. There were boxes, crates and bags everywhere. There was no organisation to the packing and it all became a mess. Nothing was labelled and so when it arrived at the house, it was just dumped in the living/dining room, which meant it had to be opened to know where it should be. Needless to say, a lot of boxes, crates and bags were not touched. I found the most important items such as the kitchen utensils, bathroom bits, clothing and bedding and made good the immediate living areas; the rest could be sorted slow time. That evening, most of our helpers left, including my family. Just a few good friends remained and they were going to stay the night and play games to seal the good vibes of our new home. The house was freezing, as we had not yet worked out how to operate the heating system. Luckily, there was a gas heater in the living room and so that was on full and heated the house nicely, it was so powerful. When it was on full, you could not sit in front of it at all. We kept all the doors open and the whole house was quite warm. We ordered in some pizza and Lloyd went to get some fried chicken for those who did not want pizza. It was a good night. We drank lots of coffee and fruit juice. (Funny that: no one drank alcohol, but then most of my friends did not). We talked and laughed, trying to keep the noise down, as the kids were asleep upstairs. It was such a happy night and the house was warm and homely, even though there were boxes all over the place. I would catch myself looking around, wanting to be pinched. It was all a dream sometimes, but it was a dream I did not want to wake up from.

Morning came and there were movements downstairs and in the bathroom. Denny and I had slept in our bed in our new home for the first night and the others had slept on the furniture downstairs amid blankets and quilts. They had eventually turned the heating off and so the house was now freezing again, but there were signs that it had been put back on as I could feel the heat radiating around the bedroom door that was left ajar the night before. I got out of bed, drew back the curtains, and welcomed the morning light, happy and content. The day ahead was going to be busy. I wanted to get rid of all the boxes, crates and bags, but first we had to sort out the hot water. Denny was already up and had sorted it along with the heating. He was so clever, but why had he not done that last night? Maybe he was just too tired to think, but nonetheless, we had hot running water and the heating was on and working. All the kids were still asleep. By now, Yvette had two children (Mike and Marcia) and of course there were my two. I tiptoed back out of the bedroom and went to the bathroom. I stood at the door in awe of my surroundings. This was all mine. I had a quick wash and got dressed. As I went downstairs, I could hear voices. Denny and Lloyd were in the kitchen making coffee. Denny was actually going to bring me up a cup, but of course I had woken up and so he did not need to. Lloyd looked really tired.

Shoy

Yvette had not woken up yet. We stood in the kitchen drinking our drinks (of course Denny had a cold drink as he never drank coffee or tea; in fact he never drank any hot drinks).

As the morning went on, everyone got up, the kids had their breakfast of various cereals, and I made a huge fry-up for the adults. After eating Yvette, Lloyd and the kids left to go and get freshened up and they would come back in the evening.

We were now alone in our home for the first time. Mercedes and Ezra were in the garden exploring and we had started on the boxes in the living room together. Denny was unpacking the items and passing them to me. My heart was racing. Would now be the time to ask him? Should I wait for the 'right' time? When would be the right time? Now is as good a time as any. I took a deep breath.

'Denny?' He looked at me momentarily. 'This house is really fantastic isn't it?'

'Yeah.'

'Now that we have our own house, how about us getting married, or at least setting a date?'

He hesitated, and then clasping his hands together whilst sitting astride one of the tea chests, he spoke. 'All in good time!'

What did he mean by that? 'All in good time!' What was wrong with now? I wanted an answer to my question, not an 'all in good time' response.

'What do you mean, *all in good time*?'

'Well, I know I said when we got our own house we could get married, but I would rather have a house in the West Indies; that would be my proper home. Then we could get married down there.'

I could not believe it. He had changed his mind. We now had to strive for a house in the bloody West Indies. Why the hell would I want to get married in the West Indies and when was that going to happen? We did not have any more money left as it had all gone towards this house and we had not even begun to pay the mortgage. He was taking the piss. I stood up away from him and just continued to unpack, in disbelief of what I had heard. He honestly did not love me. I had been told it a million times, but now I could see it. How many more times was he going to move the goal post and how far? He had dangled this invisible, unreachable carrot

Shoy

for years. Firstly, it was, 'When we get our own place'. The flat came along and then it was, 'Well we can't afford it with the two children and it would be better if we got a house'. We had got the house and now it was, 'When we get a house in the West Indies'. What would happen when we eventually got a house there? The whole day I could not think. I was so hurt.

That evening, Yvette and Lloyd came back, but by then most of the work had been done. I had made dinner for all of us. Lloyd knew something was wrong, as he had asked me a few times during the course of the evening. Yvette, on the other hand, did not notice, or at least I didn't think she did. I could not tell him. I was not ready to tell anyone. I was so embarrassed. I wished I had not bought the house, but it was too late. I had to make the best of a tricky situation. Maybe I asked him too quickly? I would leave it a while and ask him again another time, maybe in a month or so.

A few months went by and between the both of us we were earning quite a bit of money. I was still the office manager in the department in the hospital where I worked and he was still working as a metal-spinner locally. This job he had had since he left school. He was really good at it and loved it. We were managing the mortgage just fine with no problems and we were actually saving as well. I thought it was about time that I put my mark on the house.

Looking for What?

The whole house had this drab, grey-coloured carpet on the floor throughout, including the bedrooms and the bathroom. The walls were magnolia and the ceilings were white (throughout). It was like living in a mono-coloured TV set. Whilst shopping one day (which I absolutely detested), I picked up some decorating leaflets and colour charts. I was going to decorate my home. That evening after dinner, I put this to Denny. Now in most partnerships, things like decorating and buying of furniture items would be a joint decision and there would be give and take on both sides, but in this case not so. He bluntly said no. He liked the way the house was decorated and there was no need to change it. Once again, I was dejected. I would have to put up with the olive-coloured curtains, the second hand nets, the grey carpets (all over the bloody house) and the magnolia walls with no features. Even the pictures on the walls were mainly his choice. There were a few of the children, but there were none of the two of us. In all the time we had been together, there was only one time we had a photo taken together and that was on my twenty-first birthday. A group of us had gone to see Millie Jackson at Caesar's Palace in Luton and someone took a picture unexpectedly, and he looked so startled in the photo that it was not worth framing. That was the only time. The other pictures around the house consisted of Malcolm X, Martin Luther King (I know I should know about these people in great depth, but I knew very little; only what I had picked up along the way. They were of no interest to me. Oops, did I really say that?) Still, they hung around my house. There was this one picture, which I hated when it was in the flat. It was a picture, well actually a poster, of some black girl who was advertising black hair-straightening products. He would gawp at her and this hung on the wall. Can you believe it? But to top it all, I let this happen. I did not retaliate. I did not let him know how much I wanted things to change. I was not strong enough. I was scared. I did not want to lose him. I was an idiot. I was a doormat. Our, so-called 'lovemaking' went out of the window. I found myself not wanting him to touch me. I did not even want him to put his arms around me at night. In fact, I did not want to sleep in the same bed. On the few occasions that we did make love, I would fake orgasms, knowing that once I had climaxed, he would ejaculate and then get the hell off me.

Things were falling apart and the dream of a life together in our home was fading. I wanted out. I wanted to be on my own with my children. He was decorating some other girl's flat. She had been after him since I could remember and he did not hide the fact that she wanted him. His reason for not taking her on was that she was too fat and not his type. But I still believed that he sexed her just for the hell of it. She had been passing our house when she stopped by. He was not in, so I had the pleasure of talking to her on the doorstep. She wanted to thank him for all the decorating he had done for her. She (the bitch) had no idea how she wanted to decorate her flat and left it all to him; this he did and apparently it was 'spanking good.' So how did she thank him? Why was he not decorating our home?

On one particular occasion, Lloyd and Ricky had arranged for us, that is, Yvette, Denny, me and themselves, to go ten-pin bowling. I had never been before, but I was up for it. They arranged the whole thing and I arranged for the kids to stay at my parents' house. The day came and Denny was sick. He had come down with something like flu, so he was unable to go. Yvette could not get anyone to look after her kids so she could not go, and therefore it was just going to be Lloyd, Ricky and me. The evening came and then there was another problem. Denny was supposed to be driving us there, as neither Ricky nor Lloyd had a car. They turned up at the house, not realising that he was not going. But problem solved, he threw his keys at Lloyd saying, 'Make sure you don't bang it.' Great, the night was still on. We left. I sat in the back of the car. All the way I was very quiet. What could I say? My thoughts about Lloyd were far from clean. I was always thinking about him, especially as he and Yvette had grown apart and he was now a free agent. I wanted him, and what I wanted I got, but this was going to take some time. Maybe too much time. I wanted him now. I was here alone with two guys, something that

Shoy

had never happened before, and I was in love with one of them. The only thing was, he did not have a clue. We arrived at the bowling alley. It was a very cold, dry night, but the atmosphere in the bowling alley was warm and friendly. Lloyd explained how to play the game and showed me some techniques. He had to get very close to me to show me. My senses transferred to where he was touching me so I could feel every inch of him. He smelt so good. I could feel my juices running. I wanted him. I wanted us to be wrapped up in each other's arms. The bowling was great fun and I even got a strike. At the end of the games, Lloyd got a print-out for me so I could keep it as a souvenir of my first strike. As he handed it to me, I touched his hand. It was soft and warm. I did not want him to remove it, but he had to. We momentarily looked in-to each other's eyes. What was going on? Did he know what I was thinking? We were now making tracks to go home. The night was still young and I did not want to go home just yet, but I could not tell them this. We got to the front door of the bowling build-ing and could not believe it: it was snowing and very heavily. The shoes I had on had no grip on them at all. Both Ricky and Lloyd took me by the arms and walked me to the car. I was being held by both of them, one on each side. Lloyd was holding me and I was holding him. I was laughing as my feet slid all over the place. I almost brought both of them down at one point.

Looking for What?

We got into the car and Lloyd started the engine, wiping the windows. I sat in the front this time and Ricky in the back. Lloyd turned to me.

'Where would you like to go now?'

I looked at him. Where did I want to go now? 'Hmm what do you mean?'

'Well, we can go to a pub, play a few games of pool and have a drink. It's still early.' That was such a good idea. My thoughts exactly! We both turned and looked at Ricky, who was in agreement. So off we went to find a pub. Once again, they both held me to walk across the pub car park. It was nice and warm in the pub. Lloyd bought me an orange and lemonade and they both had a Budweiser. We waited for a pool table to become free, and then they started to play. I could not play to save my life. I wished I could as then I could have joined in.

'Hey, Shoy, come and play.' I laughed at Ricky.

'What makes you think I can play? This is the first time I am in a pub.'

Shoy

'So come here anyway. We will show you.' Ricky showed me how to hold the cue and hit the ball. It was easy when he was leaning over me guiding my hand, but once he left me to do it myself, that was it. I hit the table instead of the ball. I was useless. They both laughed and I felt stupid, but they made me try again and again and soon I was getting the hang of it. At least, I was hitting the balls, but they were not quite reaching the pockets. It was okay, actually, and we played another game after that one.

I sensed that Lloyd kept watching me sneakily, but I was not sure. I reckoned I was just imagining it. I so wanted him to notice me, but I knew it was stupid to expect him to. What was I thinking?

We moved from the pool table and started to play the table football. I was quite good at that and it was Lloyd and I against Ricky who still won. It was now getting late and we decided that we should make tracks home. Lloyd dropped Ricky off first and then drove me home. It was the longest, most quiet journey I have ever had. We did not even put the radio on. We said nothing to each other. On arrival at the house, I got out of the car and Lloyd followed me to the front door. I opened it and we both walked in. Denny was wrapped up on the settee.

'How was it?' He asked.

'Yeah, it was good, once I got the hang of it. We should take the kids - they would love it.' I turned to Lloyd who was still standing at the door. 'Would you like some coffee?' He always took his coffee black with two white sugars. It had to be white sugar otherwise he would not drink it.

'Yes, please,' he replied. I turned to Denny and asked him the same question. He declined. Lloyd then sat down and started talking to Denny. I disappeared into the kitchen and soon returned with the coffee. As he took the mug from my hand, I had my fingers positioned around the mug so he would have to touch them as he took the mug. It worked and he touched them for what seemed an eternity. His hands were so soft and gentle. As he took the mug he said, looking at me with his brilliant, glass-blue eyes, 'Cheers, big ears.' I smiled at him, hoping Denny had not noticed my flirting with him.

FINGERTIP LOVE

The relationship between Lloyd and Yvette was now well and truly over, even though she was expecting his second child (her third). She did not want him at all. She was resigned to the fact that she would be on her own with her children and did not need a man to be happy. I so disagreed with her. She had the best guy in the world and she could not see it.

Lloyd was so upset by everything, especially as she had been playing 'silly buggers' and not letting him see the kids when he wanted to. He spoke to me at some length in the evenings on the phone asking my advice, and then he told me, 'Look Shoy, don't tell Yvette, but I am going to leave England and go back to the West Indies as there is nothing left here for me.' What was I hearing? How could he say that? I was there. I wanted him. But of course he did not know this and would not want to know it. If he had had eyes for me and had picked up on all the little hints, he would have stayed. He would have made a move. He would have let me know that he felt the same way or a little, anyway. But there was nothing, obviously. He was still very much in love with Yvette. He was leaving. I would never see him again. I could not believe it. I had to do something. I could not let him leave without telling him how I felt and even if I lost him as a friend, at least he would have known. I then thought, what if he tells Yvette? I could not let that get in my way. Her loss was my gain and I had to act fast.

A week went by and we had spoken two or three times during that time. I just could not pluck up the courage to open my mouth and say what I had to. What was I going to say? I had rehearsed it a hundred times and still I could not get the words right or decide where to start. I felt he knew something was wrong. He kept on asking me if I was all right. I had so many chances. He was in effect giving me opportunities to open my mouth and say all the things I had planned, but I kept putting it off. I had the week off

Shoy

work and he called me during the day. I could not talk to him then as the kids were about.

'Can I call you back this evening when Denny goes out?' It was Thursday and, without fail, Denny would be out of the house. He was hardly ever in on a Thursday. The day was long and my mind was churning with words ringing in my head. I wanted to off-load all this information. He needed to know.

That evening, I called and he picked up the phone real quick. We started talking about nothing in particular.

'Are you sure that you are all right, Shoy? You sound as though you have something on your mind. Is everything okay with you and Denny?'

'Is anything ever all right with Denny and me? You lot know more about our relationship than I do.'

He did not answer. Well, that took us straight off the track. Once again I had fluffed it. There was silence.

'Look, Shoy, Ricky needs to use the phone for a minute. Can I call you back when he has finished?'

Fingertip Love

'Yeah, course you can.'

He hung up, giving me a reprieve. Moments later, the phone rang. I picked it up and answered. 'Hello?'

His voice came back at me.

'Hi there, how are you?'

'Oh, could be better, but you know how it is?' There was a silent pause as we both tried to find something to say. Why were we finding it so difficult to talk tonight? Usually, we would have verbal diarrhoea, but tonight - tonight of all nights - we had nothing to say.. I took a deep breath. 'Can I put a scenario to you and get your opinion on it?'

'Why, who is it about?'

'Why does it have to be about someone? It could just be a situation couldn't it?'

'Well is it?'

Shoy

I sighed. 'Okay, just listen. I can't tell you who it is about at the moment, but it's a situation that has to be sorted out quite quickly, because time is of the essence.'

'Okay, go ahead.'

'Right. If there was a friend of yours who fancied a friend's ex-boyfriend or girlfriend, what would you advise?

'Well, that would depend on how close I was to the friend and the ex-boyfriend or girlfriend of the friend.' Considering this was my scenario, he had totally confused me with that line. So I had to engage my brain again.

'What sort of answer is that?'

'Look, why don't you tell me the proper story? Who fancies who?'

'No, I can't tell you that because it would blow the whole thing. The person is not too sure about this course of action and she/he would be upset if it got out and she/he is not ready. Do you follow?'

'In that case, I am not going to give my opinion unless I have the full story and who is involved. That way I can give you a proper answer.'

I sighed. He was being so difficult and too clever for my liking. What was I to do next?

'Well, in that case, I will say no more.' This brought complete silence to our conversation (we were getting real good at that). 'Are you talking about your sister?'

'No, whatever gave you that idea?'

'Just an educated guess!' Well, he was totally wrong. He had totally missed the boat.

'Well, you are wrong. Look, I am gonna have to go now. Denny has just driven into the drive. I will call you back when I can, okay?'

'Okay, call me soon. Bye.'

I hung up and went downstairs. Denny was not staying; he had just come home to pick up something he had forgotten and he was

Shoy

back out of the door in two seconds. Fantastic. I went straight to the phone and called Lloyd back. He seemed pleased to hear from me so soon.

'Come on, Shoy. Carry on with the cryptic conversation that we were having earlier. I am intrigued. I want to know what you were going on about.' I laughed with him. 'Does your sister fancy me?'

I swallowed. What course of action was I going to take now? He was thinking about the wrong person. What if he fancied my sister secretly and now I had thrown them together? Oh my god! I had to turn this around, but for now I would run with this and see where it took me.

'What if she does?'

'No way. I see Stephanie as a sister and that's the way it's going to stay. She's a good kid and I would not risk that friendship for the unknown of a relationship.'

I went quiet (again) as thoughts went through my head. Should I own up to what I wanted to say or just drop the whole thing now?

'Are you all right?' There was that question again, the one that would prompt a thousand answers but never the right one from me.

'Yeah. Why?'

'Well, you went so quiet, I wondered if I had said something wrong.'

'No, you have not said anything wrong.'

'So why have you stopped talking to me now?'

'Okay. If I tell you who this person is, I want your honest thoughts on the matter, even if it upsets me, okay?'

'Carry on.' There was a moment of silence and then I blurted it out, eyes closed.

'Well, the person is me!' I had my ears half shut waiting for a response.

'I know.' I opened my eyes and my lips were smiling. My hands

Shoy

were sweaty and my heart was now running around my chest like it was on a mission around Brands Hatch searching for that black-and-white flag.

'What do you mean, you know?'

'I've known since that night we went bowling. I could feel something going on between us. I thought it was just me and I so wanted to talk to you that night about my feelings, but then I just dismissed them. Why do you think I have been calling you so much? I always knew when Denny was out and I would call you then, wouldn't I?'

'Well, what can I say?' I was so happy inside. 'Okay. Now that we know about the way we feel for each other, where do we go from here?'

'Well I think I need to come over and see you and we can talk and sort something out, don't you think?'

'Fine. Denny is going out tomorrow night. Why don't you come over then?'

'But it's Friday. We usually come over and play board games.

Everyone else will be there as well.'

Of course! I had to think fast.

'Well, I can cancel everyone else and forget to cancel you, or not be able to get hold of you and so you can turn up unaware of the fact and no-one would be any the wiser.'

'That's fine with me.'

We concluded our conversation and hung up. That night I was in heaven. I could not believe the conversation that had taken place. Nothing was going to upset me now. I could not wait to fall asleep. Wake up. Go to work. Come home. Pick up the children. Cook the dinner. Eat. Wash up. Get the kids off to bed. Denny would leave for the evening and then I would be left alone to prepare for my special guest.

The working day was long and endless. I was on a high all day. Carmel wanted to know what had got into me, but I could not tell her, not yet, anyway. She would be appalled at the idea, so I would have to keep it all to myself for a bit longer, but I was bursting to tell her. But then, what had I got to tell her? Lloyd might not turn up. He might change his mind between last night and tonight and

Shoy

so I would be back to where I had begun, just hoping for a glance, a touch, a stolen moment. I would have to wait and see.

I finally got home with the kids and sorted them out with what they wanted to eat. My mind was awash with thoughts of Lloyd. Denny started to get ready. He was a weekend bouncer at a nightclub, and they had asked him to cover this particular Friday, hence his reason for being out as this was not his usual night. He was expecting everyone still to come over. As I knew he was not going to be in, I told him that I had cancelled them earlier that day, and that the only person I could not get hold of was Lloyd. He did not bat an eyelid. Why would he? He left, telling me not to wait up, as he would be late. It was a special event and he would probably not be back until four to five o'clock. Whatever, Lloyd would be long gone before then. That I was sure of! Mercedes and Ezra were upstairs in Mercedes' bedroom playing with various games and paints, amusing themselves. They were always locked away in their bedrooms. They hardly ever watched the television. This I was thankful for. I called Lloyd. He was on his way. As he was quite nervous about the whole thing, he suggested that he would call me when he got to the top of the hill, just to make sure that I was still alone. Why was he so nervous? It was just another Friday evening and he was on his way over to play board games. Anyway, if it made him feel better then who

Fingertip Love

was I to upset him? About ten minutes later the phone rang and I jumped. I answered it.

'Hello?' It was Lloyd.

'Hi. Everything okay?'

'Yeah. Are you still coming?'

'Of course,' he replied quite quickly. 'Do you not want me to come anymore?'

'Yeah.' My voice was high-pitched. 'Where are you now?'

'I am at the top of the hill. See you in two secs.'

He hung up and I looked out of the window in the direction of the top of the hill. There was a car approaching with headlights on. Was this him? My heart was racing again and had stuck in my throat. I could hear it loudly in my ears. My throat was going dry. The car was slowing down and was now pulling into the drive. I moved away from the window and waited for the doorbell to ring. Sure enough, it did and I went to the front door and opened it, by which time the kids had come to the top of the stairs to see

Shoy

who was at the door. Lloyd walked in and the kids came running downstairs to see him. This was not out of place as they knew him very well and would always jump on him and play fight for a bit, but this night I wanted him to myself. Whilst he was clowning around with the kids, I suddenly remembered that I had to explain why he was here alone.

'Oh, by the way, I tried to get hold of you to cancel this evening, but obviously I did not manage to get you. Did Ricky not tell you that I cancelled this evening as Denny would not be here?'

'No. Oh well, now that I am here, are you going to make me a coffee?'

'Yeah, okay.' I left him with the kids and a few moments later he was in the kitchen with me, the kids having left him and gone back to their bedroom. I did not know what to say to him. I made his coffee and handed it to him, touching his hand as he took it.

'Thanks, big ears,' was his reply as always. We walked in to the living room and sat down. The television was on, but I could not tell you what was on. My mind was not on the television, to say the least. I had other things on my mind, but somehow we now needed to start talking. He sipped his coffee and just looked at me over the rim of the mug with his gorgeous blue eyes. I was melting. I could feel myself heating up. I wondered if he could see that I was sweating under his gaze.

'So, you came then?' I said, hesitantly.

'Did you think I would not?'

'Well, yeah. In view of what we are thinking of embarking on, it's enough for anyone to change their mind.'

'So, have you changed your mind?'

'No, not at all. If you don't try these things, you will never know if it is going to work out.' We were now talking and things were getting easier between us. I sat on the floor leaning against the settee that he sat on at the other end. I so wanted to move closer to him. I wanted to touch him. I wanted to feel his warm, soft hands on my skin. So near and yet so far! He placed the mug on the coffee table that was in the centre of the floor.

'Shoy, come here.' I slid slowly along the side of the settee and knelt up in front of him. His arms were around me and were pulling me closer to him. Our eyes met. Gradually we drew closer to each other. I could feel his hot breath on my lips. I closed my eyes. *'Please touch me now. Now. Now.'* I thought. At last our lips touched. His lips were so gentle, just like his hands. At first it was just a touch and we pulled away from each other. We slowly moved our lips back together and very slowly and gently we started to kiss each other, exploring each other, not wanting to part. I deserved this. He kissed me as if we were long-lost lovers, reunited and never wanting to let go of each other. I felt loved, wanted, needed, all in the one kiss. This was real and it was going to be mine. We finally parted. In a whisper, as that was all I could manage, I said,

'Should we really be doing this?' It was safe to ask that question, as I knew he felt the same way that I did. His kiss for me was just as real as mine was for him.

He answered, 'Well we are two consenting adults and we both want it, don't we?' I looked down at the floor, smiling.

'Yeah….. but ……' He stopped my words with another kiss. It was so sensual and warm. I wanted him to kiss me more and more. I pulled away and continued what I was about to say before I was interrupted.

'Look, we could stop this now, before we go any further?'

'Why would I want to do that?' He was very sure with his answer.

'Well we have to seriously think about Yvette and Denny.'

'Eh, no. You have to think about Denny. Remember, I am no longer with Yvette. We parted a long time ago and, as you know, I am living on my own. She has my children and one on the way, but I have no other ties with her. She chucked me out in no uncertain terms and made it quite clear that she did not want me anymore.'

'Well, I have to think about her. After all, she is my best friend and it would only seem that I am moving in on her man.'

'But Shoy, no matter what you think, I am not her man. Not any more.'

We both paused for a while. He spoke. 'So, what are you saying? Is this over before it has begun?'

'No, no of course not. Of course I want us to have a relationship, a worthwhile relationship one for keeps; if possible,' I paused.

Shoy

'But I have to tell you, I need to tell both of them that we are seeing each other before I have sex with you. I cannot make love to you or truly commit myself until they know. That way I am fully relaxed, it's all above board, and we can really get to know each other without wondering how it will affect anyone when they found out. Is that okay?'

'So, kissing; is that not a commitment?'

'Well, yes, I suppose it is in a way, but we have not crossed that line where other emotions are involved. I just don't want to go down that road.' In my mind, I did not want to get into another situation where I was having sex with someone that I felt was not going to mean anything in my life: just rampant sex when he wanted it and nothing else, and then, at the end of the day, I was still left with Denny and all his indiscretions and nothing to show for it. But I could not tell him this, not now. Maybe I never would. My mind returned to the conversation in hand. 'Well at the moment we have only kissed, and a kiss is just a kiss.'

'Is that what you think? That we have just kissed and it has meant nothing? Look, Shoy, I have loved you for a long time, since you were with Denny from the beginning. I have never told anyone this, but I have fancied you for such a long time. I used to watch

Fingertip Love

you walk up and down the road with your mum when you used to go shopping past the pub, and you were never aware that I was your secret admirer, but I was never in a position to make a move on you. You always seemed to be with him, never alone.' I stopped him.

'I was on my own for quite some time actually. When I went on holiday to Spain the first time, I went to forget about him. We weren't together then. Where were you?' He hugged me.

'Oh, Shoy, I am so sorry I should have been there. He would never have had another chance. I would never have let him have you back. You would have been mine – forever.'

I sat on the settee next to him and we chatted for the rest of the evening, giving each other a little kiss now and again. We talked about when we were growing up. When we had seen each other as teenagers. You see, I had noticed him when we were at secondary school. He was never at my school, but he and some other guys would always be outside the school gates when school was over, hanging around. He had the biggest afro, his hair was light brown, and he stood out in the crowd. He was one of the quiet ones, never shouting and making a spectacle of himself to get noticed, but I noticed him. I knew I was not in their league. I was ugly

Shoy

and never dressed like the other girls they were after. He would never have noticed me, and yes, I was right; when I asked him, he hadn't remembered me. He hadn't even remembered me going to Ingrid's house. He would be there sometimes, but he was always with someone else, so I knew I was not in his league. But why was he attracted to me now? I was over-weight, useless in bed and lacking self-confidence. He was going to have to work hard, or I would if I was going to keep him - if ever we got it together properly. We had a good laugh with each other. We were so relaxed and time fled by. Soon it was past midnight and he had to go. He left, but before going, he planted a big kiss on my lips saying,

'That will keep you going until we meet again, which will be soon.' I closed the door behind him and ran to the window to wave him off. I watched the car lights disappear out of sight, up the hill. I turned off the lights downstairs and went up, checked on the kids, had a wash and went to bed. Just as I got in, the phone rang. I answered it.

'Hello?'

'Hi. Babes. How are you?'

'Hi. I thought it would be you.' Yes, it was Lloyd. He was calling, as he wanted to say goodnight, which he did, blowing me a kiss down the phone. That was so sweet. I hung up with his voice in my head and drifted off to sleep.

Saturday morning came and I went about my usual Saturday morning activities, doing the shopping and spending the day with the kids. Now that we were living elsewhere, we were not going down to the library as much as when we lived just up the hill, but I would buy them lots of books and we would go into town, do the shopping and then when we had got back and had some lunch and settled down, we would read and read. Saturdays with the kids were so much fun. It was their day and I tried to make it as interesting and as wonderful as possible (always on my own).

Shopping was always a bone of contention with Denny. He would never go with me. All he would do is to hand over his half of the money, along with 'I want this and I want that,' and that would be his contribution in helping. He would eat most of the damn food. We used to (at that time) spend about forty pounds a week on shopping. For his twenty pounds he would want all these fancy fruit juices (as he would never drink undiluted juices). He would want certain cuts of meat, which had to be lean, sausages, bacon, eggs, and beans, along with some other crap things. He thought that his 'hard earned' twenty pounds would be able to purchase all

Shoy

of that and then I could put in my twenty pounds and buy the kids all their food for their packed lunches for five days each, cereal for breakfast, milk, all the fruit (of which he ate most as he was a fruit hound) and all the vegetables for the week. I would never get all the shopping with forty pounds and invariably I would spend a lot more, but I had to make sure that I got his stuff first and then with whatever I had left, I would buy what I was able to. This was so depressing for me. Once again, it was 'why do stupid women like me put up with crap men like him?' But we stayed there, simply because we either did not have the common sense to get out, or we were just blind, blind when it suited us. But my time was coming and this was not going to go on forever. To top it all, I did not drive and so getting the shopping home was costly, as I had to get a taxi each time. Denny would never help. Sometimes I would get back home and he would still be there. I would unpack the bags with the help of the kids and he would not even offer an explanation as to why he could not collect us. I would call him and ask him to pick me up and all he would say was that I should get a taxi and he would pay for it when I got home. He was such a bastard, yet I stayed there. One day I would pass my driving test, but first I had to start taking lessons and that was next on my agenda.

My job was now moving to another town, about fifteen miles away from where it was now, and the bus service to and from the hospi-

Fingertip Love

tal there was not reliable nor ran at the right times. In the interim, Carmel and I arranged that if we went with our jobs we could share the cost of the petrol that she used to get us there and back, so this was my incentive. I started driving lessons in an automatic car, as in the past, I had tried and tried in a manual, somehow I just had not been able to get that clutch/accelerator business, and hill starts. The automatic was much easier and I was sure I was going to pass first time. In no time at all, my instructor, who incidentally was a lesbian but the nicest person you could ever meet, put me in for my test. I was sure that I was not ready. I had bought my own car, which was a Mazda 323. It had a reconditioned engine and it was a metallic silver/grey. It was beautiful. It was my very own car. Whenever I could I would try to get Denny to take me out in it. This did not happen very often and so most of the time it would be standing there, unused in the driveway. Denny, from time to time, would ask to borrow it and I would refuse. Now, you would think that that would have caused an argument, but no, not at all. He would leave it. I suppose he was thinking that, if he could not borrow the car, then he would not be giving me lessons. Whatever, I was not going to give in on that one. He had had the back of his car wrecked by someone running into it and so was on foot, or begging lifts from mates.

So my test came back for mid-June and that gave me exactly three weeks. It was one of the quickest test receipts that the instructor had seen. Maybe someone had cancelled and my test request form was in the right place at the right time. But this suited me fine. At least I could then get my car on the road and not pass it every morning in the driveway, whatever the weather. I decided not to tell anyone, not even Denny. I wanted to do this alone. It had crossed my mind that maybe I would tell Lloyd, but I decided against it. I wanted to surprise everyone. If I did not pass, I did not want everyone to think that I was a failure and besides, Yvette had passed her test first time and that would be a blow. She would gloat!

Anyway, we returned from our momentous shopping trip and Lloyd called. Denny had been getting ready to go to his cricket match: the same match that Lloyd was getting ready for as well. They both played in the same cricket team and so would be together on a Saturday and Sunday. I had never been to one of these matches; there was never enough room in the cars for me to go, but I would always hear from some of the other girlfriends of some of the players of various matches they had had, and they would always want to know why I was never there. Well the answer was simply this: I was never invited. Lloyd and I had a quick conversation. It was nice and reassuring to hear his voice after the night before. We had no idea when we would see each other

Fingertip Love

again. Everything now depended on when, where and how Denny and Yvette would be told and I wanted it to be real soon, but Lloyd wanted us not to rush and to make sure of what we were going to do. So I waited. In the meantime, I had hinted to my sister that I was seeing someone else and it was someone she knew. She had guessed all sorts, but she was not even close. She had not mentioned Lloyd's name at all. She was going to have to wait and be surprised just like everyone else.

The day came for my driving test and I went to work as usual. No one knew. Not my mum. Not my dad. Not my brothers'. Not my sister. Not my kids. Not Denny. Not Yvette. Not Lloyd. I had not even told Carmel at work or any of my other colleagues. My driving instructor picked me up from work. I drove home as the practice lesson to pick my car up, as I was having my test in my very own car. The instructor had checked it over the week before and it was all right for the test. I then drove my car down to the driving test school office, parked it and went in to register. I sat there for about fifteen minutes when a very stern man came out from an office and called my name. I answered. He then asked where my vehicle was. I showed him via the window. We proceeded to the car. He took a look around it and then we got in. He explained what was about to take place and then asked me to start in my own time. I did the necessary. During the test I made a couple of small mistakes, but I was well aware of them. My three-point turn was perfect and my parallel parking was the best I had ever done. I was always good at them, and was not worried in the least. The only thing that bothered me was the emergency stop. In my lessons, I would always stall the car and of course that would mean a fail, but on this day, it all went to plan and I did not stall the car. We returned to base and he asked me to turn off the engine, which I did. He then asked me questions on the Highway Code, which I got right. He then sat there for a couple of minutes writing frantically. Well had I passed? My hands were all sweaty when finally he turned and looked at me, and for the first time he smiled. I knew it: I had done it. I had passed. I was so delighted that I flung my arms around the test instructor's neck, much to his surprise. He handed me the necessary paperwork and congratulated me. On getting out of the car, my driving instructor was waiting. She had been so nervous for me and on my return she could not tell if I had passed or not. She was ecstatic and hugged me, congratulating me as well. The first thing she ordered me to do was remove the 'L' plates that were stuck on the front and back of my car and then we sat in the car and went over what happened next, but basically I had passed, although my lessons were not yet over. I had decided that I would book in for four more lessons with her and that would be to drive down to London with her, so I could get up to speed as a new driver. Apart from that, I was a driver with my own car. That afternoon I got into my car, drove myself out of the driving test centre and stopped outside my parents' house. My mum was so happy for me. My dad was not yet home, so I would have to come back later and give him the good news. With that I left. I took myself off to see Lloyd at work. He could not believe it when I turned up.

'How did you get here?'

I was beaming at him. 'Well, I drove myself.'

He was so pleased for me and gave me a big hug and a huge kiss right outside his workplace. What if anyone saw? He did not care and just kissed me harder. I left him and drove myself to work. On the way, I was starting to become complacent, went too close to the kerb, and hit it, bouncing off. Luckily there were no cars behind me. With that, I took a hold of myself and calmed down. There was no way I was going to kill myself on the first day of taking my 'L' plates off.

I drove to work, parked my car in the car park for the first time, and walked across to the building. I walked in carrying my 'L' plates and threw them on Carmel's desk. All she did was look at me and screamed, leaping up from her desk and hugging me. I

Shoy

did not even have to say what it meant, she knew. In no time at all, the whole building knew what had happened and they were congratulating me. I felt so clever.

I left work that evening (in my own car) followed by Carmel. I had told her how I had hit the kerb on the way to work and she had laughed. I turned up at my mum's and collected the kids. They were screeching with delight at the thought of Mummy taking them home in 'her own' car. They sat in the back on their booster seats strapped in. They were a picture. By the time I got home, Yvette had heard and was outside the house to congratulate me. The only person, who did not know by now, was Denny and he was not home yet. When he came in, I told him my good news and all he could say was, 'So why did you not tell me when your test was?'

What did it matter? There was no 'well done'. He just murmured, half-heartedly, 'I knew you would pass anyway.'

Lloyd and I were growing closer and closer, but still we had not had any physical contact. When I was alone at night, I would masturbate thinking of him touching me, making me wet and making love to me. Whenever we got the opportunity, we would play with each other and kiss a lot, but it went no further. Lloyd seriously wanted our relationship to be a proper one and for us to be together. I wanted the same, but we still had the hurdle of Yvette and Denny. Yvette was now being very nice to Lloyd, as she had heard that he was possibly seeing someone else. She, being scared and shocked, came and spoke to me in confidence. Could you believe it? She was telling me what I already knew. She had no idea who it was Lloyd was meant to be seeing and, for the time being, that was fine by me. I was getting anxious for them to know and to know real soon. It was all getting too close.

We had a very serious chat one evening. We had met at a local pub and planned what action we were going to take. Our plans would take place on the same evening, roughly at the same time. That way, no one would be ahead of the other one with information. Yvette was sure to want to let Denny know what was going on and vice-versa, so this plan had to go like clockwork so that neither would have a surprise for the other one.

Yvette had now launched into fighting talk, saying she wanted Lloyd back and that she was adamant she would find out who this other woman was. I knew this would happen, sooner than she knew it. But still I could not tell her a thing. I really wanted to and so many times it was on the tip of my tongue, but I could not. It would spoil the plan. She was now spending a lot of time at my

Shoy

house and she was getting bigger and bigger with her pregnancy. Every moment she got, she was at my house and I was very uneasy with all of this. It just went to show; she did not know me at all. If she did, she would have realised that I was hiding something from her. My actions told her this time and time again, but she was not wise to any of it. She was just so wrapped up in her fight for a man she did not want. She would ask my advice. How could I advise her? He was mine and I could not tell her how to get back the man I had fallen in love with. I knew I should have, and under normal circumstances, of course, I would have helped her in any way that I could, but not this time. He was now mine and there was no way I was going to blow that. The only thing I told her was that she had to fight if she seriously wanted him back. After all what had she offered him in the last few months? Was I mad? Had I lost my mind? But what could I say? I was caught unawares this time and now I had thrown her into his arms. This was one of those moments when a revolver (not that I would have known how to use one) would have come in useful.

On the other side of the picture was Denny. I had to pull away from him. Make him guess that things were not good between us without having to tell him bluntly. I started by not having sexual relations with him. I would go to bed early and make excuses not to have sex with him. By now, I could not stand him touching me. His touch was not the same. It was not as sensual and soft as Lloyd's. We would have little disagreements about very, very stupid things and we would not talk properly for days. One evening he came home, obviously having suspected me of having sex with someone else (you see, when you have been there you know the signs) and he forced me to have sex with him. I just lay there and with that he got off. I was disgusted with him. He pushed me away saying, 'Well, whoever makes you feel good, you'd better go back to him, because you will not have any more of me.' Well, he had answered my prayers. It was never a good thing to call my bluff. More times than not, it would back fire as I would not have it called very often, but when I did, I would rise to the challenge and I would come through.

Things in general were getting really rough between us and my sister was now noticing the changes and the presence of something going on in the house whenever she came over, which was quite often. I still would not put her in the picture. I felt the less she knew, the better it was, but she was always asking and I was always refusing to tell her. The only bit of information she was given was that I was having an affair. The person would remain nameless for now.

My sister was relentless with her questions and every day she would ask, 'who is this person? Please tell me.' I knew I could trust her and so I told her. Her mouth fell open. She could not believe it. Then of course came the barrage of questions.

'When did it start? Does Yvette know? Does Denny know? Is that why things have been so bad between you?' I just looked at her, not answering her questions. She was so excited. I could see it in her eyes. 'Oh my god, I am going to leave town. Can you imagine what Mudda is going to say when she hears about this?'

'Well, Stephanie, that is the least of our problems. We still have to tell Yvette and Denny.' My sister held her mouth.

'Oh God, just make sure you tell me when you decide to do that. I am going to emigrate. The noise, man? Can you imagine?' Really, I did not want to. It was great talking to someone at last about the events of the past few months. Stephanie was such a help. She listened and came up with some useful thoughts and suggestions.

I called Lloyd that night and told him about telling my sister. He did not mind in the least. In fact, she was the one person he was looking forward to telling. He knew she would be in agreement with our being together and he was right. The first time my sister saw him after being told, she flung her arms around his neck, stood back and thumped him on the arm and said nothing more. Every time my sister saw either of us, she could not stop smiling. She was so happy for us and just wanted the whole thing to be out in the open.

All this stalling for 'the right time' had been made more complicated by the fact that Denny and I had booked a family holiday, along with my sister, to the Caribbean long before this affair started. I was going to have to tell him before we went on this holiday. I wanted out of it, but at the moment I could not see a way. Most of the fare had been paid for and it would mean losing a lot of money, and the kids were so looking forward to it. Mercedes had been before, but it was an opportunity for Ezra not to be missed. It would also have meant that my sister would lose her money as well. I was committed to this god-forsaken holiday. Why was I always in a difficult situation when it came to holidays? The last time being pregnant and now this, wanting to be with someone else? Heh, maybe I could get Lloyd to go in the place of Denny? Maybe not, after all. We were staying with his uncle, that would have taken some explaining.

The whole situation was dragging on and I was getting impatient. Basically, Lloyd wanted me to hold on until I returned from my holiday and then we would break the news, but that was not what I wanted. I wanted to know that everything had been settled. I did not want to go on this holiday, with Denny not knowing and our having to sleep in the same bed, pretending to be a couple. After all, that was what was happening. We were pretending. There was no love. Hardly any contact. We just led two separate lives.

I was now exerting pressure on Lloyd and he agreed on a time and day. It was of course going to be a Friday and we had decided on eight o'clock. By then, the children in both houses would have been fed and most of them tucked up in bed and the adults would be left alone. Denny was not working this particular Friday and so it was all systems go. For some reason, I was not nervous or scared. I just wanted to get it over and done with. It had gone on far too long and the end was in sight. Eight o'clock approached and I launched into the all-life-changing speech.

'Denny, I am no longer in love with you and I am seeing someone else.' I paused, knowing that he would ask who. Sure enough he said,

'Who are you seeing?' He looked vulnerable and lost. His eyes were different. They were searching for an answer.

'Well you are not going to like this, but.......' I could not bring myself to say it, but I had to. Just about now, Lloyd was telling Yvette the exact same thing and I had to do it, before the phone rang and it would be her, interrupting. 'Well it's actually Lloyd that I am seeing'. He stood up and just looked at me in disgust. For the first time that evening I was feeling scared and sick. I had hurt him and I could see it. But I felt nothing, nothing at all. This was for all the hurt and pain. For all the lonely nights I had lain awake wanting to know where he was and with whom. This was for all the times I had wanted him to be a father to our children and he had never been there, always letting them down and leaving me to make up plausible reasons as to why he was not there for them. This was for me. He did not even know what to say now. How could he? He had not even seen this coming. Even though he had commented on me seeing someone else, he still had not seen this one coming.

The phone ringing broke the oppressive atmosphere. I knew who it was immediately. I stretched to answer the phone, but Denny snatched it out of my hands and answered it. It was her. I could hear her voice from the receiver. She was crying. He invited her over and replaced the receiver. Oh great. Now the two of them were going to be here in my house and she would be slobbering all over the place. I had to get out before she came down. Denny

Shoy

went to the toilet and I took my chance and left the house. I had to find Lloyd. I needed to talk to him. I drove around to his various haunts, but could not find him. I drove up to Ricky's. He had not seen him all day, but was well aware of what was taking place that evening. He was happy for us, but right now all that was on my mind was to find Lloyd and talk to him. I needed to know what he had said and how she had taken it and whether we were still going to be an item. I returned to the house, not having found Lloyd. Yvette was no longer there. I walked into the house and into the living room. It was dark and quiet. I turned on the lights and saw Denny sitting there. He had been crying. He stood up and came towards me.

'Shoy, please let's talk. We need to talk. You left without giving me a chance to even talk to you.' I sat down and waited for him to talk. Now he wanted to talk. Now I got his attention. This would have to be real good. I was hard and I was not going to be an easy pushover. I knew where I had come from and I knew where I was going and where I wanted to be and he was not part of that picture, but I would listen.

He asked me loads and loads of questions, some of which I could not answer, would not answer. He did not push me for answers. He was quiet and shaking. He was a small shadow of a man. I had never seen him this way before, although I obviously had got his attention, but this was a battle he had lost and no amount of sucking up was going to get me back. I had given him the best time of my life and now there was nothing left for him. At various intervals he would let a tear drop which would move on to a crying state. But, you know, it made me happy to see him in this state. This just made up for all the hard times he had put me through. For all the little presents he had given me and I was left to rid myself of them secretly as if I were the one to blame. This was for all the lonely nights I lay by myself in that big double bed, wanting him by my side and knowing that he was at the side of someone else. This was for all those months of receiving malicious phone calls, taunting me and driving me almost insane all because he had put himself about and everyone else wanted him so badly that they had tried to scare me off. He continued to talk. He made quite a lot of sense really, but it was falling on deaf ears. It turned out to be a very long night and eventually we went to bed. He lay there and I fell asleep almost immediately. After all, tomorrow was going to be an even longer day. That I was sure of!

Bright and early the next morning, Yvette was there on the doorstep with kids in tow. She walked in as though nothing had happened and this was her house. The kids went upstairs and we were left alone in the living room. She looked at me.

Shoy

'Well, when were you going to tell me?' Did she really think that she was going to get a conversation out of me that day? She kept on. I turned the television on and ignored her. She had been told and there was nothing else to it. Where the hell was Lloyd? I had not heard from him all evening. I did not want to talk to her until I had spoken to him, but now he was nowhere to be found. After she had calmed down, I decided that I could hold a civilised conversation with her and we talked a little, but I was still very reluctant to say much. After a couple of hours or so, Lloyd turned up. He kissed me on the cheek at the front door. God knows what had happened and what had gone on between them, but this was not the same person who had left to tell her that he was moving on and with whom. My mind was working overtime. I needed to talk to him and told him so as he walked through the door. We arranged to meet a few hours later in the usual pub. Denny took the kids to the park at the top of our road and the three of us were left there. We were silent. I turned to Yvette and said, 'Yvette, I would appreciate it if you could go now. I want to get on with what I have to do and I don't want you here.' She then replied in a manner that said 'I am the queen of the castle here'. 'How can I go when the kids are not here?'

'They are in the park at the top of the hill. You can drive up there and pick them up. If not, Denny can drop them over when he gets back.' I looked at her waiting for some smart aleck reply, but she disappointed me and just got up and left. I then asked Lloyd to leave saying I would try to get away later and meet him for a talk. We said nothing more. It was an unreal situation.

The next couple of weeks went by. Denny and I had not resolved anything and neither had Yvette and Lloyd. All four of us were in a stalemate. We had not moved any further forward and we had not gone back. Something had to happen. But what? Unbeknown to Lloyd and I, Yvette and Denny had decided that all four of us would get together and talk the whole thing through, especially with this holiday coming up. Throughout this stalemate business, we somehow managed to keep it just between the four of us (well, with my sister and Ricky knowing, but that was it).

So the kids were once again carted off to my parents and Yvette's were staying with hers. Lloyd and Yvette came over to our house and we were going to have this 'talk' on presumably their terms. Lloyd and I were now not really talking, not as we should have been. I sensed that Yvette had got to him and that he was now backing out, but that was fine. I was strong enough to go it alone. I did not need him and would not beg him and put him in a situation that he did not wish to be in. I waited to see what the outcome

Shoy

of this meeting would be. That evening, the four of us ended up in my bedroom as when Yvette and Lloyd arrived I was up there and Denny took it upon himself to bring them straight up (prat).

So here we were. The three of them sitting on my bed and me gazing out of the window. This was a conversation I did not want to have. I was clear where I wanted to be and I really did not know why we were talking again. Denny called over to me.

'Shoy? Do you have anything to say?' Well, with that I spun round and faced them.

'Why the hell do I have to say something? Did I call this fucking meeting?' Yvette then decided to open her mouth.

'Well, there is no need for language.' I turned on her. It would have made me feel better to slap her, but she was still pregnant.

'Why the hell don't you just shut your mouth? This is my room and you are in it without being invited, so don't you dare talk to me about language.' That shut everyone up and Lloyd started.

'Okay. Why don't you and Denny………..' He was looking at Yvette. 'Why don't you two tell us what it is you want and we can then get a picture of where we are?' What the hell was that? We knew where we were and they did not need to take the floor. Why was he confused? I just looked at him. I knew he had changed his mind, but he did not have the guts to tell me and now this was his forum and he was going to use it to tell me. I waited with bated breath. Still there was nothing. I turned back to resume my gaze out of the window. In the distance I could hear sirens and they were getting louder and louder. Suddenly, there was a speeding car hurtling down the hill and it was closely being followed by three squad cars. Everyone came over to the window and we watched as the car and the flashing lights disappeared down to the end of the road.

'Well that was exciting. You don't see that every day.' For a moment I had forgotten why we were there, in my bedroom. The silence returned and I carried on looking out of the window.

'This is ridiculous. Why are we all sat here if no-one is going to say anything worthwhile?' She spoke and that was all she could come out with. We had already worked that line out. With that I turned once again and faced them.

'Who asked you to come here anyway? You're the ones who wanted to talk, so talk.' I looked specifically at Yvette and said.

Shoy

'You think you are so clever? You think that if you put me on the spot, I will cave in and then I will settle for second best and you can have your precious Lloyd back? Well guess what? That is not so.'

'Don't shout at her. She's here to try and sort this mess out, just like the rest of us.' Denny came to her rescue. Well that figured. He would always rescue someone else, but never me.

'Oh yeah. The mess that I caused!' Lloyd now found his voice at last.

'What do you want, Shoy? Do you want us to give it a go or do you want to give things a try with Denny?' I raised my eyebrows.

'What do you mean by that?' In my mind we knew what we wanted and now he was asking me 'what did I want?' Had I missed something over the past couple of weeks? She had got to him and changed his mind and he no longer wanted me. I could see that now. I had been so stupid. I lowered my voice as if in submission.

'Lloyd, you make your mind up and let me know.'

Denny now piped up,

'Shoy, I don't want to lose you and the kids. I do love you and I need you. Look, in front of these two, I promise to treat you better and to take you out. I will landscape the garden the way you want it and we will decorate the house anyway you want and change whatever you want to change. Please just stay and give me another chance. I deserve a second chance'. That was not a good thing to say. Not now, not at this moment in time.

'Oh yeah, that's just fantastic. So wah? You want me to throw my arms around you, kiss you, and tell you that everything is going to be okay? That will never happen. You see, Denny, all those years I wanted you, you never wanted me. I was fine as the' little wife' in the house, who would have your clothes washed and ironed, your food on the table when you got home, lie down and fuck you when you wanted me to please you and now you have the nerve to tell me that you need me? I would have lived in a tent in a field in the middle of nowhere, if it meant that I would have you to myself. I didn't need a house with a landscaped garden and decoration to suit. I just wanted you. I wanted you to myself. I did not want to have to share you any more and fight off all these bitches that would lay claim to you over me. Me, who gave birth to your chil-

Shoy-

dren! I tried everything possible to get your attention as a woman and as the mother of your children, but you were blind, blind to all of it and now you have finally opened your eyes. Hmm... Go to hell. Furthermore, I have nothing else to say to anyone. I want you all out of my room and right now. This conversation is over and I want you all to get out.' The room fell silent again. Denny came over to the window and drew the curtain across to stop me looking out of it.

'Oh wow, drawing the curtain. Do you think that you are my father in days of old when he would draw the curtain so hard that it would drop off the edge of the rails and I would be too scared to touch it? Well look!' I drew the curtain back and continued looking out of the window. I turned. They were all still there sitting on my bed.

'I told all of you to get out of my room and leave me alone.' Even with that, Lloyd still had to go one step further.

'Well I think that we should give Denny and Yvette another chance to prove that they want us. I personally feel that I should give Yvette another chance, after all she is having my child and I would like to see it born and give us a try.' He was talking to me. He had bottled it. He had been taken in by her once again, but I would see the day when he would be thrown to the kerb and this time there would be no way back for him. He was spineless. He brought tears to my eyes for the first time in ages. I was hurt, rejected.

'Well, you do what you have to, but there is no way that Denny and I will get back together. It is over and I am moving on. Now for the last time, can you all get out and leave me alone.'

'Can you give us a moment?' Lloyd asked Yvette and Denny to leave us alone. They went and he came over to the window where I had been standing the whole evening. I looked at him with tears rolling down my face.

'How could you do this to me? I thought you said that you wanted me? You have humiliated me. You did not have to wait until now to tell me and even then you did not tell me that you did not want me anymore. Why?' My voice was harsh, but I looked at him with pity, pity because I knew that she would drop him like a lead balloon when she was good and ready, and he would feel that pain harder than any other pain he had felt before, and it would hurt him for a long time. Best of all, I would be there to see it. I suppose I should have been feeling upset or numb or something, but looking at him, I just felt very, very sorry for him. He could not see what I saw. He did not want to see it. He did not feel what I felt for him, but one day, mark my words, one day he would beg me to come back to him. Denny and Yvette were happy with themselves downstairs. Their voices could be heard upstairs.

'Shoy, I am so sorry for what I just said. I thought it was what you wanted?'

'How did you arrive at that? Did I ever say to you that I wanted you to get back with Yvette and give her a second chance? Did I ever say to you that I wanted to get back with Denny and give him a second chance? Well?' I waited for his reply, but there was none coming. 'Well there you go. NEVER.' I was now poking him in the chest real hard and he was backing away from me. I pushed him away totally. 'You will regret what you have done today and what you have put me through.'

I pushed past him and went downstairs. Denny had put the kettle on and was making me a cup of tea. Obviously from the look of things, Yvette was not going anywhere. She had already taken her shoes off and was settling in for the night with the television on and remote control in her hand. We all sat in the living room and the three of them talked about this and that – a load of rubbish. It was unreal. There we were, two of us had started off the evening

Fingertip Love

by wanting to be with the other (or at least I thought we had) and by the end of it all, we were right back where we started, except that I was not with Denny now, but Lloyd was back with Yvette and that stung me more. Denny left to pick the kids up from my mum's and I was left alone with the two of them. I now wished that I lived near the railway station like I did when I lived at the flat. I used to disappear at night and sit on the platform for hours, just reading. I got to know the guards at the station really well and they would keep an eye on me, especially when they knew that a train or freight train was due, just in case I had an idea about jumping. I was not that deranged. I just needed somewhere to sit and think and if I did not want to think I would read. This time there was none of that escape and even if I wanted to, Yvette's car was blocking me in, in my own drive.

Denny returned with the kids and I was so glad to see them. I gave them something to eat and drink and then took them up to bed, getting them washed and undressed, and then tucked them up and read them a story. Whilst I was up there, Lloyd came up to say goodnight to them. He waited for me to finish the story and then we sat at the top of the stairs. I did not say a thing. I could not find the words I wanted to say. There was no point now telling him how much I was falling for him. How much I wanted to make love to him. None of that was going to happen now so there

Shoy

was no need to go there. Yvette and Denny had decided to get the Scrabble out. How could they play games at a time like this? Lloyd joined in the game, but there was no way I was going to sit and play any games with them. I sat at the other end of the living room and just flicked through the channels, looking for something to watch. I offered to make some more coffee for whoever wanted it. Lloyd was the only one who wanted another drink. Yvette followed me into the kitchen. She looked at me and I looked at her. I switched the kettle on and got the mugs ready. I thought I had better say something.

'Look, Yvette, I am not sorry for what I have done. Given the chance, I would do it all again. You know that you don't really want him, so why are you pretending? And what's with all the 'I took him away from you?' You were already broken up. Anyway, your pretence will be found out.'

'Shoy, don't you think that my kids need their father?'

'Huh, you should have thought of that when you chucked him out and played with his head. What if it was not me? What would you have done then? How would you have fought to get him back? Don't even bother to answer. This time you have been lucky, but next time, and believe me there will be a next time, you will end up the loser.'

'Yeah maybe, but this time, you are the loser.' The bitch, she stood there in my face and said that. This was all just a game to her. I could hear it in her voice. She again escaped another slap, which would have wiped the smirk off her face. I took a deep breath and took the coffee in to Lloyd. Denny and Lloyd just looked at both of us as we walked in. They knew we were having words and they were waiting for further reactions, but there was none to come. I was too tired and I could not be bothered. All I had to do was wait. Wait very, very patiently.

KNOWING WHAT YOU WANT

Time has a way of moving on. Life returned to 'normal' for Yvette and Lloyd (well almost). He had moved back in with Yvette and the kids, but still he had his foot halfway out of the door in that he had not given up his room at Ricky's. For Denny and me, well, what can I say? It was never going to be the same. Unlike Lloyd, I knew that I did not want him back. I did not want to be with him, but it was difficult. I had no money and I had no-where to live other than this grey and magnolia 'castle'! Effectively, I was trapped, but I was planning to get out. It would take some time, but I would succeed, even if it took me five, ten years.

Despite all the promises that were made at our so-called 'adult talk', nothing was forthcoming. There was no landscaping of the garden. There was no decorating. No carpet changing. Nothing. A big nothing! What was he waiting for? If he wanted me, why did he not just get on with the changes and please me? Actions speak louder than words and in this case the words were the loudest thing going on.

Within a month, Lloyd started to call. I had not made any attempts to contact him and I did not visit Yvette's. I wanted to give them the chance to get back together properly. I never felt that he should have been there, but if it was what he wanted, then I was going to do all I could to give them the chance that they wanted. I knew that the moment I spoke to him again, we would be right back to where we left off. To begin with, I kept our conversations to a minimum. I deliberately kept him at arms length. I could not trust him again. I wanted him back, but I had to play it cool. I had to let him make all the right moves. He was not happy with Yvette. He was always talking about what she did or didn't do (not that it interested me in the least), but I had to let him talk, let him get it all off his chest.

Shoy

I was becoming the 'devil's advocate.' As I had passed my driving test and, of course, was driving my own car, I invited myself along to their cricket matches. I would pack lunch and snacks for the kids, games and their bikes. They had had second-hand bikes bought for them. Denny, in the past, would not let them have bikes at all, even though I found out that he had bought Nigel one for one of his birthdays. It was always one for the others and something else for mine, but he was not going to have things his way now. I decided on second-hand ones because they had never had them before and it would give them a chance to learn how to ride and bang them around, and then for their birthdays we could buy new ones. This was my plan and Denny was going to have to go along with whether he liked it or not.

So here we were one day, all packed up and following the convoy of cars to the cricket grounds. Denny, of course, did not come in the car with us; he still went along with his mate. All in all, he did not really want me there, but now he could not stop me. We arrived at the cricket ground. There were lots of other children there and the kids had a great time. There were swings nearby and most of them had something with wheels. Lloyd was so surprised to see me there. He had no idea that I was coming. I watched the game with interest. Lloyd looked so good in his whites. He would throw glances at me and I would sit there and stare at him.

Knowing What You Want

I so wanted to touch him. I knew that my feelings for him had not changed in the slightest, but because he had been out of sight, he was not on my mind that much. That day, Lloyd told me that he had played his best and he had done it for me. He had scored ninety-nine runs not out. The other guys started to tease him. They had never seen him play that well before. One of them even said maybe it was because it was my first time there and he wanted to show off in front of 'Humphrey's' girl. Little did he know how truthful that was, but they still had no idea what had gone on between the four of us. Denny's mates used to call him Humphrey. It went back to when BT had their little Humphrey character in their adverts and Denny's family had newly put in their phone and Denny was always on the phone to everyone, so of course they called him 'Humphrey.' Yvonne was always at the cricket matches. She would be, more times than not, the scorekeeper.

At one of the matches that I went to, she asked me if I would like to learn how to score. Why not? I thought. It was quite easy to learn and then we would take it in turns to score the matches. I got so involved with the cricket, to the point where, on one occasion, I had been asked to cook the evening 'cook-up' for all the players. I agreed, but when it came down to it, I was so nervous. What if they did not like the way I cooked? Anyway, I got on with it. On the menu was:

Seasoned chicken pieces. These were seasoned with loads of onions. Spring onions. Tomatoes. Green peppers. Red peppers. Ground black pepper. Turmeric powder. Paprika. Mixed herbs. Parsley. A touch of curry powder. A touch of West Indian hot pepper sauce. Salt. Mustard powder. Splash of vinegar. And tomato puree. It was then left overnight, marinating. The smell that erupted from the removal of the lid was just amazing. I always loved the smell of seasoned meat. To cook the chicken I then had to find the biggest pot (which of course my mum had) and in it I poured some vegetable oil and about three pot spoons of sugar. It needed continual stirring over a high heat until the sugar turned completely brown and was bubbling. The chicken would be added and then left to simmer over a medium heat. Most of the time the chicken or whatever meat was being cooked would be cooked in its own juices, but because I had so much for the cricketers, I had to add in some liquid in order to cook the chicken properly. It was a wonderful smell. I had to cook this at the cricket grounds in the kitchen and everyone who came in said how really good it smelt. But was it going to taste good? I would taste it periodically, but I felt that there was something missing. I was so nervous. Along with the chicken I cooked another large pot of plain white rice (nice and easy). I made a mixed salad to go with it all. These men could eat you out of house and home. During half time, they

Knowing What You Want

had devoured chicken in breadcrumbs, which had been made by Yvonne with home-baked bread served with hot pepper sauce and also the usual array of filled sandwiches. There were drinks galore. Even the kids had so much that they would be refusing food (which is unlike most kids). It had been a long day and now the time had come when they would be eating what I had prepared. I could not stand it and I asked Yvonne if she would serve it all up for me. She laughed. She could not see the problem. She had already eaten some of the chicken that I had cooked with some of the rice and she thought it was good. To have her approval meant so much, but still I was nervous. Anyway, she served it up. I stood there from the hatch in the kitchen, watching all of them eat. It was going down really well and some of them wanted more. Half-way through, one of the other guys from the 'losing' side shouted out, 'Who is the cook?' Should I own up? Or was he going to complain? The decision was taken out of my hands. Yvonne and some of the other girls that were there pointed at me. If I were white I would now be a dark shade of red.

'Well-done, little lady. This is the best rice and chicken I have tasted for a long time.' With that came moans of agreement from some of the others. It was a success, but there was no way I was doing it again. That was too nerve-racking. Lloyd looked over at me with eyes of admiration. During the whole day, he would slip

Shoy

little comments to me about how good I looked and how much he wanted me. I had him where I wanted him, but he was going to have to wait just that bit longer. After all, like they say, 'absence makes the heart grow fonder,' and this was certainly happening in his case.

Of course, where there are large cook-ups, there is a large amount of washing-up. Yvonne and I were well prepared and had bought the washing-up gloves and started to make in-roads on the mounds of plates, dishes, cups, knives, forks, spoons and those large pans. In no time at all, we had it all sorted and dried. It was a long day, but it was good. I got to see Lloyd and most of all he got to see me. He would slip me the odd wink and even take chances and touch me. He even managed to kiss me on the stairs. We just happened to be there at the same time and could not resist.

The next week, of course, Yvette turned up with the kids. She seemed so surprised to see me there, but I knew she knew I was there because Lloyd had told me that he had told her. Hence her reason for coming. She did not trust the situation and wanted to be there to keep her eye on things. I totally ignored her. I had the scoring to get on with, so I did not have to talk to her at all. Denny was now getting more amorous with me and he would openly put his arms around me. I was so uneasy with this. He had never done anything like it before and we were not suited to it. I could not just push his arm off and I would spend most of the time trying to think of a way to move so his arm would slip off. Junior (who was actually one of Mercedes' godfathers and who was also nicknamed 'Moonface' - the reason for which I never found out) was very suspicious of the whole situation and questioned quite openly in front of the team.

'How come you two are here and everyone is so 'lovey dovey' with each other?' By you two, he meant Yvette and me. What could we say? I just shrugged my shoulders, Yvette laughed, Ricky just looked amazed and waited for a response, which never came, and Lloyd and Denny never said a word. So it was being noticed. Junior would never miss a trick. From there on in, he had his eyes on all four of us. He would ask Lloyd questions and in turn he would tell me what everyone was thinking and saying. Junior knew something had taken place. His guess was that Denny and Yvette had been caught together and Lloyd and I had given them ultimatums and so hence their behaviour. But how wrong he was. You see no one would expect little, innocent me to ever be unfaithful to Denny. HE was my soul. HE was my life. HEEEE was a bloody waste of time!

Lloyd and I were now having numerous conversations whenever

we could. I would be very careful what I said to him. Although we had kissed again and obviously that chemistry was still there between us, I was not going to be the one to make the first move again. If he wanted me he was going to have to make that move. That day came during one of our conversations. We had been talking about some unimportant subject when he said, 'Shoy, I am miserable without you. I know what I did was wrong. I want you and only you. Do you think we can give things another go and this time we tell Denny and Yvette what we should have told them the last time around?'

'So how are we to do it this time? You saw the reaction we got last time. Do you really think it is going to be any easier this time? They are, I am sure, expecting something like this. You may have been playing happy families with Yvette, but me, I have not been any different.'

'What are you saying, that you and Denny have not been having sex?'

'No, I did not say that. We have been having sex, but not in the way two people in love with each other would. It has purely been a satisfaction thing – for me anyway.' I could tell that he did not like the fact that I had even had sex with Denny, but he was no better. He had been 'making love' to Yvette and I am sure that he revelled in it.

My holiday was drawing nearer and nearer and this was upsetting Lloyd more and more. He did not want me to go as he expected me to make good with Denny and not want him when I returned. He was so double-edged with his thoughts and comments. He had taken Yvette and the kids on holiday to Canada the year before and there was no thought about me then. He had quite happily gone off and had a good time. He reckoned that he kept thinking of me and had told his uncles about me. Was I to believe this?

During the week leading up to the holiday, I had packed three suitcases for the four of us. Knowing that suitcases getting lost in Barbados were a regular occurrence (my mum had hers lost on two occasions), I decided to pack a bit of everything in each of the cases instead of dedicating one suitcase to each of us. I had picked up my sister's case and also Tanya's case, just to make sure everything was in one place. On the Friday night, Tanya and Stephanie stayed at our house so we were all in the same place. We were being picked up in the morning by one of Denny's brothers and one of his friends. The kids were all excited, including my sister, but my nightmare was growing. I really did not want to go on this holiday. I spoke to Lloyd very sneakily on the Friday night just to tell him goodbye until I returned. He was very sombre and hardly said anything to me. I hung up prematurely. I could not be doing with that sort of attitude. So, okay, he did not want me to go and I did not want to go, but we were just going to have to get on with it and get on with our lives once I returned. There was nothing else for it.

I was awake early on the Saturday morning. Everyone was ready and Denny's brother was late. I was pacing up and down wondering where the hell he was. I hated relying on other people, but there was no way around this one. None of my brothers could oblige and so I was stuck with Denny's relatives and friends. They were never reliable at the best of times, so I really don't know why I had expected anything to be different that day. Finally, he turned up. There was no time for pleasantries. I showed them the suitcases of which there were five, along with the little items of hand luggage. I got the kids into the cars and we were off. The keys for the house were being left with the neighbour, but they were out so Denny posted them through their door. There was quite a lot of traffic on the way and I was getting rather anxious. I loved going to airports and on this day there was no exception to that feeling. We arrived at the departure building and piled out of the cars.

'I cannot believe it!' Everyone looked at me. Had I gone mad? I

Knowing What You Want

could not believe it: one of the suitcases was missing. I glared at Denny's brother. He was such a prat. I could not stand him and now he had given me more ammunition to hate him. 'So who's going back to get it?' There was no way I was leaving without the other suitcase.

'Whose suitcase is it?' Denny asked tentatively.

'It's YOURS actually, so if you don't want to go back for it then you will be without clothes for the whole of the holiday'. It was a lie, I know, but in the missing suitcase there was all the new clothing I had bought for the kids and myself and also there were some photos Lloyd had wanted me to deliver to his mother. You see, if Denny had helped me pack, he would have known what was in what, but of course that would never happen. There was a quick discussion and it was decided that Winston, who drove the fastest and safest, would go back for the missing case. So he hot-tailed back. The neighbour should be back home by then and so they would have the keys to open the door. Off he went. In the meantime we went over to the checking-in desk and explained what had happened. They checked-in the suitcases that we had brought with us and once we received the other one, that would be checked-in as well. But if for some reason the case did not turn up, then it would have to be booked onto the next flight and we would have to collect it from the airport in St Vincent the next day. It would not be a disaster, but still I was up in arms about the whole thing. It was a sham already. We waited and waited. The flight had been called once and we were still waiting. In the nick of time, Winston came screeching around the corner. He had made it. Denny took the case, it was booked in, and we boarded our flight. Finally, we were on the flight and I could calm down. The flight was about nine hours long. There were various things to amuse you. They showed videos, you were fed a few times and I had taken games, pens, colouring pencils, colouring books and lots of paper for the kids to keep them occupied. The kids were so well behaved. Denny slept most of the way. My sister was quite excited as she did not really remember a lot about the West Indies from the last time as she was only two then. So to her this was a new adventure and a lovely hot holiday away from our parents. To me, it was taking me away from the one I loved and I was not sure that I was going back to someone who would feel the same way I did. It was all too hit-and-miss.

We landed in Barbados and transferred to the Liat, which was going to take us to the island. This Liat was unbelievable. There was about twenty of us and our luggage was going to be brought over on one of the larger aircrafts, as this one was not big enough. It was really cramped inside and the pilots were just there, in front of us. We could see everything they were doing. I felt so unsafe in this aircraft. When it took off it dipped, making me feel sick and Ezra clung on to me real hard. Mercedes was sitting in the seat across from me and I held out my hand to her. The wheels were not retracted in this aircraft and Ezra could see them and kept giving me a running commentary about them turning and turning. I tried to keep his attention from the wheels, but it was no good. Thankfully, we landed safely and, not having to wait too long for our luggage, we proceeded through immigration via the gate marked 'ALIENS.' This was what they called non-nationals. Somehow, whenever I travel, I always get my luggage searched and, true to form, I was pulled over. The suitcases that I had were the biggest ones and they were packed tightly. To shut it, I had my sister and Mercedes sitting on it and now this man wanted me to open it, firstly putting it on to the table. I stood there looking at this guy who had a smug smirk on his face.

'Look if you want me to put this suitcase on the table, you will have to put it there yourself or you will have to search it on the floor.' He was not amused by that suggestion, but came around from the other side of the table and lifted the case up onto the table. I opened the case. He was taking things out and placing them in to the lid and prodding about. Of course, there was an assortment of clothes, he was very curious as to why I only had two

Shoy

children with me, and yet I had a man's clothing in the cases. I explained my packing sense. He then told me to continue.

'So, do you think I am going to be able to shut the case, now that you have upset everything? I need some help with shutting it.' I quickly put everything back as best I could and asked for his help to shut the case.

'That is not my job. Madam!'

'Well, if you want me to move from here now, you will have to help me. You separated us from the others by calling me over and now I have only two small children with me who can't help shut the damn thing.' I was now struggling and getting hotter and more bothered. I was ready to cry and my voice was getting higher and higher. At least if the suitcase was on the floor I could attempt to shut it, but on this bloody table, there was no way. Reluctantly, the man with his screwed-up, attitudinal face helped me. We emerged through the doors to be greeted by a load of faces and then finally Denny's cousin who, of course, I had never met before. She was full of hugs and kisses and showed us the way to where the vehicle was waiting to take us to where his uncle lived.

It was getting dark and it was quite humid. On the way, we had

Knowing What You Want

the windows open and the different smells were quite intoxicating. We could smell breadfruits being roasted. Sweet ripe mangoes. The sea air. The smells were all so different.

Firstly, we were going to stop off at Denny's mums house and give her a surprise. Unbeknown to her, we were bringing her other grandchild, Tanya. She had no idea that Tanya was coming with us. The drive was long but finally we got there. By now, all the kids had fallen asleep and my sister was quiet. Here we were, at the house. She was so pleased to see us but most of all, her granddaughter. She hugged everyone and even started to cry. His dad was really happy to see us as well, and also his brother Ronald. Ronald was one year older than me, but he had the mental age of about ten to twelve. He was such a nice person and I had got on really well with him before they left England to live in St Vincent. I turned around and our cases were on the floor. Turning to Denny, I said, 'Why are they taking the cases out?' He looked very sheepish.

'Well, because it's late, we thought it would be a good idea if we stayed the night at Mum's and then go over to my uncle's in the morning.'

'So when was this decided?'

Shoy

'While we were waiting for you to come through immigration.'

'So why could you not tell me before? As usual, I am the last to know. Where are we staying? Your mum has a two-bedroom house and there is all of us?'

'No problem.' She had another room built on specially since she knew we were coming.'

'Oh, so this was all planned? We were never going to stay at your uncle's house, were we?' We helped get the cases out of the van. By this time, a crowd of children had gathered around the house. Mrs Noble (Denny's mum) came out and chased them away saying, 'Aal you never see people before? Go bout aal you business. Aal you too nosey!' This surprised me. She was so angry with them. After all, they were only children. We went into the house and immediately Mrs Noble launched into showing us around the house and wanted on-the-spot comments about the house and the contents (the contents of which I had seen already as it was exactly the same furniture she had had when she lived in England), but I humoured her and told her it was all great, fantastic. There were originally two bedrooms and she had had a third one added on about three weeks before we arrived. They were really large

Knowing What You Want

rooms with fitted wardrobes and all the usual bedroom furniture. The bathroom was strange insofar as there was just concrete on the floor; no lino or carpets as we were used to and there was no bath. She had had a shower fitted in what looked like a bath, but it was so deep and just made of concrete so none of us would ever attempt to take a bath in it. The only things that looked normal were the toilet and the washbasin. The kitchen was a great size, but there were no fitted cupboards as I had expected. When in the UK, Mrs Noble always talked about her fitted kitchen with all the 'mod cons', but there was nothing in this one except the sink and a few cupboards on the wall. The living room was roomy and looked comfortable. As it was dark we could not see out into the garden, but there was always tomorrow. I was so tired and all I wanted to do was sleep. She had made an array of food for us. At eleven o'clock at night, the last thing I wanted to do was eat fried fish, rice, fried plantain, and dumplings. I just wanted a hot drink and my bed. She showed us where we would be sleeping. The kids immediately got changed and were in bed. My sister was sharing the bedroom that Mrs Noble was also staying in along with Mercedes, Ezra and Tanya. There were two large double beds in there, along with a single bed in one corner. Mrs Noble had the single bed and the others shared the other two beds. With all this furniture in the room, there were still bags of room. It was the largest room in the house with windows on both sides.

Shoy

Mr Noble was sharing one of the other rooms with Ronald and of course Denny and I were left sharing the third bedroom that she had had added on (brilliant, so good of her to do this). My sister went out into the garden to have a cigarette and I decided to go to bed. I had had enough. I did not want to stay here for the whole five-and-a-half weeks, but it looked as though I had no choice in the matter.

The next morning, I was woken up by the sound of a cockerel right outside our bedroom window. It was so annoying. As there was no way it was going to stop, I got up. Denny was fast asleep. I did not even hear him come to bed. I got my wash bag and bits and pieces and went along to the bathroom. As I left the bedroom, I encountered the strangest smell. It was dinner. It was about seven o'clock in the morning and I could distinctly smell dinner. I sneaked into the bathroom. I stood there with the door locked behind me and just looked around. This bathroom was the worst I had seen. It was cold and uninviting. The window was so small that the light hardly came in. I just wanted to be in and out as quickly as possible. I hated bathrooms at the best of times and this one was no exception. I turned the tap on in the washbasin and there was just a drizzle of water. It was cold. I thought I would have better luck with the water in the shower. As I drew the curtain back around the shower, I encountered a huge, and I mean

Knowing What You Want

huge, spider in between the two panes of glass. I screamed and Mrs Noble came running to the bathroom door, knocking on it and shouting to me to open the door. I quickly unlocked the door and she came in. I told her about the spider. She laughed and said.

'It's been there for a long time now. It not doing anyone any harm. In fact she's pregnant.'

I could not believe that they were having showers with that thing just there in the window. I was mortified. There was no way I was going into the shower with that near me. This was turning out to be a nightmare, just as I thought it would. I washed as quickly as I could, bearing in mind that the water was practically non-existent. I wrapped the towel around me and left the bathroom, making my way back to the bedroom. By this time, Mercedes and Ezra were awake and in the living room. I returned dressed. They were already out in the morning sun, munching on chunks of homemade bread. I sat out on the patio, which was actually the front doorway to the house. It was cool, but already the mosquitoes had had their breakfast, leaving their telltale marks dotted on the lower parts of my legs. It was hard to resist the scratching/itching/scratching-cycle thing. Ezra was climbing up the garden gate, wanting to see what was going on down the little roadway that ran past the house. There were voices all over the place. It might have been

Shoy

early in the morning, but there were already arguments and abusive language being hurled through the air. Mrs Noble appeared at the door, offering me some breakfast of fried fish and homemade bread. I really did not want the fried fish, so I just had the bread and a cup of tea. Forgetting to tell her that I did not drink milk, she had made it full of milk. I had to throw it away. I had bought with me some dried milk and made another cup. By now, my sister and Denny were awake and mulling about. Everyone woke up so early. The smell of dinner woke Denny and he opted for the dinner of red fish soup, containing dasheen, yams, sweet potato, carrots, dumplings and loads of boiled-down soup at eight o'clock in the morning. It all looked really good, but at this time in the morning? I didn't think so.

I was ready to go exploring and take the kids out. They wanted to go down to the beach. For some reason Mr Noble did not think that it would be a good idea to go down there. As he said, 'It's not what we do around here.' Well, quite honestly, I did not give a damn what people did around here. This was my holiday; I paid for it (well to be honest, I could not even afford it really. I had borrowed the money, including the spending money of three hundred pounds, from the husband-and-wife doctors that I worked for at the hospital. I had told them all about the problems with my relationship and I think they must have felt so sorry for me. I was

Knowing What You Want

desperate to go at the time of booking the holiday, purely because I did not want Denny to go again (on his own). But by the time it came round, I wished I had not tried so hard). I was determined to make this holiday one to remember and to make sure that my kids had a good time. If they did not want Tanya to do things with me, then that was their problem; I was not going to get between them and their favourite grandchild. My sister, hearing the conversation, wanted me to wait for her and we would go together. We left with looks.

The beach was not nearby and we had to walk about twenty minutes to get to it through the village and down the main road, but we got there in the end. The sand was completely black due to the volcanic activities that took place some years previously, but to the kids, it was a beach. They ran up and down the beach looking for shells. There were some other kids there (the so-called beach that they 'don't do around here') and they made friends with the kids. There were some guys training, running along the beach and doing acrobatic stunts. I sat there watching and taking in the scenery and watching the noisy waves as they lapped the shore. The breeze was cool, but then the sun was not completely up and it was slightly overcast.

On returning to the house, the first thing we were greeted with was

Shoy

Mrs Noble sitting on the veranda saying, 'I hope you lot don't think that you are walking into my house with all that sea water on all you?' I looked at her.

'Our feet are dry and we were going straight into the bathroom to wash the salt off anyway. How else are we to get rid of the salt?' Obviously she had not thought through her statement and was now cornered.

'Well, aalright, but there is no water for all of you to have a shower.' With that, Mr Noble came out of the house. Now Mr Noble was a very quiet, tall man. He had nothing bad to say about anyone. He would mind his own business and would only comment when the time was right and he had thought about it at great length. He smoked a little and would always disappear for a walk, in order to get some peace and quiet from you know who.

'What you mean there is not enough water? Water don't run out around here it just run out of the taps all day.' He disappeared into the house and came back. 'So is wha wrong with di tap? Noting coming out of di tap at all.' He waited for an answer. I could see that this was going to be just great. Denny had, of course, gone out by now and I was left here with his pedantic mother. No matter. I went into the bathroom (much to my amazement the spider had been removed) and I positioned the plastic tub that was in the shower for dirty clothes under the shower (which incidentally had no shower head on it; it was just the end of the pipe which had no swivel on it whatsoever). When I turned the taps on, the water just trickled. This was going to take ages. So I left it running and went to the kitchen to heat up the kettle. She was not at all pleased with this, but there was no way I was going to wash my 'English' children in cold water that they termed as 'warm.' It was as warm as drinking water from a tap with an ice cube in it. I washed all three of the kids down and washed myself down as well with the same water. We were all clean now. What were we going to do for the rest of the day? The kids were fine because they had found new friends and were out playing with them. This was another bone of contention with Mrs Noble already. She did not want them to mix with the local kids, but I soon pointed out that if I lived there, these were the kids that my kids would have to mix with. She could not tell me what to do with my own children. She never mentioned the episode again, but I knew she was not at all pleased.

I was missing Lloyd so much. It was only day one, but I wanted to go home. I hated this place. I was already a prisoner. My skin was creating. I had been bitten to shreds already and was scratching every opportunity I got. My sister had gone off exploring on her own and I was left in the house with Ronald. He was not at all well. He had a very bad leg and was limping a lot. It would bother him from time to time, he explained. The other kids around would call him names, purely because he was not as bright as them for his age. Ronald was a good bloke and very kind and it was so easy talking to him. Denny was not seen the whole day and late that evening, long after the kids were put to bed, he returned, recapping his day with his dad on the veranda. My day did not matter. I sat in the corner watching the television that did not even have a clear picture. Why was it that this family who once lived in England and were used to a high quality of living, and now they were back 'home' they put up with all this inferior standard of work and service? It was just beyond me.

That night Denny and I went to bed at the same time, more or less. He had other things on his mind, but I was not interested. I just wanted to be left alone. I put on a pair of pyjamas that covered me from head to foot. I also put on a pair of socks. The only parts of my body that were not covered were my hands and my face. All of this was to ward off those pesky mosquitoes. Denny huddled close to me in the night. I was so hot. I even had a fan on the whole night, but I was just so hot. I thought I would self-combust. I had to give in and remove the socks, but I would remain wrapped up in the thin sheet that was our covering. I could not get used to this thin piece of material. I just wanted my continental quilt. I did not want him near me, but it is difficult when you are in the same bed. He kept trying to touch me and it just conjured up images of Lloyd and me in my head. Thinking of Lloyd just aroused me, so I gave in reluctantly, and we had sex for the first time in ages. It felt good. It felt right, almost as if my body had been craving it and now it had been satisfied, but afterwards I felt so guilty. I was betraying Lloyd.

The next morning came just as the one before and Denny had made plans for us to visit various members of his family consisting of an assortment of cousins and aunts. His family was huge. Our family was practically non-existent compared with his. Of course, we were introduced to so many, that, no sooner were we told their names, it was just in one ear and out the other. Everywhere we went, we were being offered food and drink. How much did these people consume? They were all so friendly and they all thought that I was cute, nice, or beautiful. We (being me and my sister) would get winks and they had this way they would 'pssss' at you. I so hated that. As far as I was concerned, you used that when you wanted to shoo a menace chicken. That 'pssss' would just warrant a look of disgust and this would make them more determined to get our attention, which was never forthcoming.

Shoy

As the holiday wore on, my life was getting more and more unbearable. Within the first week I wanted to return home. I called the airport to find out when the next available flight would be leaving. The one thing that stopped me from getting the flight home was the fact that Ezra was on my passport and if I wanted to go home, he would have to come with me. I could not spoil the holiday for him. He was having such a good time. He would be out with his little friends, climbing trees and rolling around in the sand and getting soaked under the standpipes of which there was one at the end of each road (if you can call the little dirt tracks road). He was a child that was free and happy and there was no way I could spoil that. He would never forgive me, so I was stuck. I had to stay. Most days I was left alone in the house with Ronald. He was getting worse and his leg was giving him a lot of pain. He had a district nurse and she would call in every couple of days to change his dressings. It was all very confusing what exactly was wrong with his leg, but when I saw the wound, it could only be one of two things. It was either a leg ulcer or it was cancer. Whatever it was, it was just eating away at his skin. Because he had been wearing long trousers since we arrived, you could not see how much the calf of his left leg was swollen. It was tight and then there was this open wound that was oozing pus and smelt terrible. As the nurse changed his dressing he would scream with pain. I felt for him and it made me so sad. He needed to be in hospital.

Knowing What You Want

All this dressing changing was not getting him anywhere. There was no way it was going to get any better. I spoke to Mrs Noble about his leg, but she just felt that if he got up and walked about, it would increase his circulation and so aid healing. I could not believe her archaic thoughts. They were not those of a loving mother. Had I been his mother, I would be beside myself trying to get all the help and advice that I could and there would be no way that he would be at home waiting for some nurse (as good as they are) to come and just change a dressing that I could do myself. But who was I to comment? Ronald and I would talk a lot about England. He so wanted to go back. He hated the West Indies. In England he was not teased and had lots of friends. He even had a job at one of the big schools in the town washing up and he was good at it. But because of his mental age, he had to come back to St Vincent with his parents. Poor guy.

NIGHTMARE IN PARADISE

The carnival preparations were well under way and the whole island was buzzing with talk of it. Denny had hired a jeep so we could get about more easily, but I hardly ever saw him. He was always out, even more so now. We had arranged to go into the town one evening to one of the many events leading up to the final day of the carnival that were being put on in the main park. My sister and I were busy getting ready when he came back. I had not seen him all day. He walked into the bedroom saying, 'Where you going?' What sort of question was that?

Nightmare in Paradise

'We're going to the park to see the beauty pageant.' This was the first round of the beauty pageant and there was going to be girls from other islands competing for the title of 'Carnival Queen.'

'So who you going with?' I laughed, expecting him to laugh. Surely he was joking?

'We are going with you. Remember? We arranged it last week'

'No, I am taking my cousin and her daughter. It's her birthday and I promised I would take them. The jeep is full and so there is no room for you and your sister. Maybe you could squeeze in, but your sister definitely won't be able to get in as well. If not you could catch a van.' A van was the equivalent to a bus. I could not believe it. But there again, I should have guessed. I was never first in his life. There was always someone else who warranted his attention more than me. I was never taken out. I was never the one he wanted to be seen with. I was so hurt. I could not speak. I pushed past him and went to tell my sister. She was cussing as we spoke. I tried to calm her down. She was not upset at the fact that she could not go, but that he had the nerve to put someone else in front of me. She knew I did not go out much and that it had taken an age for me to agree it and this was to be my first night out. I was already dressed, my hair was done, and I was really, really looking forward to it. I could see from her bedroom window the others sitting in the jeep, waiting for him. Obviously he had just come in to get changed and go off again. I heard him pass the bedroom door and was making his way out to the jeep. I ran out after him. I was not letting this one go. I had to say something. Just as he got in to the jeep, I held on to the door.

'I don't believe what you have done to me. How could you arrange to take other people instead of me? Since we have been here we have not even gone into town once together. I am left all day to my own devices with your brother as his keeper while everyone else is out having a good time, and then when I get the chance to go out for the evening, you arrange to take your cousins, birthday or no birthday.' I was now shouting and he was looking more and more embarrassed. I stood there. His cousin apologised and started in on him. She could not believe that he had done this. She wanted to get out of the jeep and not go, but I insisted that she went because there was no way that I was going now. I turned and went back into the house past his mum and his dad who did not have a clue what was going on. I stayed in my bedroom all evening in front of the fan, reading a book.

The next morning I just had to talk to Lloyd. I waited until everyone was out, except for Ronald, and then I sneaked a phone call to

England. Lloyd was at work and it was a long wait whilst they got him to the phone. 'Hello?' came his voice. He sounded so close, as if I could put my hand down the receiver and touch his face. I wished it were that simple. 'Hi there.' I had to whisper just in case there were ears around.

'Hi Babes. How you doing?' His voice was happy and pleased to hear from me.

'Not good. I was going to come back.' I explained the palaver to him.

'So where is my letter?' he asked. Before leaving we had promised to write to each other at least one letter a week. As he would not be able to post his letters to me, he would keep them until I got back and then I could read them all.

'Well, I have written a letter to you, but I have not been able to post it as I don't know where the post office is and of course I have to be careful. We don't want Denny to find out what I am up to. But I will post it soon. Actually, you will probably get three in one go, so be patient'. He was satisfied with that.

'Have you written anything yet?' I asked.

Shoy

'Sort of. I started, but you know I don't write letters'

'Rubbish. You just have not had a reason to. So get on with it. I am expecting at least five letters so you'd better get a move on. Look Lloyd, I have to go now. Don't want to run up this phone bill, but I am having a nightmare here and just want to come home. I will try to call you again. Don't know when, but I will try, okay?'

'Okay Babes. Take care. Shoy? I love you.'

'I love you too.' I hung up reluctantly and returned to my nightmare in the daytime of the tropical sunshine and heat.

The mosquitoes were having a heyday with my skin. Nothing new there, then! The bites were now infected and very painful. They got so bad that I had to go to the local hospital and they sprayed some iodine solution on them, which then made them worse because I was actually allergic to it (being an iron preparation). The thing was, they did not say what they were going to spray on my legs and just carried on regardless, and then there was a big rush to wash it all off as quickly as possible. Back to square one and in more pain than when I first arrived. They gave me some antibiotics and some sort of mosquito repellent cream to help the itching and pain. It all helped the pain and the itching (very temporarily), but the swelling got worse and worse, to the point where I could not walk properly. It even hindered my getting sandals on, as skimpy as they were. What else could go wrong with this bloody holiday?

All of us, including the kids, went into the town for the main event of the week: the procession. It was so colourful and this was the first time I was ever going to a carnival. I had not even gone to the one in Notting Hill, albeit practically on my doorstep. So this was a first for me and I was going to enjoy it in all its glory and this sunshine. My sister had arranged to go with her friends, but she knew I was terribly unhappy and decided to come along with us to keep me company and give me moral support, for which I was grateful. At least with her coming along we could have a laugh and if necessary lose Denny for the day and have a good time with the kids. Talking to Denny was such a chore. It was all a front just for the kids. I did not want to spoil anything for them and if they knew that we were not talking, there was no telling how it would affect them.

The procession was spectacular and it went on for hours and hours.

Shoy

The kids ate and drank for what seemed like all day. They were all so skinny. It made you wonder where they put it all. Mercedes had asked her friend Inez (this was the girl that I would pay to post my secret letters) to come along. She was thirteen years old and she had never ever been into the capital. They only lived about ten to fifteen miles away, but she had never been. How sad was that? She was in awe of the whole place and to top it all, on this very special occasion, she was there. It was so nice to see her face light up. She started to cry tears of happiness. It was all too much for her. We all gave her a hug and told her to just have a good time and fill her head with memories that would last forever. We found a space where the kids would be safe to watch the procession and also dance. The music was so loud and all our favourite tunes were being played. The kids would dance and dance and every time Denny put the camera on them, they would go all shy and stop, but he managed to get them when they were totally unaware of what he was doing.

The processions came to an end and there were loads and loads of people just milling around, talking, laughing, shouting, eating and there were even some people that were so intoxicated either with drink or just the events of the day that they had fallen asleep where they fell and others would just step over them. We made our way back to where Denny had parked the car. Amazingly, we did not lose anyone. On the way home in the jeep, the kids were chatting non-stop about everything they had seen, eaten and done. It was so nice to hear them talking and laughing. Inez had had a great time and could not wait to get back and tell the rest of her family. She felt so lucky and did not want us ever to go home. In fact she would have liked us to adopt her and give her a 'great life' in England, but of course this was not possible.

When we arrived back at the house, my sister went out and soon returned. Denny and I were in the bedroom having a discussion, when she came in.

'Denny, can you take me and Shoy into town for the second part of the beauty pageant as we did not get to see the first one?'

'Yeah. No problem.' I sorted the kids out for the evening and got ready to go out, just like the last time. Denny went and got the jeep and came back for us. Astonishingly, it was just the three of us in the jeep making our way to town. But this surprise was all too short and too good to be true. Sure enough, we got to the stadium and started to hang around.

'What are we waiting for Denny?' I asked, knowing full well that a stupid answer would be coming.

Shoy

'Umm. I told my cousin that I would meet them here.' I looked at my sister and she looked at me. The look between us said it all. Sure enough, they turned up and we made our way through the crowds to get our tickets for the stadium. As we approached the ticket kiosk, I moved back so Denny could get the tickets (after all, he was paying), but to my utter dismay he turned to me and said, 'I hope you and your sister have money to pay to get in?'

'What do you mean? Are you not paying for me? You know I don't have a lot of money'

'Well if you don't have enough money, then you'd better go home or wait in the car.' Surely he was joking. He could not be serious. My sister was amazed, but I glared at her, the glare that said 'don't say anything'. Luckily I had some money on me and so did she. We never went anywhere without having our own money. I could not believe what took place then. Denny actually paid for his cousin and her daughter as well as himself, right before my very eyes. Once again, I had been a complete fool. I was mortified, but I was here now and paid for my ticket. We walked in and they were deciding where they were going to stand to get the best view of the stage. Considering my sister and I were not very tall and they were, their chosen spot was far from ideal; we could not

Nightmare in Paradise

see a thing. All these tall people dwarfed us. So the two of us decided to move without telling them. They were too wrapped up in themselves to notice that we had moved, anyway. My sister was trying very hard to cheer me up. I was okay. After all, I was in the town and at a live recording of the beauty pageant. I was now determined to have a good time and if, at the end of it, we could not find them to get home again, then we would just have to get a van back. The pageant started and the girls were so beautiful. Halfway through I felt this arm around my shoulder. I shot round ready to do battle, thinking it was some nasty boy wanting to get off with me, but it was him! It was Denny. What did he want? He had actually found us.

'Hi. What do you want?' I asked him in a low, thinking he was crap, sort of voice.

'Well that's nice.' He moved his hand from my shoulder. 'I walk all over the place looking for you and this is the greeting I get?'

'Well what did you expect? You told me that I had to pay for myself to get in, not mentioning it before leaving home. What if I had no money, eh? What then? Would you have just left me to make my own way home? I can't imagine that you would take me back after driving all this way. And then to top it all, you pay for

Shoy

them. Who are they to you? I am the one you brought to this god-forsaken place that is eating me alive and you just abandon me to my own devices.' I was now crying. Something I had not done in front of him for the longest time and now I had reduced myself to this in front of loads of people. I felt disgusted with myself. He was hugging me.

'Shoy, I am sorry, but I had promised them that I would pay for them. You see it is the second part of her birthday present and it cost so much. I mean it's twenty-five dollars each to come in.'

'Don't you think I know that? I just paid it for myself.' I pushed his hand away from my shoulder. He sat down beside me. I ignored him for a while and just watched the pageant. My sister, in the meantime, had spotted some of her friends in the crowd below and gone to join them. She did not want to leave me, but I insisted. There was no need for both of us to miss out on the fun. After a while he turned to me and said, 'I wonder where the rest of them are?' I pretended not to hear him. Why on earth was he asking me that? Did I really care? Would I lose sleep over it? He repeated the question.

'Look, if you want to go and find them, then go. You seem to be worried about them so go and find them and put your mind at rest. After all, they don't live here and they don't know how to get home and they don't know anyone here.' He looked at me, puzzled.

'Okay, I will go and see if I can find them. Don't move from here. I will be back.'

'Yeah. Whatever.' Sure enough he found them and brought them back with him with some other people in tow. Oh great. I totally ignored all of them. This night was just the pits. To top it all it was starting to rain. Luckily we were under cover, but those that were below had to run for shelter under the stadium roof. The stage itself was made for the occasion and they did not have a cover over it, so of course the pageant and all the other festivities that were taking place had to be put on hold, as the rain and electricity did not mix – for obvious reasons. How stupid. You would have thought that they would cover the stage just in case? With all the downpours, the show kept being started and then it would be halted again. Some of the dancers would slip and slide and the routines would go out, simply because the stage was soaking wet, and in between performances there were people sweeping the streams of water off the stage. It would all dry off quite quickly as the night was still very humid, but the rain was persistent and kept on coming back. When the whole pageant was over, there was

Shoy

free-for-all music and lots of steel bands, playing calypso music. This was my favourite. With that, I joined my sister, went down to the bottom of the stadium, and started to dance. First of all we were just there by ourselves dancing and before you knew it, there was a group of guys around us and they were winding and going down with us. It was great. We had a great time. Denny, in the meantime, I could see, was just watching me from where he sat. I would glance over at him and could see that he was still watching, but I did not care. What could he say? What could he do?

Of course, Denny offered to take his cousin and her daughter back home, as they could not find their ride. Once again, he was priceless. When we got back to the car, Denny decided that I should sit in the back of the jeep with my sister and the cousin's daughter, but his cousin was not having it. She told him off right then and there saying that he did not deserve someone like me. Who did he think I was that he could treat me that way? Under no circumstance was he to put someone else in the front of his car and put me in the back. That was not the way relationships were conducted. I was stunned at her words, but she was nice and they were so true. So I sat in the front. They all fell asleep in the back, but I was awake all the way. We got back home and I just jumped out of the jeep, went straight into the bedroom, and went to sleep. I heard him come to bed, but I pretended to be asleep so I would not have to talk to him.

Even though the procession was all over, the actual carnival spirit was nowhere near over. There were events planned for the evening, so to that end, Denny, my sister, a couple of Denny's mates (who were also from England and staying in the same village) and I went back into town for all the dancing and musical events. The streets were buzzing, even more so than earlier in the day. I was not feeling too good and wished I had not come. I was quite tired, but carried on with the dancing and winding. I can remember dancing with my sister and could not wind down (as you do) because of this pain in the tops of my legs. I felt such a lightweight. Usually I could dance and dance, especially when calypso was playing, but that night I could not manage it. The next thing I knew, I was sitting in a doorway with Denny and my sister standing over me, frantically fanning me. I had fainted and now I was freezing. Freezing in the hot, tropical night air. I was shivering and all I had on was a short-sleeved t-shirt and a pair of shorts. I just wanted a continental quilt and a soft, inviting bed so I could snuggle down and go to sleep, but instead I was sitting in this doorway freezing, knowing that we were quite some way from home. Denny took off his t-shirt and put it over me. It was not much, but it was all he had. Even though I was not feeling well, I still felt an air of surprise at his action and glanced up at my sister and we both exchanged a look of hmm, 'what's he up to?' Denny then suggested that he got me back to the jeep and put the engine on to warm me up. He laughed, as he could not believe that I was so cold, but he could see that I was shivering. He helped me up and supported me whilst I was walking. He offered to carry me, but I declined. Just as we were moving off, his friends caught up with us, wondering if I was okay. I told my sister to go with them and I would see her later. Denny and I were left to walk back to the jeep. I got in and he switched on the engine. In no time at all the car was toasting and I was feeling a little better. I reclined in the front seat and got hold of my sister's jacket that she had left in the back, wrapped it around myself and gave Denny back his t-shirt. He sat in the car for a bit, but it was just too hot for him, understandably. So he stood outside keeping an eye on me. I then tapped on the window and asked him to turn the engine off, as I wanted to go to sleep. He sat there with me for a while. I woke up and he was still there. The noise of the night could still be heard.

'Look, Denny, there is no point you staying here. I will be all right. Just lock the jeep doors, leave the keys with me, go off, and find the others. I will be fine.' He was not sure he wanted to leave, so promised that he would come back at intervals to keep an eye on me. It was such a tender moment. He hugged me.

Nightmare in Paradise

'You sure you are all right? I can take you home if you want and then come back in the morning for the others.' I would not have it. The journey there and back would be too much. I would be fine.

'Please, just go.' He left.

The next morning, I had a rude awakening. Right where the jeep was parked was the yard for the sound systems and they were all tuned up and testing their systems. It was so loud. My head was hurting and I was now hungry, but I was feeling much better. Denny had come back to the jeep at some point. I did not even remember letting him in, but he was lying in the drivers seat with his mouth wide open, fast asleep, even with the racket that was going on. He could sleep through an atomic bomb blast. Soon afterwards, who should be knocking on the window of the jeep, but my sister. She looked ragged, but was beaming. She was drunk, and still singing. She had had a really great time with the other two guys, but now they were tired and ready to go home. Denny awoke. They got in and we set off home in the light of the early morning sunrise. I had missed a fantastic night.

During the weeks leading up to the carnival, there were various song competitions and only one could be the winner for the Road March on the final day. We had heard on the radio on the way

Shoy

home that the chosen song was Kangaroo. Denny liked another song called Whistle, but my sister and I, along with the kids, knew that Kangaroo was the better song and it would win. So during the last night in the park the band that sung Kangaroo would be handed their trophy and they would play the song, live on stage in its entire glory. I hoped that I would be better to go back that evening and see the last night's events. We would have to wait and see. Denny, miraculously, hoped that I would be okay, as he wanted to take me back. What had taken place? Was he all right? Maybe my illness had rubbed off on him and made him soft in the head.

Once again, the heavens opened on the night and the stage got soaked. You would have thought that they would have done something about that considering the problems it had caused when they had the beauty pageant. So once again, the bands would start and then they would have to get off and so it went on. This meant that the whole thing was longer than it should have been, but I would never complain. It was a great night and would be in my mind for years to come.

Unbelievably, there were many good things that happened, but because my feet were so swollen all the time, I was limited as to what I could do. I still tried my best. We went on an excursion to

Nightmare in Paradise

the falls on the island. The only way you could get to these falls was by sea and the journey there was just diabolical. You had to do what I would describe as a trek, over rocks and boulders down to the shore and then the long boat would back up to the rocks, as close as they could, and you would jump on to the boat with the help of the men that were going to row it around the bay to the falls. That was so exciting, but the sea was rough and I did not like that. But it was well worth it, because the falls were beautiful and it was just something you should never miss. Two of the men on the way over jumped off the boat with harpoon-like spears to catch our lunch. About half an hour after we arrived at the beach near the falls, they came in with a catch of beautiful fish of which we took some photos. Denny had the video camera and filmed most of the day. It was spectacular what they had caught and it tasted just as good as it looked. We took the kids to various places of interest, but one of their favourites was the Botanical Garden in the town. There was so much for them to do and they just loved the quiet and the different species of animals and fauna. On that particular day my feet were really bad, and so most of the time I just found somewhere in the shade to sit, trying to recover.

There came a period during the holiday where I felt it was about time I went to see my side of the family. Of course, not being able to drive a gear car, I was at a disadvantage, as I could not drive

Shoy

the jeep. So once again I was totally dependent on Denny. He was reluctant to drive us about and wherever we went, he would always be in a hurry. There was always something better to do somewhere else. He took us to see my dad's niece who still lived in the village where my dad was born and raised. When we saw her she was just the spitting image of my dad. She knew we were coming and had prepared a feast for us to take to the beach.

We arrived at her house and found that she was in the middle of washing which was not going to take long to complete. She gave us some drinks made of fresh lemons, sugar and lots and lots of crushed ice with a hint of essence. This was my favourite drink. The children amused themselves with the puppy that she had running around the yard, which was named 'Puppy'. We moved from the porch and sat on a garden seat under a lovely shady tree with beautiful pink and yellow-flecked flowers all over it. Her house was situated at the top of a hill and the view was absolutely breathtaking.

You could see the sea to the left with its gentle, rolling waves kissing the beach, stretching around the bay and out of sight behind the rocks and boulders in the distance. There was the meandering road in the hillside opposite with the cars and buses weaving their way down to the village. You could see the village stretching back

Nightmare in Paradise

into the distance with a backdrop of mountains shadowed with greenery, thick forests and banana plantations. How could this not be paradise? As we sat there soaking up all the exquisite beauty with just a gentle breeze, a tiny hummingbird flew up to one of the flowers on the tree. It was so close. You could see the magnificence of its colours and could hear the muffled hum as it gathered the sweet nectar from the various blossoms. All this beauty was captured on the video that Denny was recording at the time.

The pure, serene tranquillity of the moment was broken by my cousin's voice calling us. She was now ready to make a move. She had planned to take us down to a local beach instead of the one that you could see from her house. This beach was 'the crème de la crème' and was over the hill around the other side of the island, which meant a little walk up the very steep hill and down the other side. As my cousin had prepared so much food, Denny thought it would be a good idea if he took all the pots and pans in the jeep and parked it as close to the beach as he could. The rest of us decided to walk, as it was such a beautiful day. Of course, the going down was easy. That beach was just out of this world. The sand was white and the sea was an icy, clear blue. The setting was a little bay and there was a large sailing ship anchored just off the beach. Whilst there, some fishermen came in with their catch and we watched them pull the catch in. The kids, for the

Shoy

first time ever, saw the fresh fish jumping about in the nets. Ezra was squealing with excitement. My cousin bought some of the fish and roasted them right there on the beach and we ate them. As if she needed to do anything else to go with all the nice things she had prepared. There was a mango orchard that we had walked through to get to the beach and we had picked some ripe, sweet mangoes. It was mango heaven. The day was hot and my feet swelled even more. So much so that I could not get my sandals on at all. I tried standing with both my feet in the water with the waves lapping over them, trying to cool them down and get the swelling down, but it was not working. It felt good, though. It was time for us to leave so I asked Denny if he would get the jeep so I could go back in it as my feet were in no fit state to walk all the way back. His answer was just a flat, 'No.'

'What do you mean, no? Look at my feet. I can't walk back. There is just no way. Come on please?'

'If you want me to get the jeep, then you will have to pay me.' I laughed, thinking he was joking.

'So how much would it take?'

'How much have you got on you?'

'Hmmm, about fifty dollars.'

'Yeah, that will do.' Surely, he was joking.

'Yeah, right. Go and get the jeep.'

'No, hand over the dosh now. Then I will get the jeep.'

'You are joking aren't you?'

'Do I look like I am joking?' He was not and I was in too much agony to decline paying.

I handed over the fifty dollars and off he went. No one was witness to this, but I now knew that there was nothing between us. Nothing left. Why was he like this to me? What had I done to him? Before we left England he would have done anything for me, even though I did not want it. In a way, I suppose, he was paying me back for wanting to leave him for Lloyd. I cried my lonely tears and he arrived with the jeep.

For the rest of the holiday, of which there was not much left, I only went out as far as the town or the beach near where his parents lived. I could not go very far because my feet and the infected mosquito bites anyway. I was living a nightmare. During the last week of our holiday, Ronald got really sick and it was suggested that he went back to England to get his leg treated, as they could not do anything for him there. Mrs Noble and Ronald left about two days before we were due to leave. Ronald was so looking forward to going back. He was looking forward to his friends visiting him in hospital and he vowed that he would not come back. He was planning, when he got better, to run away and they would not be able to find him. In my mind, I did not think that he was going to make it. He had now lost a lot of weight, even in the short time that we were there. I wished him well and promised to go to see him in the hospital as soon as we got home.

Mrs Noble was now gone and Mr Noble let us play the music as loud as we wanted and cook whatever we wanted. We were now normal people on holiday not suppressed in any way. It was the best two days of the whole thing. On the day she left, Mr Noble found out that she had turned the water supply down and hence the reason for the trickling water from the taps. He could not believe that she had done that. She was so mean. There were so many things that she did that were uncalled for and mean. I had bought a crate of Ju-c™ for the kids as they drank a lot and she took it upon herself to open all of them in order to get the lids as there was a competition running leading up to the carnival. This then meant that the drinks would go flat. Needless to say, I made her buy another crate. She would hide food even when I had bought and paid for it. She turned down the thermostat in the fridge and it would take four days for ice to harden. I had always thought that she was a nice person, but I now saw her in a different light. I felt so sorry for her.

Finally, the holiday from hell was over and we were on our way home. The kids, of course, did not want to leave. Ezra had had such a great time with his little friends that he had worn away the bottom of his shoe where his big toes were and he had been climbing and running around with his shoe in this state for most of the holiday and had not said a word to anyone. They would have lots of good memories and had made some really nice friends.

We arrived back home on the Friday morning real early and Denny's brother and his friend were waiting to pick us up. It was cold, so much colder than what we had been experiencing over the past five-and-a-half weeks, but it was nice to be back home. Home to the things we knew.

I was now back. Back in my own home the first person I wanted to speak to was Lloyd. I called him when Denny had popped out.

Shoy

He sounded very distant and not at all pleased to hear from me. My fears were turning into reality. Had he found someone else in my absence? Or had he gone back to Yvette and was now dreading telling me?

'Hi Lloyd, I'm back. Did you miss me?' There was a slight hesitation from his end.

'When can I see you?'

'I will come and see you probably Sunday some time. Is that okay? If I can come sooner, I will call, okay?'

'Yeah. If you can spare me the time?'

'What do you mean by that? What's up?'

'We will speak when I see you.' He hung up. Well, what was that all about? I was anxious to find out. I had to see him that day. There was no way I was waiting until Sunday. I took the kids over to see my mum and somehow got away from them and went to see Lloyd. Ricky answered the door, let me in, and then left. Oh boy! Obviously something was wrong. I went in to the kitchen. There he was, just as gorgeous as when I left. I walked over to him, but he walked away. Okay, so this was going to be tricky. I thought I had better start the conversation.

'What's wrong?'

'You mean to say that you don't know?'

'Know what? I have only just landed this morning. What am I to know?' There was silence and he just watched me with disgust. What had I done to deserve this? 'Well spit it out. Obviously I have done something or someone has said something to make you hate me so much that you can't even bring yourself to touch me. What has happened since I left?'

'Well, where would you like me to start?' He was now pacing up and down the kitchen.

'How about the beginning? After all, I haven't got anywhere to go in a hurry. I am all ears!'

'Are you sure you want me to tell you?'

'Of course I do. How else am I supposed to defend myself if I need to, because I am sure that whatever it is, Yvette is at the bot-

Shoy

tom of it? Have you told her about us again and have you changed your mind?'

'No.' I sighed a big sigh of relief. At least he had not changed his mind. Or had he?

'What is it then?' I was now getting impatient. I needed to know.

'Do you want some coffee?'

'So it's going to take a long time then?'

'Well, that would depend on your answers.' I looked at him, puzzled.

'Okay, I will have a black coffee please.' He went over to the sink, filled the kettle, and plugged it in to boil. Whilst he was getting the cups, I thought I would say something to change the atmosphere. He looked so cold and frozen. It was as if he was not the same person. But why?

'By the way, did you write me any letters whilst I was away?'

'Maybe.' It was a snapped 'maybe'. Oh boy. Things were serious, whatever they were.

'Well, surely you should know whether you wrote to me or not? I wrote to you. Did you receive them?'

'Yes I did.'

'I was getting quite worried here. I thought that you had not received any and that's why you are so upset. It was quite difficult to write more. I would have liked to have written more, but there was always someone around and then there were the problems of getting them posted. As you know, it's not as easy as just dropping the mail in a post-box. You have to walk to the post office and my feet were so swollen I could not walk much. After the second week, I paid one of Mercedes' friends to post them for me. She was really nice and I really liked her. She would sit and talk to me for ages about all sorts of things. She was only 13, but..........' I was interrupted

'Quite finished?' Obviously he was not interested in my drivel about posting letters.

'Yes.' I so wanted to touch him. I had been in the house for half

Shoy

an hour now and still he had not been near me; not even a peck on the cheek or a touch of his hand. Nothing. He placed my coffee on the table, sat down across the table from me, and just looked at me. There were tears in his eyes. But why? What was he going to say? I dare not ask another question. It seemed better to just shut up and wait for him to say whatever it was he had to say. He sighed.

'Where shall I start?' I shrugged my shoulders. We had been here already. I wished he would just get on with it, but I had to be patient.

'Whilst you were away on holiday, I heard some interesting things about you and your sister.'

'Me and my sister,' I repeated in a high-pitched voice. What did my sister have to do with me? 'What sorts of things did you hear?'

'Did you have a nice holiday?'

'I told you earlier. It was okay. It would have been better if it had been with you, but that was not possible, so I had to make the most of a bad situation. Why are you asking me about the holiday now when you were about to tell me something else?'

'Did you and Denny get on?'

'Sometimes, but most of the time not. He did some really nasty things to me and made me cry a few times. He was really unbelievable. Most of the time I was in the house with Ronald as my feet were nearly always swollen and I could not walk far before they would start to hurt something chronic.'

'Hmm. Did you have sex with him?'

'Yes, about twice, maybe three times, but I did not really get into it. Don't know why I bothered really. I suppose it was just wanting to be wanted and you were not there, but I was thinking of you.' He laughed. His face softened.

'He must have felt really good then, if you were thinking of me?' I smiled back.

'Hmm, never thought about that.' The questions continued. I felt like I was on trial. For what exactly? All would be revealed, that I was sure of!

Shoy

'So what did your sister get up to?'

'Most of the time, I really could not tell you. She was not there with us as she had made friends of her own and she was out most of the time with them. Usually I would only see her when she came home for a change of clothes or for something to eat or to find out if we had arranged to do anything. Anyway, Stephanie is a grown woman and she does not need our permission to come and go. So what's with that question?'

'Did you go around with her at all?'

'Hardly. I told you, my feet …..' He interrupted me again.

'Yeah, yeah, yeah. You said your feet were swollen.' There was an air of disbelief on his part in that statement. I raised my eyebrows. He did not believe me for some reason and I was now getting impatient. I did not need this.

'Well, whilst you were away, someone who had just come back from yard told me how he saw you and your sister with different men each night and how you spent time down on the beach and various other places, but each time he would see you with someone else and you were revelling in the company. You and your sister made a name for yourselves around the village and Denny's parents were not pleased with you and your sister.'

'So what did Denny say about all these goings on? Or did your source not stretch to that one?' I was now shouting at him. My voice had risen a few octaves and the coffee was pushed away from me. Otherwise I might have thrown it at him. 'How could you believe what you heard? Would I have bothered to write to you, taking all those chances, if I was gallivanting about with 'all' these different men as you are insinuating?' I was eyeing him up and down. 'Well, so wah? Cat got your tongue now?'

'So are you telling me that it is not true what I had heard from this person?'

'You are such an arse. Do you know something? I am not even going to answer that because you probably decided what the answer was going to be before you even talked to me personally and just wanted me to come here in front of you and confirm some….. some….. rumour, because at this stage, that is all it is. Well guess what? I am going to let you believe what you want, but I tell you this: if this is the way that things are going to be in our relationship, then it's not worth going there. I don't want anything like this where once again other people are heard above me and other people's views are more plausible than mine.' I got up from the table and started walking towards the door, grabbing my jacket from the chair as I went. I was opening the kitchen door when he said,

'Shoy, please don't go. I am sorry. Please close the door.' I continued out into the hallway and started to open the front door. Before I knew it, his hand was slamming the front door shut and he was now standing behind me with me facing the door. It was like a scene out of one of those Hollywood movies. My mind snapped back to the matter in hand.

'I am so sorry. Please forgive me? I should have known that you would not get up to anything like that, should have believed in you, and not have listened to anything that anyone had to say. You see the thing was....... the thing was, I was so jealous. I so wanted to be there with you and just kept thinking of you.... you and him lying on the beach or walking hand in hand, staring into each other's eyes in the sunshine without me and I just kept thinking that you had forgotten about me already.' He turned me around to face him. He was drying my tears. I pushed his hand away and he continued.

'Look, Shoy, all I need to hear is that you never got up to anything

Nightmare in Paradise

with anybody and that will be the end of this stupid episode…… I promise.' I wiped the tears from my face myself.

'Well you know what? I will not give you the satisfaction of saying what you want to hear. You can carry on thinking what you like. I will not confirm or deny anything. Okay? And another thing! What if I turn to you now and say…… it's all over….. forget the whole thing……. eh? What would you say then? You know something? I am so disappointed in you! I never thought you were like that. The fact that you questioned me the way you did as if I were a criminal….. nah….. that was not good at all. That was darn right nasty.'

'Shoy, I know. I am so, so sorry. Please forgive me and let's start this conversation again and forget that this happened. Please?' He looked so boyish standing there in front of me, tears in his blue/green eyes. I reached in to my bag and handed him a bundle of envelopes.

'Here are the letters that I wrote to you and did not get the chance to post. They continue from where the last one left off, which you should have received. Where are mine? Or did you not bother to write any at all especially after your little newsflash item?'

Shoy

'Yeah, I wrote, but I am not sure that you want to have the letters.'

'Why not? What's wrong with them?'

'Well they started off okay, but I got so lonely that I could not think what to say. After all, you are the first girl that I have ever written a letter to and I did not know what to say without sounding foolish. Also, after I heard what was supposed to be going on down there, I stopped altogether because I thought, what's the point? Especially if you're not even thinking about me. I thought you had found better things to occupy yourself with. Sorry.' He looked at the bundle and raised his eyebrows; obviously impressed at the amount of letters he was going to have to read.

'All the same, let me have the ones that you have written and the rest you can write to me and I will collect them over the next few days. You are not getting off that easily.' We laughed. At last a smile and he looked so much better. But there was no way that I was letting him off the hook that easy. He went upstairs and got the letters that he had written and handed them to me. I started to open them and he stopped me.

'Don't read them now. Read them when you are alone.'

Nightmare in Paradise

Okay, I will read them when I have a moment alone; probably in the bath tonight when I get home.' The pupils of his eyes were now much wider and his face was now soft in the way he watched me. I could feel him wanting me for the first time since I walked in the door.

'Shoy? Come here.' I smiled and teased him. I knew exactly what he wanted.

'Why?'

'I have something for you and you have to come over here if you want it.'

'Now, what makes you think I want what you have?'

'Oh you do. You know you do. Anyway, curiosity will get the better of you.'

'Oh will it now?' I stood there for a bit and then thought better of it. I could not resist him. I wanted his arms around me. I wanted his lips touching mine. I wanted him to make love to me. I just wanted him. I walked over to him, dropping my jacket as I went.

Shoy

He flung his arms around me and kissed me, gently at first and then he was pressing his lips so hard against mine. I was where I wanted to be: where I should have been two hours back.

Our lips finally parted. 'So how was the holiday?' He finally asked.

'Well, where would you like me to start? It was the worst experience of my life.' Lloyd was listening intently and had tears in his eyes. He gave me a hug - a tight one.

'I am so sorry for what I put you through when you came to see me. Instead of giving you the welcome that you should have had, I played the arse and gave you even more crap. I am so sorry, Shoy.' He sighed heavily. 'I do love you. Don't go away from me again like that.'

WHAT THE HEART WANTS

Yvette, by now, had had her third child. He was the cutest little boy and they named him Nathan. Lloyd was the proud father and once again, I was put on the back burner while they continued their game of happy families. Despite that, he would still see me on the quiet. That suited me fine, because I was getting what I wanted out of it and I suppose he was getting the best of both worlds in that he could see his kids and see me at the same time. I was quite getting used to this now, but nothing had changed between Denny and I. We were just ticking along and I was biding my time, waiting for the day when either he would

Shoy

leave or I would.

The day came when Yvette and Lloyd, again, had a barney and he was out. And by all accounts this was it: the final fling. Things got back on a more permanent footing for both of us.

Sex with him was wonderful. He would make me feel good about myself. He adored my body and would tell me so. Every minute I could, I would spend it with him.

The first night we had sex it was an unforgettable experience. It was like no other I had ever experienced. We had been out that evening for a Mexican meal and then made our way back to his place. Ricky was out for the night and so we had the whole place to ourselves. As we walked in through the doorway, we started kissing. Our embrace was tight and lingering. At this point, Lloyd attempted to sweep me off my feet and carry me upstairs, but this I did not like, so instead I held his hand and we walked up the stairs, me following. He led me into his bedroom and I closed the door. We stood there in the middle of the floor, holding each other. We started to undress each other. Firstly, I had to remove his light brown leather jacket, which I flung across the room on to the chair that was under the window. Underneath he was wearing a white t-shirt. I could smell his aftershave and I kissed his neck, inhal-

What the Heart Wants

ing the smell that I had become so accustomed to. He was now removing my coat and it fell to the floor around our feet. Slowly, he started to unbutton the red dress that I was wearing. The buttons went all the way down the front. The buttons came apart so easily and the dress slid off my shoulders and onto the floor. I sat on the edge of the bed and undid his belt that was around the waist of his jeans. This I struggled with a bit, but with his help it was now sliding out of the housing. The front of his jeans did not have the conventional zip, but fasteners. These I could not undo and I was tugging away at them and the moment was being lost as we began to laugh.

'Have you lost something?' he asked, teasingly.

'No. I know exactly what I am looking for and give me……' I tugged at the last fastener and the trouser was now free. 'There, I knew I would get there in the end.' I slid his trousers down past his knees and he stepped, one foot at a time, out of them holding on to my shoulders with his hands. So here we were in our underwear. He pushed me back onto the bed and then lowered himself on top of me. We paused for a moment and slowly our lips touched. His tongue was rhythmically rotating in synchrony with mine. I could feel his penis hardening against my thighs. His chest was warm against my nipples. With a start, he rolled me over on top of him, our lips still locked in erotic pleasure. His hands were fumbling around my mid-back, trying to undo the clasp of my bra. I felt the material ping free, like a catapult releasing. Our lips parted and I snuggled my head into the pit of his neck kissing it gently. I kissed my way down. He gasped as my lips touched his nipples. I teasingly bit them, encircling his areola with my tongue. He was now breathless. As I made my way down his body, I could feel his hard, erect penis against my stomach. I had only touched it before and now I was going to see it and taste it, but that moment was halted as he stopped me and pulled me up towards him and pushed me over onto my back. His tongue was now exploring me like an anteater searching for that tasty grub in the mound of earth, and his fingers gently massaged my swollen vulva. I whispered embarrassingly, 'Oh Lloyd, it's wet.' Of course it was going to be wet, but it had been such a long time since I had been this wet that it came as a surprise to me. We both laughed at my words. He pulled me to the bottom of the bed by my legs and kneeling down he parted my vaginal lips with both his hands and touched my bud with his tongue. I watched him briefly licking me, not wanting to miss a drop of my sweet juice. I swung my head back on to the bed and, grabbing hold of a pillow, pulled it across my face, not wanting to make a sound. It was so intense. I was struggling with the touch of his tongue on my sensitive clit, my legs closing around his head. He could feel my climax mounting. He pushed

What the Heart Wants

open my legs, thrusting his tongue deep into my vagina. I came violently, my body vibrating under the power with which I came. Without a moment's delay he was pushing his hard, erect penis into my vagina, extending the orgasmic delivery. I pushed the pillow away. With my mouth open and my back arched I moved my hips, gyrating with his rhythm. He pushed himself up on to his hands and closed his eyes real tight. I knew he was about to ejaculate. I could feel him getting harder and harder inside me, and his movements quickened. With a sudden jerk, he had released himself fully, pushing his penis right to the heart of my soul. He collapsed beside me, and, both panting; we lay there, our juices now mingled as one. This was the first of many such encounters, not always that intense, but always satisfying.

THE WORTH OF LIFE

My relationship with Lloyd had now moved on to another level and we wanted to be together as a couple. We no longer wanted to be two people finding pockets of time, sneaking a kiss here, and making love there. I knew in my heart that my love for Denny had completely dried up and no longer existed and I wanted out of the set-up we were in.

Lloyd and I talked about ways in which we could be together. We thought about getting a mortgage of our own or renting a place of our own, big enough for both of the kids and us. Of course,

The Worth of Life

through all of this it went without saying that I came as a package with my kids. There was no way I would ever leave them behind. They were my life and my reason for living and putting up with all the crap Denny had dished out in the past. This Lloyd understood and would not have it any other way.

We had gone to a few estate agents and the whole picture was of doom and gloom. There was no way we could get a mortgage as he had some debt problems and I was already committed to another mortgage and would have to get my name off the existing one before things could progress. It was all going to take too long, so we had to think again. Somewhere along the line, we came up with the idea of offering Denny a sum of money for his share in the house that we owned together. Lloyd and I planned our proposal to put to him and had worked out what would be a good financial offer. As we had not been in the house that long, I knew it was worth ninety thousand pounds. So I halved that and then took off the deposit money that was offered to me from the housing association that amounted to fifteen thousand pounds and then took off the amount of money I spent on land searches, solicitor's fees and stamp duty at one percent of the value of the house, which roughly came to about two thousand five hundred pounds. So, based on my figures he was going to be offered a total of twenty-seven thousand pounds, with a leeway of a thousand pounds in case he wanted to negotiate. We would take out a loan for this amount. It all seemed simple. I arranged a meeting between the three of us for a Friday evening.

My car had been playing up all week. It kept spluttering and would not start properly. Yet another bill I would have to fork out for. Denny had been uneasy with me the whole week, understandably. Whenever I could I would leave the house, not necessarily going to see Lloyd, but just so I was out. He wanted to talk one evening and I did not want to. I grabbed a jacket and got my keys. He chased me to the car trying to stop me from leaving. I locked the car doors quickly and of course the stupid car would not start. Eventually it did, but by this time, he was hanging on to the door handle shouting for me to open the door. Did he really think I was that stupid? I backed down the drive and he was still hanging on. There was no way he was going to let go. He was enraged. As I swung out of the drive, he jumped on the front of the car holding onto the wipers. I kept shouting at him to get off: I could not see as he was blocking my view. I tried jerking the car as I drove forward a bit and then slammed on the brakes, but still he was hanging on. Then I reversed, which he did not expect, and he shot off the front of the car. I grinned. He shot off at such a speed and he disappeared in front of the car. He then jumped up and just as he was going to jump on again, I turned the steering wheel hard

The Worth of Life

right and tried to go around him, but I drove the car over his foot. In the rear view mirror, I could see him limping. Shit! What was he going to do when I returned? I could not think of that now: I would deal with that later. I went home quite warily, not knowing what mood he was going to be in. But he was already in bed complaining about his foot. I was sorry, but it was stupid of him to jump on the car. Who did he think he was? Superman?

The next day when I was with Lloyd, I was dropping him home and he could feel the car shuddering, just like I had told him. When we got to his brothers' house he opened up the bonnet and took a look in the engine. As soon as he opened it, he could see that the distributor cap had been partially taken off and that was why the car was not working properly.

'Look, Shoy, the only way these things come off is if someone takes them off. This has been purposely loosened.'

'So why would anyone do that? No one has been driving the car other than me. Who would have done that?' We both knew who it was, but now the car was fine, there was no need to do anything about it. (I felt that way, anyway)

Friday came and Lloyd arrived at the house, bang on time. I

Shoy opened the door and let him in. He kissed me, but I could see and feel that he was not looking forward to this encounter. We both walked in to the living room, closing the door behind us. Denny was already sitting in one of the single armchairs near the window, so we both sat on the settee opposite the fireplace. Being too apprehensive to beat about the bush, I started the conversation quite quickly and bluntly.

'Well.' I sighed heavily. 'The reason we….' (I pointed to both Lloyd and myself) 'wanted to have this meeting with you…..' I was looking straight at Denny and he straight at me, 'was to put a proposal to you.'

'Yeah, and what proposal is that then?' He said very sternly.

'Well, we would like to buy you out of the house, offering you……' Before I could complete my sentence Denny interrupted, his voice now raised.

'You can't afford to buy me out. Where would you get the money from?' Of course, in reply to his raising his voice, I raised mine.

'Well, that is no concern of yours. The question is would you accept us buying you out?'

'You bitch. You call yourself a 'best friend' to Yvette and this is what you do to her?'

Astonished by this answer, I replied 'What the hell has she got to do with any of this?'

He stood up and at that point it was as though time stood still, but he carried on moving, moving towards me and I knew he was going to do something to me, exactly what only the next few moments would reveal. As he drew closer, passing Lloyd, he punched out and my reaction meant his punch caught me in the side of the head instead of my eye. Following that, he grabbed me around the neck and dragged me out of the chair. By this time, Lloyd had grabbed hold of him and was trying to get his hands free from my neck, but to no avail. He released one of his hands and with that punched me in the stomach. My legs went limp and I was hanging with him still holding me by the neck and Lloyd still trying frantically to release his hand from my throat. I could not breathe. I could not even make choking noises. Lloyd, I could see, was punching him about his body and he finally released his grip from my neck, but had hold of my clothing. I was gasping for air and choking. The pain was extreme. Before I knew what was happening, Denny had dragged me full length over the wall

Shoy

that divided the living room from the dining room and as I crashed to the floor, scraping my body and legs as I went, they both fell on me. I once again returned to the desperate state of not being able to breathe. They were squeezing my life away. My eyes darkened and I could not see. My hearing was disappearing and all the noise and commotion was now distant. The grim reaper was approaching, but I was not ready. My children were upstairs asleep and I would never ever see them again. I did not even say goodbye. I did not want to go. I could not go. The next thing I knew, Lloyd was full in my face shouting for me to get out of the room and he was shoving me towards the kitchen out of the dining room. Where was Denny? I still had to think about him through all this commotion.

'Shoy, get out now! Get up. Come on girl, move.' He was roaring at me. I was disorientated, my throat throbbing, and I was spitting and spluttering, still gasping for some air to reach my lungs. I tried to take a deep breath, but, doubled up with pain, could not manage it effectively. I started to crawl towards the kitchen door, leaving them entangled on the floor. My back was towards the two of them when I felt this hand grab me back and lay into me on the floor again, punching me about my back. I could not take anymore. I was hurting and real bad. I kicked with every ounce of strength I had left, kicking Denny in the face and breaking free once again. This time I was determined he would not get hold of me again. I crawled to the kitchen and stood up as best I could, but it was not as easy as my mind wanted it to be. I somehow made it to the front door and down the path to the phone box that was right opposite the house. I lifted the receiver and dialled '999'. Hysterically, I somehow spoke to the lady on the other end. I came round on the grass bank outside the house with a woman police officer bending over me with an ambulance crew on the other side of me. I lifted my head slightly and saw squad cars and Mariah vans. What had I told them to warrant all of this? The neighbours were now out and wondering what had taken place. I was being asked a barrage of questions, but I could not speak. I was hoisted off the floor by two of the officers and helped into one of the squad cars. In the house, there were still scuffles going on and the police had decided to arrest the two of them, as they would not calm down. As I sat in the car, I saw first Lloyd being led out of the house and then shortly afterwards Denny, and they were both placed in separate cars and taken away. I was now worried. Where were they being taken and for how long? The police officer I asked could only say that they would be taken to the local police station, and advised me to give them a ring. She left me the number. Looking at me, the officer said, 'I think we should take you off to the hospital and seriously get you checked over.'

Shoy

'No, I can't go. My kids are asleep in bed.' They were not aware that there were kids in the house and were really surprised at the fact that they had not woken up. They helped me into the house and one of the officers went upstairs to make sure the kids were all right. They were. I was now finding it really hard to breathe, but I insisted that I would be fine after taking a couple of painkillers.

I closed the front door and heard the cars and vans disappear. What a night. I walked upstairs and looked in on my children. Miraculously, they were still asleep. I bent over and kissed them both. Funnily enough, they were sleeping in Mercedes' bed. They would sleep together quite often, as Ezra did not like being alone. They looked so peaceful and beautiful. That was the way I wanted life to be for them.

I left their room, leaving the door slightly open. As I walked into my bedroom there was an almighty bang, bang, banging at the front door. I had no idea who it could be. But then I went cold. Oh my god, was it Denny come back to finish me off? I went over to the window and peered out cautiously. It was Yvette. Her car was parked in the driveway and she was standing back from the door, looking up at the window. I drew back, holding my side as I moved. The bitch. How could she know what had gone on so quickly? I bet Lloyd called her and did not even call me. I

The Worth of Life

went downstairs really quietly (would you believe it, there was I sneaking around in my house like a thief). Getting the number the police officer gave me, I returned upstairs, jumping as she banged on the door again, shouting through the letterbox.

'I know you are in there because your car is still here. There is no way I am leaving until you open this door. One way or another you will let me in, because I am not going anywhere.' Well, she was in for a long wait, because there was no way I was going to open the door to her when I was in that state.

I called the police station and asked if I could speak to Lloyd. The officer who answered informed me that they could not take phone calls at the moment and that they would be released later that night. I slumped on the bed.

'What time are you letting them out?'

'Probably about one o'clock, but we will not let them out together.'

'Is there any way you can let me know which one you will be letting out first?'

Shoy

'Well, not really, but what I can do is, if you tell me which one you want out first, then he can give you a call and you can come down and pick him up and we will let the other one out half an hour later. How's that?' I thanked him gratefully. Yvette, once again, shattered the silence, at the door. Was she ever going to get sense in her head and go away? But there again, she did not have any sense in her head, otherwise we would not be in this situation, because Lloyd would have been with her and there was no way I would have intervened ever.

I so wanted to get hold of Ricky. He would come over and help me out now, but my phone book was in the car and of course Yvette was camped out behind my car in her car. I was trapped. I had to sort something out. There was no way I was going to stay in the house and wait for Denny to come back and finish me off. I had a couple of hours. I started to pack. This was all hampered by the fact I was in so much pain and I was now getting dizzy spells, which came and went quite frequently. I was in a state really, but I had to pack some things and get out of the house and take the kids with me. I got a case down from the wardrobe and packed mostly the kids favourite clothing, school uniforms, underwear and a few other bits and pieces that I thought they would need. I threw in a couple of items for myself, but I was just more concerned about them. I then dragged the case down the stairs as best I could. I got a couple of black bin liners and started putting in items of toys that they liked best, along with colouring pencils, paper, colouring books and felt tips. The phone broke my frenzied, manic packing. It was Lloyd.

'Hi, babes. Are you all right?' I was crying now and gasping for air. Just hearing his soft, sweet voice reduced me to tears.

'No, I am not okay. I am in pain and I am packing.'

'Packing? Why?'

'Well, the police told me that they were letting you out first and then him and of course he is going to come back here. After what he has done, do you think I can stay here tonight?'

'No. That's why I am on my way. I have called Ricky and he is on his way down now to pick me up and then we are coming over to you to get you out of there. Shoy, I am so sorry for what has happened.' What was he sorry about? He had not laid a finger on me.

'Oh, by the way, Yvette is outside the house in the car with the kids wanting to come in. She has been banging on the door at

Shoy

intervals, shouting at me.'

'Don't worry about her. We will sort her out when we get there. Are you completely packed?'

'Yeah. I just have to wake the kids and get them wrapped up in their quilts and put them in the car.' The phone went dead, but I figured he was calling from a payphone and the money had run out. I ran through my in head once more all the items that I would need to be away from the house and try to lead as normal a life as possible until I was able to get some of my things again. The thought of leaving my home made the warm, salty tears roll down my face once more, but I did not have time for this now. I looked out of the window and sure enough, Yvette was still there. Did she not care what she did with her kids? How could she just sit out there in the cold at one in the morning?

I was now clock-watching. An engine started and there were screeches of tyres outside the door. I went to the window and peered out. Yvette was disappearing up the hill. She had given up. Within the next couple of minutes there was a knock at the door and voice shouting, 'Shoy, it's, me. Open the door.' It was Lloyd and Ricky. I opened the door and he came in and hugged me.

The Worth of Life

'Ahhh.' My ribs were in agony. As we stood there talking, Ricky was busy loading up my car with the cases and bags that I had managed to plonk at the door.

'Shoy, Ricky is going to go and stay with his girlfriend tonight and so the kids can have his room and you can stay in with me.'

'No. No. I am going to stay with my mum. I have caused enough trouble and I think now I need to depend on my family for help. If I came to stay with you and Ricky, how long would I be there and it would be such a disruption for the kids.' He knew I spoke sense and so agreed. Time was getting tight, we went upstairs, and I tried not to wake the kids up too much. Ricky lifted Ezra out of bed, wrapping him up in his quilt, and Lloyd lifted Mercedes doing the same and they put them in the back of my car. They hardly woke. Mercedes opened her eyes, but after being reassured that everything was all right and that I was going to be with her, she soon closed her eyes and went back to sleep. Just as I was about to leave the house, I remembered their lunchboxes, went to the kitchen, and grabbed them along with a carrier bag containing the bread, ham, salad, drinks, fruit and snacks. In fact, I just went through the cupboards taking all the things that I knew the kids liked and would have for their lunch. Lloyd could not

Shoy

believe how my mind was working, but the happiness of my kids was paramount and I would never, willingly, try to upset them in any way.

I got out of the car, leaving the kids wrapped up in it and went up to the front door of my parents' house. Ricky had followed us down to my mum's and was waiting for Lloyd in his car. It was now almost one-thirty in the morning and, not wanting to wake up the neighbourhood, I gently tapped the knocker, turning and looking at Lloyd for support. My mum was always a light sleeper and I knew that she would hear it. There was a light at the top of the stairs and footsteps descended and her shadow appeared at the door:

'Who is it?'

'It's me, mum.' She opened the door.

'Shoy, what's wrong? Are the kids okay?'

'Yes, they are in the car. They are fine. Mum, there has been a bit of trouble. Can the kids and I stay here tonight?'

'Of course! Go get them. I will wake your dad.' I was not so keen

The Worth of Life

to hear that bit, but I supposed he had to know sooner or later what had been going on and tonight was going to be the night.

The kids were put straight to bed by my mum and she then came downstairs and made me a hot drink. Lloyd had been invited in and he told Ricky that he would call him when he needed to get home. We sat in the living room and I started my story telling to my parents. First of all, my dad was seething with anger that Denny could do something like that to me. He then completely changed what he was saying and came to the conclusion that I asked for it.

'If you had not gone behind his back…….' I cut him off mid-stream and made sure he understood that I had not gone behind his back in anyway. This was now my opportunity to put them straight on a few things that they knew nothing about. All the years I had been with Denny, they were not aware of the ups and downs, the numerous women, the lonely nights, the feeling of being a one-parent family with a lodger. They were so surprised, but tonight I was going to come clean with everyone and they were astonished at what I had put up with.

'Well, I think it's about time you got off to bed. You don't look too good anyway.' My mum then turned to Lloyd and told him to

Shoy

call me in the morning. I walked him to the door, we kissed momentarily, and he left, deciding to walk home to clear his head.

That night I could not sleep. I lay there with the events of the night turning over and over in my head. I could not get comfortable as I was in so much pain. I could not breathe properly and had to sit up most of the night, which made it easier but not altogether better. My ribs were sore. My head was pounding. My face was burning and the rest of me just felt a wreck. Morning came all to quickly and still I could not breathe properly. I sat hunched over the dining room table with my hand supporting my ribs on the left-hand side. My mum, being a nurse, was not at all happy with the situation, but I still did not want to go to the hospital. She made us some breakfast, but I just could not manage any of it. I tried to drink some tea, but not even tea, my favourite drink, would go down.

The doorbell went and I could hear it was my Aunt Opal. We called her Aunty as we had known her for a good few years, but she was not actually related to us. She was the kindest person I knew and she would always have time to listen to you. She came in to the dining room and immediately she walked in, she hugged me. With me wincing in her arms, she was not at all happy with my reactions and told my mum to get dressed and take me off to

The Worth of Life

the doctors. I did not want anyone to go with me and made my way down to the emergency surgery.

I was not long in the waiting room when the on-call emergency doctor called my name and the room number I was to make my way to. I walked in and sat across the desk from him. He was not my own doctor and so I was not at ease.

'So what can I do for you, Shoy?' His words gave the go-ahead for the tears to well up in my eyes. I was trying hard not to look down, as I knew that action would just release all the tears again and I would run the risk of not stopping.

Like an express train racing through a dark tunnel I started. 'Well, I have been beaten up and I can't breathe and I am aching all over and my head hurts and ……..'

'Woe, just slow down. Let's start from the top. Now you say you have been beaten up. How did this happen?' I recapped the whole event from start to finish. The doctor was so comforting. He came around the desk and handed me a bunch of tissues. Kneeling on the floor beside me, he listened completely. He then examined me as best he could without causing me more pain than I was in already. He was not at all happy. He called an ambulance

Shoy

to take me to the hospital. Whilst waiting for the ambulance, I telephoned my mum. She and my Aunt Opal would be on their way over to the hospital.

I was already sitting up in a cubicle on oxygen when my mum and Aunt Opal arrived. The doctor had not yet done her bit and within moments she came in and started her examinations. I was in so much pain: pain I could not begin to describe and it hurt me to breathe. Every breath I took radiated around my body, all in the wrong place. She ordered me to have some x-rays so they could see more clearly what was going on with my ribs and other organs around. I returned to the cubicle, pushed in a wheelchair by a porter and my mum carrying the x-rays.

The doctor turned and looked at me and then looked at my mum and my aunt.

'Well, young lady, you have had a narrow escape.' She turned, looking at my mum and aunt. 'I am not going to mince my words as I know that you two ladies are both nurses. Shoy was very close to dying. She has sustained three broken ribs of which one is about an inch and a half from her lung.' She held up the x-ray to the imaging light and showed them what she was talking about. From where I lay I could see quite clearly the ribs that were bro-

The Worth of Life

ken. (Not too sure where the lung was, though). 'She also has a couple of cracked ones.' Turning the conversation around to me she continued: 'You are going to experience quite a bit of pain for some time, but there is nothing we can do, except prescribe very strong painkillers and plenty of rest for at least a couple of weeks. No running about. No lifting. No dancing.' I tried to laugh, but the pain stabbed me again. 'You are very, very lucky to be here today.' I thanked her for what she had done and she left.

I looked at both my mum and my aunt. My aunt could no longer contain her sadness. She had removed her glasses and was openly wiping her eyes.

'How could he do this? How could he hurt you this bad? Did he want to leave those two beautiful children without a mother? He is a bastard.' I was so shocked. That was the first time ever that I heard my aunt swear. She was such a meek and mild lady and would never say a bad word against anyone, let alone swear. My mum just remained silent with her thoughts. We left the hospital in a taxi and went home.

Later on that day, Lloyd called to see if I was okay. I did not speak to him as the phone was situated in what was the front living room, but since my parents had had the conversion done to

Shoy

the house, the two rooms were now one. I was in no pain now for the first time since being beaten and did not really want to move, so my mum spoke to him and told him to come over if he wanted to speak to me. All day, my Aunt Opal was in shock herself. She just could not believe what Denny had done to me. When Lloyd arrived, they wanted him to go over the whole story again. My mum had tried several times to call him, but there was no answer. The kids seemed okay and my sister, who lived in her own flat just up the road from my mum, had taken them out for the day, just so they were not around to see the goings on and therefore not being scarred with memories of pain between their parents. Despite what he had done to me, I still wanted his children to love him. He was their father and he was good to them, when he bothered to be a father, but most of all, they loved him and I did not want to destroy his image in their eyes. If when they got older they wanted to do that for themselves, then that was up to them.

By lunchtime, my brothers knew what had happened and they had all arrived at the house. They were enraged but I made them swear to me that there would be no reprisals. I did not want them planning anything untoward against him. I was going to deal with it my way and I did not want them interfering in any way. Besides, he was not worth one of them doing time. They reluctantly promised, but walked out of the living room moaning under their breath. They were not at all happy. The whole day, there was no word from Denny. Okay, so he was not bothered about me, but he did not even try to find out where his kids were. Nothing.

I did a lot of thinking that day and came to the big decision that now I was out of the house, I was never going back. No matter how much he begged me (which I did not expect him to do anyway), I would not be tempted. I knew what I wanted and I was on my way to achieving it. My big plan in the sky did not include Lloyd. He was a great guy and good to the kids, and me but he was not reliable at all. Now that my relationship with Denny was well and truly over, Yvette would be fretting around him again. I had noticed that whenever things were good between Denny and me, she would play the arse with Lloyd, but as soon as she got wind of trouble between us, he would be made a fuss of and have his feet back under the table. She was such a bitch to him and he was just so stupid he could not see what she was up to.

Over the whole weekend, as word got out that I had been beaten up, various people were pestering my sister. She had been asked so many questions, but she did not know a thing. Only what she was told by me, and that was hardly anything. I tried to keep her out of it. Under pressure, my sister would crack. She so loved me, and would defend me against anyone and if they said anything

Shoy

she did not agree with, she would put them right and that I did not want. I did not want my business bandied about.

Another problem was looming. I had been booked in through my place of work to attend a computer-programming course in Birmingham, which started on the Monday morning. My brother, Clarence, was taking me up in his car, but obviously this was not going to happen, as I had to rest. I had no choice but to call my boss. All day I kept planning what I was going to say, but I had to tell him as we had paid for the course that cost quite a lot. That evening, I finally called him. I explained in floods of tears what had happened and, of course, he entirely understood, but was very concerned about me. Before ending the conversation he enquired as to who knew what had happened. At this point, no one knew, but I was going to call Carmel and let her know. He ended by saying, 'If there is anything you need, make sure you call, okay? Take care and see you soon. Don't rush back. Make sure you are completely better.'

A week of my life flashed past and still there was no word from Denny. I had to contact him. I needed some items for the kids and also myself, so I called. The phone rang and rang. Finally, he picked it up.

The Worth of Life

'Hello?' I said immediately.

'Hello. Umm, I need to come over and collect some things for the kids.'

'Yeah, well I am not stopping you. You still have your key, don't you?' I really did not know what to make of our conversation. What was he thinking?

'Okay, I will come over tomorrow.'

'Fine.' There was a moment's silence.

'Well, don't you want to know how I am, or where I am, or how your kids are?'

'Look, Shoy, you are the one who left. If you want me to care, then you should be here, not wherever you are.' Well, what was I to say to that?

'Well, I tell you this for free: I am never coming back. We have to meet at some point and go over what is happening with the house.'

Shoy

'What do you mean, what's happening with the house?'

'Well, you can't stay in it by yourself. I have the kids and I have to have somewhere for them to live.'

'Well, that's tough. I have worked hard to get this house and there is no way you and your man are getting it from me. If you try to get it from me, you will never see it.' His statement concerned me.

'What do you mean I will never see it? You can't do anything to me. I have a court injunction out against you.' He sucked his teeth and laughed.

'That is just a piece of paper. Do you think that bothers me? You carry on trying to get this house and all I can say is you will see. I know a lot of people in a lot of places and, put it this way, you'd better watch your back. Where there is a 'gang', there is a way.' He then hung up. I had heard about various gangs, but never had had anything to do with them, or with anyone who had. It worried me that he could threaten me in this way considering he had almost killed me the previous weekend. I resigned myself to the fact that I would not fight him for the house. My kids needed me and no bricks and mortar would be worth the risk of leaving them motherless.

A few weeks had passed and I was now feeling a lot better, although still there were pangs of pain if I laughed too much or moved quite suddenly. So there was a constant reminder of that almost fatal weekend. I needed somewhere to live as living with my mum was becoming unbearable. I had gone to the bank wanting to cancel the standing order or direct debit (whichever it was) for the mortgage as I was paying out four hundred and ten pounds a month and I was not living in the house at all. The bank informed me that I could not just cancel the mortgage without a letter of confirmation from the mortgage company that I was no longer liable for the mortgage. After looking into the whole thing, I found that I could not just get my name off the title deeds without going through a solicitor, as it was a legally binding document. Oh, Christ, what was I going to do? I was paying out all this money, trying to run my car, feed my children (even though I was living with my parents) and to top it all, my mum had started charging me rent at one hundred and ten pounds a month. I know this does not sound a lot, but when you only got about seven hundred pounds a month, no matter how you looked at it, there was just not enough coming in. At the end of the month, Denny was having a laugh. He sent me the bills, stating that I had to pay my half as I was living in the house when such and such was used. I

Shoy was appalled. I suspected that between him and my mum, they had conspired to bankrupt me and therefore force me back, but I was more determined than ever that this was not going to happen. I had to get out and fast.

Now working at the hospital, part of my job was to sort out information for the new doctors joining the department and find them somewhere to live, so I knew that there was accommodation available for them. Would the department that housed the doctors, consider me? After all, I had worked there for some years and now I needed some help. I called the Housing Department and asked the question very shamefacedly. To my surprise they replied that all I needed was a letter of recommendation from my boss and then they would be able to accommodate the kids and me. It was so simple. Of course, my boss wrote the letter and by the weekend I was looking at a house in a little village just outside the town where I lived. I had gone along with Lloyd and Ricky.

We drove up to the house and we could not believe that we had the right address. It was a detached old house with so much character. The house looked as though it had landed in the middle of the garden. There was a drive that went past the house and halfway down the garden to a double garage. To the left of the driveway; with its roots just breaking through the drive, was a large tree,

The Worth of Life

which overhung both the drive and the neighbours' garden. I wondered what kind of tree it was, but I loved it. The garden was about two hundred feet long and about eighty feet wide. It was huge. It was split into three parts. There was a lawn at the front of the house with mature shrubs around the edge and to the side of the house. The second part of the garden extended from the patio doors to a lush lawn, which was higher than the driveway, and all around it was a wide, mature rockery. Towards the middle of the lawn, at the bottom, there were three rock steps that led down to a huge pond, but it was all overgrown and needed a lot of attention. To the back of that were three tall fir trees that hid a secret garden. Walking down the path, which lay, between the trees and the garage, the rest of the garden stretched out behind them. There were two apple trees, blackberry bushes that lined the left hand side of the fence and at the bottom of the garden; alongside the greenhouse there were strawberry bushes. To the right was a lovely ready-to-use rhubarb patch with a long stalk sticking out of the middle. This had obviously been a vegetable garden as you could see ridges where potatoes had been grown but it was now overgrown. I planned to return it to just that: a beautiful vegetable garden. Of course, being winter, I would have to wait and see what appeared next summer, but the wait would be exciting.

Leaving the garden, we entered the house. As you went through the door, you had the impression that you were walking out of the under-stair cupboard into the house. There was a bit of a hallway. To the left of the door was a large room, which was obviously the living room. It had a fireplace, which meant that for the first time in my life, I could hang Christmas stockings up for the kids. The next door led to the kitchen. It was small, but for the three of us would be more than big enough. There was nothing in it except a pantry cupboard, a cooker (which was just like the one my mum had when we were very small; one of those New World types with the pilot light hooked onto the side of it), the kitchen sink (of course) and a cupboard which was near the door and so high up that I could not even see the bottom shelf. We went out of the kitchen door, which took us to the side of the house, and to the right of it was another room. This was obviously the washroom, which consisted of a deep, white porcelain sink with running hot and cold water and electricity points for the washing machine and tumble-dryer. There was also an abundance of shelves. One part of the room was doing absolutely nothing and could be used for anything. It was like another bedroom. Opposite this was a good-sized garden shed. The next room was at the front of the house and this would be the dining room. It had such character. The windows were large and were of a bow design but three-sided, and there was also a smaller window on the other side, which meant lots of light. We made our way upstairs, which wound around to

The Worth of Life

the right, and on the left was a large bedroom which spanned the whole length of the house from left to right, overlooking the back of the house. There were beautiful views out over the fields in the distance. It had slanted ceilings on both sides and a fireplace in the middle opposite the windows. Across from the stairs was an airing cupboard with lots of storage space and a huge tank (the largest I had ever seen). On the other side of the hallway was another room, which was the smallest of the lot but still not a conventional box room. This, too, had a slanted ceiling on one side and an alcove of shelves. The third room was opposite the bathroom and next to the toilet. It was a great size with the slanting roof opposite to the smaller room. Basically, the two rooms mirrored the larger room on the other side, were just divided into different sizes, and overlooked the lawn at the front of the house and the unmade road. It was just perfect.

The house was completely empty, except for some well-worn carpets on the stairs and some really rough, matted carpet in the living room. The house dust mites must have thought they had a holiday retreat. I had very little to fill this beautiful house with, but I was going to make it our home in the months to come. There was no doubt about it; I was going to accept it. We got back into the car and hurried over to get the kids. I so wanted them to see what I had found for us.

Arriving back at the house, I made them close their eyes and led them to the door. It was dark by now, so they could not take in the vastness of the garden, but I wanted the maximum impact as they saw the house. As they walked in through the doorway, I said to them, 'Okay, open your eyes.' They stood in the doorway briefly then they took off in different directions, calling to each other as they explored. They both ran upstairs and immediately chose their rooms. They came running out of their rooms and flung their arms around me together.

'Oh wow, Mum,' said Mercedes, 'this is like a mini mansion.' I was so glad that they liked it. It was so important to me for them to like it.

'When are we going to live here?' Ezra asked.

'Well, I would say by the weekend. I just have to sign some papers, then they will hand over all the keys to me, and then we can move in. I will bring you back tomorrow in the day so you can see the garden, which you are just going to love.'

On leaving the house with Lloyd, checking that all the doors and windows were closed, Ricky turned to me and said, 'Girl, you

The Worth of Life

are so lucky. You have definitely landed on your feet here.' This I knew and could not help but beam with delight. I had been handed a mini mansion all of my own. My thoughts turned to the fact that I would definitely need some furniture and I was going to have to sort something out with Denny, as all the furniture was not his. In fact none of it was his. By rights, it was all mine, but I knew he would kick up a fuss. So it dawned on me that I might end up with nothing, but we would have to see.

I called Denny and arranged a day that week when I could meet him and go over what he would let me have. I had given him my good news, which went down like a leaded pair of shoes in a deep river. For support I took my sister with me, as I did not want to be there on my own with him. This was the first time I was actually going back to the house since that night. I had not been able to bring myself to go before, even though I had needed to. I was so anxious and just wanted to get in and out as soon as I possibly could. He opened the door and invited me in. He acknowledged my sister as affectionately as he always did and she did the same. After all, our arguments were not hers and I made it quite clear that everything was to continue as normal where he was concerned. I did not want any taking of sides with their not even knowing what had gone on. We walked into the living room and I stood at the door. I could not bring myself to sit down.

As we went through the various items that I could and could not have, Denny asked me if I wanted a cup of coffee. What was he up to? I accepted and my sister had a drink. I still could not sit down. He looked at me, smiling, and said, 'I am not going to touch you. You have this injunction out against me and I don't fancy going to prison, so you can relax.' He stood up and came towards me, and taking me by the hand, he led me to the settee and sat me down. 'There. Now, isn't that better?' A deathly silence fell on the room. No, it was not better, but I did not move.

He had decided that I could have the following items:
- Mercedes' double divan bed with drawers in the bottom
- Ezra's pine-wood slatted single-bed
- The pine-effect book case (as I had collected an array of adult and children's books over the years along with two complete volumes of encyclopaedias)
- An assortment of pots, pans, cups, glasses and cutlery (even though I had bought the whole lot prior to leaving home and since living in the flat)
- The ironing board that I had had since I lived at home with my parents
- Various pictures off the wall
- My plants (well, most of them)

The Worth of Life

- The TV and video (as it was rented in my name)
- The washing machine (as that, too, was rented in my name)
- The upright freezer (I would have preferred to have the fridge as that would have been much more practical)
- The Japanese-style rug
- The sheep skin-rug (mainly because it made so much mess)

Basically, I could take whatever belonged to the children. He would not let me have any part of the three piece suite, none of the dining room set, the TV and video cupboard, the mahogany effect wardrobe set with dressing table that I had bought when we moved in to the flat. He did not even need this as he had fitted wardrobes in all the bedrooms. He would not let me have any of the heavy curtains (not that I liked them that much), but I insisted in having all the nets as they were from MY mum. So, list complete, we said our goodbyes.. As I left the house, he said, 'Look, Shoy, can we talk alone?'

'No. We have nothing to say to each other. You got what you always wanted. You planned it real good and it paid off.'

'Huh. Don't you think I miss you and the children?'

'No. Not at all! If you missed them you would have found out where they were the day after we left, but you did nothing. So there's your answer.'

Now all I had to do was arrange 'a man with a van' to help me move the bits to my new home. Somewhere, well after seeing the house, I told my mum. I neglected telling her in the early stages, as I did not want her contacting Denny or Yvette and their putting their oars in. I wanted my plans finalised with the minimum of fuss. Clarence offered to get a van for the day and he would help me move all my bits. We arranged the whole thing for the Saturday when Denny would be out at cricket and so he would not be in the way. Once I had removed all the things I could have, I was supposed to post the keys back through the door, but I had made copies – just in case!

We were in. It was the strangest feeling ever. I had not had a chance to disinfect the bath, sink or toilet and that night I got one of the kids' baby baths and we all had a wash in the baby bath, which I put in the bottom of the deep-old-fashioned bath. We all slept that night in the one double bed. Ezra's bed was in pieces and I did not have any screwdrivers to put it together. There were so many things I was going to have to get, but for the time being,

The Worth of Life

we would have to make do. It was cosy, anyway.

Early the next morning, the doorbell rang. I woke wondering where the hell I was. It quickly came back to me. I jumped out of bed, leaving the kids still fast asleep, as we had been up late that night talking, laughing, and playing singing games and I-spy games.

'Who is it?'

'Who are you expecting?' It was Lloyd. I let him in. I could not offer him a seat, as I did not have any, just two beanbags. I disappeared back upstairs and had a wash, returning to him. He looked perturbed as he slouched on one of the bags.

'What's up?'

'How was your first night?'

'Yeah, it was fine. Come on then, tell me what's wrong.'

'What makes you think something is wrong?'

'Come on, I can tell. I have seen that face so many times.' He got

Shoy

up from the bag.

'You want a cup of coffee? Or have you not got anything in the house yet?'

'No, I did a bit of shopping last night.' I did not have a kettle and he had to boil the water in one of the pots. Everything was still in boxes as I had not cleaned anywhere, but today was going to be the day.

'So what did you lot eat last night?'

'Oh, we went down to the fish and chips shop on the green and had something there.'

'Hmm. Did you not miss me?' I knew that was it. He expected me to call him to come and stay the night. I knew I wanted to be with him, but my first night alone with my kids was too important to me and I did not want anyone else here, interfering with that. I had to settle them in before introducing another man into my life. So I told him as much.

'So, you see me as just someone else now?' I could not enter into this kind of conversation. I did not want any man living with me just yet, contrary to what everyone's perception of me was. After telling him exactly how I felt, I knew he would not understand and he left. I suppose he was hurt and felt used, and to be honest, he was right. I had used him, but he would now have to play the game my way, or no way at all.

By the end of the day, the house was clean and the little I had was in its place. The kids had had a great day out in the garden and had been down to the park nearby on their bikes. All was well.

That evening, Ricky and Lloyd came over and Ricky ordered in a takeaway for all of us. He was really good like that. As we ate, Ricky asked.

'What's your telephone number?'

'I have not got the phone in yet; can't afford it. I will put one in when I get the settlement from Denny.'

'Well that's crazy! You can't be out here in the middle of nowhere, where the nearest phone is down at the park and you have two kids. What if they get ill in the night?'

'Well, for now, I would just have to go over to the neighbours and

Shoy

ask to use theirs. I went over there today and introduced myself to them.'

'Nah, we can't have that. I will get you the money. Arrange to have the phone put in as soon as possible, okay?' He was so thoughtful, and I think in his thoughtfulness he narked Lloyd off, just a little. I could see it on his face. He would have wanted to suggest it himself or even pay for it, but I was not expecting it from him at all. After all, he was not moving in. Not yet anyhow.

Another week went by and I had an appointment with another solicitor. I had fallen out with the one I had as I owed her ninety-nine pounds for the injunction and could not afford to pay her that, so she decided that until the bill was settled, she was not going to act on my behalf for the settlement of the house. It was getting more and more ridiculous. So in my frustration as I walked back from her office, I stopped in at another one. I got a half-hour free consultation right there and then with a really nice guy.

I brought him up to speed on all the events that had taken place (amongst the tears and snotty tissues). He was just so sympathetic. He was extremely disgusted with the treatment that I had received from the previous solicitor and confirmed that he would accept full payment once settlement had been reached, so there was no need for me to worry. He would be in touch as to the settlement. As I got to the door he said, 'It's a shame you did not come to me sooner. This would have all been over by now and you would not be in this situation today, but never mind, you are here now.' I left feeling a whole lot better.

Sure enough, within the week he contacted me personally asking me to come to the office. That I did. He had been in contact with Denny's solicitor who had submitted a settlement figure of five thousand pounds. Of course, my solicitor laughed. There was no way he was going to accept that amount of money. I sat forward in the chair, clenching my lips with my teeth.

'Look, Mr Leopold, I have to accept that amount, because he has already said that he has no money.'

'Well that is kind of tough. We will force him to sell the property and give you the share that is owed to you. Or, we go to court, get him out, and move you back in with your kids. Either way, this five thousand pounds is an insult'. I knew I could not go any further with this. I would have to accept the money that had been offered.

'No, really, please just accept that amount. I want to be out of

Shoy

debt, I want to get my name off that title deed and cut all ties with him.'

'Why are you doing this?'

Hesitating I began. 'Well, he has threatened me and bearing in mind he almost killed me, I am not about to take chances. I don't want my kids growing up without a mother. There is no-one in this world who could look after them the way I want to, so to that end I will accept.'

'But there are laws that would protect you and get around this mess. At least we can try for the house.'

'No. Please just accept the settlement.' He was so disappointed with my decision, but my hands were tied. I was not running the risk of not knowing who was going to be lying in wait for me on a dark and cold night. And would they harm my children in the long run? He wished me well for the future and gave me a hug, just like a father would.

Not long after that appointment, I had the money in my account and all debts were paid off. The rest I left in the bank. After going through all of that knowing that I had been swindled out of

The Worth of Life

everything, I was distraught and there was no Lloyd around. He was never around when it mattered and, when he finally turned up, he did not even care to find out what I had been up to or been through. All he would want was something to eat, a bath and sex. I was bored with sex with him. It was always the same. Always what he wanted!

My mum was not really talking to me now. The kids were still going back to her house after school and when I arrived to collect them, she would keep conversation to a minimum until one day it got the better of her.

'So, this house you have. How you can afford to keep the house, run your car and look after the children all by yourself?'

'Well, I am working and I got some money off Denny.'

'So how much you get from him?'

'Not enough, but I will manage.' There was no way I was telling her. Everyone would get to know and my business was my own.

'Well, I still think that you should have gone back home. Denny would have had you back. All you had to do was ask him.'

'Ask him? What, to take me back? No way! After what he did, there was no way I was going back. He knew that it would only take laying one finger on me and then I would be off, so by the fact that he did it, he made the decision and he knew how to get rid of me. Get used to it, Mum. I am not going back – ever.' She sucked her teeth.

'So, in all of this where does Yvette fit in?' I could not believe the question. My own mother was asking me about that bitch.

'What do you mean, where does she fit in? What has she got to do with me?'

'Well, you see that is how you have turned now. She used to be your best friend and now you have upset everything. She is upset, Denny is upset and where is Lloyd?' I walked away. Obviously they were all in cahoots with one another and I was the centre of their conversation. Well, it was nice to know that I held the anchor to all their lives. Now they would all be free, free to sink or swim. The only people that I was going to be answerable to were my children and I was going to prove to them that they did not need anyone else except their loving mother.

The Worth of Life

Christmas was fast approaching and the village was coming alive. There was a lady who lived a few houses up the road from me who would bake cakes and there was always one for us. She had a little sausage dog called Monty, who was so scared of other people that, even when he went past the gate and we were out, he would take a wide berth. You could never get to touch him. On the green they had train rides taking the kids around. There were various stalls selling all sorts and games to take part in. The night was really cold, but it was so fantastic to belong to a village and feel the village spirit. I was not in the village a lot due to work, but I loved it when things like this were arranged. The kids were now in a different community. Yeah, that was it; they were in a community and everyone looked out for us. The green was the centre of the community and, as the main road ran right past it, if anything was happening you got to know about it quick-time. We left the green with torches in hand as there were no lights along the road leading up to our house. This excited Ezra and he kept waving his torch all over the place. They were both in their wellies and warm coats, hats, gloves and scarves. I never took any chances letting them out in the elements. We got in the house and I left them at the door, fighting to get their wellies off, whilst I went to put the kettle on. Out of the blue, the house was plunged into darkness. We quickly switched the torches on. I was so scared, but I could not let them know. I had to be brave for them. They huddled close

Shoy

to me. Okay, this was going to be tricky. We would probably have to go to bed in the dark as the fuse box was in the outhouse and there was no way I was going out there in the dark. As we stood there contemplating what course of action I was going to take, that is, to get a warm drink for each of us and then go up to bed and read in the torchlight, the doorbell went. Needless to say, the kids screamed and I was not far behind them. I could see through the frosted glass window of the door that there was someone out there with a candle. I opened the door. It was the neighbour. There had been a power cut in the whole village and, as he knew I had not been in very long, and that I would not be aware that this was a regular occurrence in the winter, he had brought me over some candles, matches and a kettle of hot water for drinks. I thought that was so special. He was there in his house minding his own business and he thought of the kids and me. It brought a lump to my throat. I declined the water as I had a gas cooker, but was grateful for the candles and matches, as sure, enough; I had not got any anywhere. A couple of hours into the power cut everything returned to normal. All was well.

Christmas came and I was in a dilemma. I was still not talking to my mum and it was going to be our first Christmas alone. Lloyd had informed me earlier that he was spending Christmas with his kids, which meant he would be with Yvette. Fine, I thought. So

The Worth of Life

I planned Christmas just for the three of us. I dug out the little silver Christmas tree that I had had when Mercedes and I were at the hostel and the kids dressed it. I bought them quite a lot of little things. They did not amount to a lot of money, but it looked loads to them, which was the most important thing. On Christmas Eve, we had an unexpected phone call from Denny. He wanted to pop over and bring the kids their presents. That was fine with me, but I so hoped that he would not hang around when he arrived. Sure enough, he came in, but as there were no chairs he could not make himself comfortable. My saving grace! He, as usual, was spending Christmas with his mother and his sister. Just what he relished. I was keen to get rid of him, but tried not to make it too obvious. Late in the evening, Lloyd came over and brought our presents, which the kids placed under the tree, totally unexpected. I had not bought anything for anyone except my sister and the kids. For the first time in ages, he kissed me and I felt myself weakening again. I was on my own so much now and it was getting me down. I wanted adult company, and a man's touch, and this would do for now. I gave in to him and let him stay the night. We had made love once. It felt different. We lay next to each other chatting for a while. He rolled over onto me. Obviously, he wanted us to make love again. This time though, he wanted to have anal sex. There was no way this was going to happen: not under any circumstances. He was being forceful and I started to

Shoy

get hysterical under him. I was having severe flashbacks of the pain I had endured at the hands of Roger. How could he do this? How could he? As my hysterics mounted, he got off and switched the lights on.

'Shoy, what is wrong? Why are you like that?' I lay there flat on my stomach with my head buried in my hands and I was sobbing, images darting in and out of my conscious brain. Images that I thought I had lost a long time back. He had brought them all back again.

'Shoy, I am so sorry.'

'Yeah, you are always sorry. Why can't you just listen to me for a change? I told you no and you just kept telling me that it would be all right. You would be gentle. What the hell has gentle got to do with it when I told you no?' He had nothing to say. I sat up in the bed, covering myself with the bedding.

'Look, I am going to tell you something that I have never told anyone else before. When I was younger I was abused, and that was one of the ways in which I was abused.' There, I had dropped my bombshell.

'Oh my god Shoy, I did not know.'

'No. Why would you know?' He began asking me questions, but I was not about to answer them. The only thing I made quite clear to him was that it was not my dad. We left it at that.

A FORGOTTEN MILESTONE

After Christmas and that unspeakable night, Lloyd was now spending more time with the kids and me. My birthday was fast approaching and Lloyd wanted to treat me to a night out that I would never forget. For Christmas he had bought me a dark green suit that had a fully lined well-fitted jacket and a beautifully made skirt, also fully lined. It had three gold buttons down the front of the jacket and three smaller gold buttons on the sleeves. As he was taking me out somewhere special, I had to find out what sort of clothes I should wear. After all, I would not want to be dressed wrongly. He suggested that I wore the suit that he had bought. I felt and looked good in this suit. I had lost lots and lots of weight and it fitted me like a glove. I felt so sexy in it. This was going to be a good night. We had planned that I would collect the kids as usual from my mum, along with my sister who was going to baby-sit, and then I would pick him up from Ricky's with all his gear in tow. Everything was going as planned. I arrived at my mum's and got the kids coated, shoed and out. I was a bit bemused, as there were no cards or birthday wishes from either my mum or my dad. They never ever forgot my birthday, but obviously this year I was not important enough in their life. All I would hear about was how upset Yvette was and how she was bordering on a nervous breakdown. So bloody what? She was not my problem, but some how my mum had lost sight of who was the daughter and who was just the mother of one of her grandchildren, but no way a blood relative of any sort. She was always hanging around my mum's house. Apparently, during the day she would be there, crying and carrying on with her crocodile tears, about how hard done-by she had been. She needed to open her eyes and get a life of her own, outside of our family.

Anyway, tonight was going to be special, my sister and I were now sitting in the car with the kids, and we were chatting away wondering, where he was going to take me. I started the car and attempted to pull away. There was this strange scraping noise.

Shoy

'Oh god, I forgot to take the brakes off.' But as I looked down at the automatic gear lever, it was in drive. I pushed it up to park and then back into drive and tried moving off again. Still it made the same horrid sound. So I slammed it in to park, switched off the engine and got out of the car. Now I was out of the car walking towards the front as if I were a trained mechanic knowing what I was going to look at, but it was all too clear: I had a puncture. Okay, so that was easy, I had done this before and knew what I had to do. It was messy, but it was possible. So the kids were sent back inside and my sister and I struggled to get the spare out of the boot, along with the jack. Whilst walking round to the front of the car from the other side, there was another flat. How could this happen? Okay, so changing one tyre was not going to work. The garage at the end of my mum's road was still open and I ran down there to see if they had a couple of tyres, so I could get them changed. They sure did. So I ran back to the car where my sister was waiting. She then pushed and I steered the car, standing alongside it and helping her push in a way. It got a bit tricky when we reached the corner, as we had to go down the hill slightly. So I got in just in case I had to break suddenly. I steered the car in to the garage and they set to it. As they did, one of the guys noticed that the back tyre on the passenger side was a bit low, so he hauled the pressure pipe to pump it up. As he did, he noticed that there

A Forgotten Milestone

was a two-inch slash in the side of the tyre. This was now beginning to look suspicious. With suspicion in mind, they checked the other tyre. Yep, our suspicions were right. This had been done on purpose. There was no way the tyres could have been slashed, just from driving them. Not being able to afford four new tyres, they abandoned fitting them and replaced the slashed ones. With their help, we pushed the car back outside my mum's house and went in to tell them what had happened. Straight away, my dad exclaimed, 'It had to be Yvette! Nobody else!' In my mind she was the culprit as well, but how would I prove it? The main thing was how was I to get home and obviously I was not going out that night, so there was no need for Stephanie to come home with me. I called my friend, Sunil, and he took me home. On the way home, I told him all about the evening, so far, and how with the tyres being slashed, it had spoilt my birthday celebrations. He then revealed to me that he had seen Yvette's car driving off about the time I thought the car had been vandalised. He did not think much about it, because it was near the school and he thought that maybe she had been seeing someone at the school. See, everyone had their suspicions and that was without any names being mentioned or fingers being pointed. I chose to forget it as there was nothing I could do, but thank god I was not able to drive off with the kids in the car and then lose control and .... Well, it does not bear thinking about. Once home, I called Lloyd who was wondering where I was. He did not say a lot, but we had to sack it for the night. Even though we were not going out, he still would not tell me where he was going to take me. A couple of hours after getting home and having something to eat, Lloyd turned up.

'There was no way I was going to leave you all alone on your birthday.' I was really, really pleased to see him. He was so concerned about the car and what had taken place that he advised me strongly to log it all as a crime, just in case there were any repercussions because if someone were after me, then at least the police would be aware of it and investigations would be started more quickly, if it came to that. It frightened me a bit, but it made sense. Once all of that was out of the way, we had a bath together and the night went on from there. It turned out to be a good night after all and made my thirtieth birthday real special.

The next morning, he left to sort out my car. He was meeting Sunil who had promised to get me some tyres cheap. Not too long after, he was back with my car and four new tyres. I never asked him where the money came from and did not care. All I wanted was my car, as I needed it to get about. Lloyd had visited Yvette whilst getting the car and had spoken to her about the incident. He was convinced that she had done it, or knew something about it. She did not deny it and when he told her how I had nearly crashed

A Forgotten Milestone

the car with the kids in it (which was obviously a lie), she filled up and he left disgusted with her. He told her that the money now needed for the tyres was hers, and because of what she had done there was now no money for her. I felt no way about that. Whatever was happening with the two of them was nothing to do with me. As long as I was getting what I wanted, I did not give a damn about anyone else.

MINI MANSION

By now I had found myself, and rather than sitting in my 'mini mansion' with sod all inside, I decided it was about time I spent some of the money I had had to grovel for and make our house into a home. I went out to a few carpet shops. There was one design of carpet that I wanted and none other. I had seen this carpet in an Indian restaurant when I was in Birmingham on the course that I had postponed due to 'unforeseen circumstances', and this was the one I was looking for. It was navy blue with delicate little pink flowers over it. The pink flowers were not obtrusive and just blended in as a colour most of the time. I had found it and not just in one shop. I arranged for three quotes and they varied in their price ranges according to which sort of underlay and the quality of the pile itself. Within two weeks, I had chosen. It was going to cost me six hundred pounds to have the two downstairs rooms, the hallways (both top and bottom) and the stairs done but, of course, it was going to be the cheap underlay that usually stuck to the floor. Whilst waiting for the carpet to be made up, which was going to take about four weeks, I was busy trying to find, in my lunchtimes and any other time I could find, some furniture. Cheap. We had been managing to eat off a set of patio furniture that had a wobbly leg. So the first thing I wanted to get was a table and some chairs. I used to go to all the car boot sales around the area and at one of these I picked up a folding table, which was in perfect condition, for a fiver. By this time, I was back on talking terms, of a sort, with my parents, and my dad offered to give me four chairs, which they had stored, in the shed. These chairs would always come out whenever they had a party or barbecue. My parents were great barbecue lovers and my dad was very good at them. So there it was, my dining room furniture for next to nothing. With all this 'new' furniture and new carpets to come, the house needed to be freshened up. There was a drab grey colour on the walls and some of the ceilings had the paint or the ceiling paper peeling off. I went to a DIY store and picked up some paint cards. Back home I looked through them with the kids. It's funny how, straight away, you know what you don't want. Knowing the design of the carpet, but trying not to tell the kids, as I wanted to surprise them, I chose a 'white with a hint of rose'; that way, the hall would be nice, light, and inviting. This was going to be an experiment as I had never thought of using pink on anything before, but I just fancied it. The living room and the dining room I selected from the same range, 'white with a hint of blue', in keeping with the navy of the carpet. Ezra chose a slightly darker blue for his room. On his floor was the rug with the Japanese-style decoration. It was the full width of his room and went slightly under his bed, so that was ideal. Mercedes chose for her room a lilac. She had always been a 'pinkey/purpley' girl and on her floor she had the sheepskin rug that was huge and took up nearly all the floor.

So now I had all this paint, I had to get it on the walls and somehow get the ceiling looking good as well. Lloyd was never about when I needed him and we were arguing all the time, and it always stemmed from Yvette and what she was saying and who was telling him what. He just could not think for himself and he could not decide what, or who, he wanted. I guess I always knew that he really wanted Yvette and now I had accepted that.

I started painting the kids' bedrooms. I got paint all over me.

Using those rollers would splash the paint all over the place, but I was managing. I suppose I picked up that skill from my mum, as she was the one who would decorate the house whenever it needed it. The kids rooms were complete, windows and ceiling included and now I was stuck. I wanted to start the hallway, but I knew I could not reach to the top of the long wall, so I did not want to start and leave it half done. Carmel, always knowing what I was up to, arranged to come over to my house one weekend, and unbeknown to me, she bought Val and her husband Ricky to help with the decorating. Ricky was very tall and got to work on the ceilings in two downstairs rooms and the hall, repairing all the torn bits with ceiling paper and rubbing off all the flaky paint and repainting the whole lot. He painted the window that I could not reach above the stairs and, of course, painted the hallway from top to bottom in my beautiful pink (which turned out not to be white with a hint, but just a bit more than light pink, but it looked fine). He was brilliant. Val, Carmel and I dragged the gopping bits of carpets out of the house and down to the back of the garden and laid it out for the kids to play on. We swept, cleaned, and painted walls all day. My sister was chef and chief tea and coffee maker.

By the end of the day, the house was almost painted, bar a few windows that I was going to do the next day. There were windows everywhere. Carmel was so good to me and I would always be grateful to her. She was my rock in a raging sea.

I had put together Ezra's bed at last and instead of my sleeping on the mattress on the floor in the corner of the bedroom with the two of them sharing the double bed, I bought myself another bed, which was not expensive at all. Argos and B&Q supplied all the chest of drawers. It took an age for me to work out how to put them together and the bits were so heavy. One time, when Denny came over to pick up the kids, he saw me struggling and offered to put them together for me. Problem sorted. The best bargain of all was the three-piece suite. There was an advert in one of the local papers, which offered three-piece suites for one hundred and fifty pounds; the only snags were that you could choose the material you wanted but not the style, and you had to wait about four weeks for it to be made. So I did.

Three weeks into the waiting for the carpets, I got a call to say that there had been a problem and the carpets would now take a further four weeks. I was so looking forward to my carpets that I made out I was thoroughly disgusted with the service. Okay, so they were cheap, but I was still the customer. I had paid my money and now I had to wait even longer. To that end, the guy on the phone (who was in fact the owner) decided to do me a deal. He would not charge me anything extra, but he understood my dilemma, as I arranged all my furniture delivery to coincide with the carpets. To that end he would deliver the Hessian-backed carpets, which were the best quality, (provided I agreed) in about a week. Was I really going to turn that down? In all, I had delivery of about a thousand pounds' worth of carpet for only six hundred pounds. I did not tell the kids about the carpets or the settee and arranged for the settee to be delivered on the same day as the carpets. When I brought them home from school, they could not believe their eyes. They flung their arms around me. There was no more clump, clumping up and down the stairs and all through the house. They lay on the carpet and rolled about. They rolled all the way from the living room, through the hallway and into the dining room. They were so funny: they kept doing this most of the day. Ezra cracked his head a few times on the woodwork as he rolled, and even fell down the step at the front door, which made us laugh.

So now my house was a home, freshly painted, carpeted and furnished. My kitchen had taken on a new look as well. It happened that my mum had kept all her old kitchen units when she had the house extension done and her new kitchen fitted. So now I had a kitchen. John, my youngest brother, came over with his coping saw and cut the work surface to size. Within a few hours, he had my kitchen fitted. I now had cupboards and work surfaces. My mum had given me her old cooker, which was not that old, and a

Shoy

friend of the family fitted it. My home was complete and all was well.

CONFESSIONS OF THE HEART

So my yoyo wound-out relationship with Lloyd had now re-wound itself and he was back, stronger than before and now spending a lot of time at the house: so much so that I was getting worried that he would want to move in. I still did not want him to live with me, although I had given him a front door key. He was not the one; not made of the ideal, sustainable material needed for my future man, but he was good for satisfaction, for good feelings and calming. Basically, I was using him and I did not care. As long as he thought he had me where he wanted me, then I was ahead of the game.

Shoy

Yvette, on the other hand, was still banding about. I would get back from work to pick up the kids from my mum's and she would be there. I would go to visit them at the weekend and she would be there. Late in the evening, I would call and she would be there. Did she not have a family of her own? And did she not have her own home? What the hell was her problem?

So, inevitably, I got home from work one day to find her there. Not wanting to hang around, I started to ready the kids.

'Shoy, I would like to have a civilised talk with you on your own somewhere quiet, if possible.' No. It was not possible. But I was intrigued. What could she possibly want to say to me?

'Why?'

'Please. If it was not important, I would not be here asking you.'

'Oh really? But you are always here, so what's new?' That was a bit below the belt, but so what?

'Well, it's taken me this long to pluck up the courage to ask you for a chat.'

'Okay. Fine. Where do you want to go?'

'I thought we could go to the park in the car.'

'Okay, we'll go in my car.' We made our way to the park and I stopped, switching off the engine. I took off my seatbelt and turned to look at her.

'So here we are, talk.' Before she could open her mouth, I interrupted. 'Do you know anything about the sabotage on my car that took place around my birthday?'

'No.'

It was a very quick no and nothing else to follow. She did not even ask any questions about it, or why I had even asked. I left it at that. She started on her important talk.

'Shoy, it's so hard at the moment knowing that Lloyd is with you and prefers you. I know you make him happier than I ever could, but I am begging you to give him back to me.' Well, my mouth fell open and I began to laugh. It was sad to see her beg me.

Shoy

'Look Yvette, if you want him so bad, then talk to him. It has nothing to do with me. I have not got him tied up or gagged. He is free to do exactly what he wants.' She continued to bore me with accusations such as 'taking food out of her children's mouths and feeding mine.' Well, she should have thought about that before she wrecked my tyres and put me to the expense of getting them replaced. During her drone, I just had to stop her.

'Is this all you wanted to say? Because if that's it, then this conversation, is well and truly over. You need to talk to him and not me.'

'Well, there was something else I needed to say to you.' I looked at her, intrigued. Was this yet another one of her so-called 'important' chats that would drone on and on? 'For a long time now, I have wanted to tell you something, but I never knew how to tell you and I think this is as good a time as any.'

'Yeah, well get on with it then; I have children to get home.'

'Do you remember when I used to collect Ezra from school at lunchtimes, before he went full-time?'

'Of course I do. And?'

'Well during that time, Denny used to come home at lunchtime and he would come on to me.'

'When you say *'come on to you'*, what exactly do you mean?'

'Whatever you want it to mean?'

'What bloody kind of answer is that? You'd better start talking, and no cryptic one-liners. If you have something to say, just flipping say it.' I was now shouting at her.

'Okay. To begin with, we used to just mess around.'

'Mess around?' My hand movements gestured a need for more information. 'There is no way I am going to make this easy for you. You started in on this conversation and now I want it all. So just cut all the stalling and crap and spit it out.'

'Okay. Like I said, we started out just kissing and then one day he asked me if I would have sex with him. I told him that if I did he would have to take you out more often and treat you better, because you deserved it. He was also talking about leaving you for me and I told him not to do that. I told him to stay with

Shoy

you.......'

Her hand was now reaching across to touch me. I hit it back. She continued holding her hand.

'You were so unhappy at the time and this was a way I could make you happy. Do you remember when he started taking you out more often?'

She had the bloody nerve to ask me that after what she had just said? What was I to think? How would that make me feel? I held my head in my hands and laughed but then, quickly turning back to her.

'So all this 'Yvette, the hard done-by' act going on with me and Lloyd being the villains, you and he had already done your dirty deed at my expense and I was made to look the fool. I had been living a lie, thinking that he loved me. So how many times did this happen?'

'Only the once!'

'You're a fucking liar. For one quick lunchtime poke, he was taking me out all over the place and he *stayed* with me. You were quite cheap then?' I turned back and looked out of the car window. Remembering that almost fatal night, I shot across at her and straight in her face I shouted, 'Do you know what his last words were as he lunged over to me and punched me in the head? Eh? Well I will tell you: *'how could you call yourself a friend to Yvette, when you are taking her man away?'* That's what he said. You bitch! In effect I got two broken ribs as well as a few cracked ones, concussion, bruises everywhere, NOT TO MENTION the fact that I nearly lost my life, for YOU. Because deep down he wanted you and this was his way of showing you what he would do for YOU. Well, I tell you what you deserve to lose everything. I was more of a friend to you than you ever were to me. At least Lloyd and I told the both of you about us before we slept with each other, because I felt it would not be fair to you if I went behind your back. It was never going to be easy, but we can't help who we fall in love with.' I paused. 'Well, think again, bitch. If you want him you will have to fight for him.' She was now crying and I was in pain again. I would still get bouts of pain from my ribs whenever I got over-excited or sexual tension was too much, but this pain, now, was from anger and rage. I would have smacked her in the gob, but I knew it would probably cause me more damage than I could do to her. She was not worth it. I started the engine and drove back to the house. All the way back, she was crying. Huh, I wished she had had a good reason to cry.

Shoy

If I had smacked her as I wanted to, then I could have understood. I got out of the car, not saying a word to her, and collected my kids. She just sat in her car and did not come into the house whilst I was there.

When I got home, still fuming and full of disbelief, I called Lloyd and asked him to come over that night. Then, I revealed to him her little confession of the heart. He for some reason went into one. It now became apparent to me that he was wondering was she carrying on with Denny whilst they were together? Hmmm interesting!

THE TRUTH WILL SET YOU FREE

Why, oh why, was I taking so long to get a grip of my life? Did I really need a man in my life so much? And if I did, why was he the choice?

My life had, once again, gone from content-happy to the usual unhappy-crap. Yvette, once again, had wormed her way in between us. For some reason, namely my mother, Yvette and I were talking (of a sort). This was the most dangerous thing I could have done. She would now be telling me where Lloyd was taking them and what they were getting up to 'as a family'. Okay, so he was taking us out too, but there was this constant comparison on her part. Inevitably, I was going to get drawn into something and it was not long when this inevitability took place.

She called me one afternoon when I got in from work and started on about how someone (who she wanted to remain nameless) came to her house and told her that she was to hang in there, because it was only a matter of time before she would get Lloyd back for good, and that the only reason Lloyd was with me was because I was ill and he felt sorry for me and was finding it hard to break away. As you can imagine, this got the better of me. Most things I could turn my back on now, but when it came to my illness, huh, no way. Lloyd, of course, came over as usual that evening and I was in the middle of ironing the kids' clothes. Yvette's words just rang through my head like Big Ben striking the hour, every hour. As Lloyd lay there on the bed, I watched him from across the ironing board. Could he be so shallow to just stay with me because I was ill? I tried to answer the question myself just from looking at him, but it was no good. I was going to have to ask.

'Lloyd?' His gorgeous blue eyes were looking at me. 'I had a phone call today…..' Why on earth did I say that?

'Yeah, from who?'

'It does not matter who. The fact is they were saying how you want to go back to Yvette, but the only reason why you are not with her is because you feel sorry for me, with my illness and that. Is that true?' He was now sitting up on the bed. I could see he was not going to swallow that one too easily.

'So, tell me. Who is this person? If you don't tell me, then we don't have anything to talk about.'

'So is there something to talk about?' He totally ignored me. So I left it at that and never said another word. Time got the better of him and he had to ask again.

'Who is this person?' I shook my head. I could not say, because I had totally turned the story around. He was now standing in front of the ironing board. 'If you don't tell me who this person is, then I am leaving. I am going to Ricky's and I will not come back until you tell me. Its up to you!' He started to put his shoes on. He was serious then! Oh Christ, this was all going wrong. Why could he not just answer the flipping question?

'Okay. Don't be mad with me.'

Shoy

'Carry on.'

'Hmm. What happened was Yvette ……..'

'I knew she was behind this.'

'Look, just listen before you go off on one. Yvette called me today and told me how someone had gone to her house and told her that you would be back with her real soon, and that you were only with me because you were sorry for me with my illness. Hence the reason why I asked you the question!'

'So why did you say you got a call?'

'Well, I know how wound up you can get and I did not want you to go charging over there and shout your mouth off at her. We have both had enough of all this bickering and we both want it to stop.'

'So did she say who this person was?'

'No, she would not tell me.'

'Well, I am going to find out.' I just knew that was going to happen.

'Can I borrow your car?'

'No. Do you think I am going to lend you my car so you can go charging over there?'

'Well in that case I will walk.' I did not really expect him to, but nonetheless, he left. It turned out that he had phoned Yvette from the call box and she had picked him up. Later on that night, he came back and took what little things he had at the house, saying.

'You lied to me once too often and now it is over. I asked Yvette what went on and she said that you called her and said that so long as you were ill, you had me where you wanted me. I don't like being used. I never expected this of you.' He had tears in his eyes, but for what?

'Lloyd, I have not lied to you. I just know what you're like and what Yvette said hurt me. That's what hurt me.' But he was not listening. As he left, I looked out of the stair window and I could see her car. She was waiting for him. Enraged by what she had done, I had to prove once and for all that I was not lying. But

Shoy

how could I do that now? He was gone and there was no way she would retract what she had said. The battle was over.

I went to work as usual and all that was on my mind was the fact that Lloyd called me a liar to my face. I had never lied to him. What reason would I have? I sat at my desk typing the audio-recorded clinic letters and the tape was not good. The doctor whose tape it was had left the machine on in his pocket and all I could hear was his footsteps, who he spoke to and even when he went to the toilet. It went on for ages before he realised that it was on and then he did not even wind the tape back. That gave me the idea of the century. I was going to tape her, but I had to try it out to see if it would work. I got one of the recording machines and put a tape in it. I then went to one of the empty offices and called Carmel on her phone. Sharing the earpiece with the machine, I spoke to her about whatever and hung up. I then rewound the tape and played it. I jumped off the chair. It had worked and it was so clear! Carmel had been told of the events of the past evening and I called her back and asked her to come to the office. As she walked in, I played the recording I had just made. She could not believe what I had done. She thought I was so clever. She knew I had not been lying, but she said that obviously I felt strongly about being called a liar and that was why this idea had been sent to me. Boy, was she right! My plan was gathering momentum. The

The Truth Will Set You Free

only problem I had now was that Yvette's phone had been cut off, so how would I get her to a phone? I could not turn up with the machine in my pocket. It suddenly dawned on me that I had the telephone number of the payphone on the corner of her road. You may think this strange, but whenever Lloyd was there, in the early days, he would call me from it and I would call him back. The only problem now would be getting her to the box. I had to sort this now, today. I grabbed a handful of blank tapes and returned to the empty office to complete my task. I called the phone box and it rang and rang and, finally, some guy picked it up.

'Hello?' came a very surprised voice on the other end.

'Oh, hi there. Is there a girl called Yvette there?'

'Eh. No.'

'Well, she was supposed to be standing there waiting for my call. Do you think that you could do me a favour?'

'Yeah. Sure.'

'Okay. She lives at number 56. Can you possibly call her to the phone for me?'

Shoy

'Number 56 you say?'

'Yep. That's it. Just across the road. Thank you very much.'

'Is that the one with the 'For Sale' sign in the garden?'

'Eh, no. The house is not for sale, but it might be the one next door. The number is on the outside of the door, though.'

'All right, I will go and knock on the door. Do you want to hang on?'

'Yes, please. Thanks a lot. Oh, by the way, her name is Yvette.'

'Okay. Yvette.' With that I was left with my heart in my mouth. Would she come? Would she even open the door? I waited some time and thought this was not going to work, but I so wanted it to. I could now hear the conversation the stranger was having with her. As I sat there waiting, I never really expected her to come over to the phone, but as she had been using the phone as her own, she would be tempted. Oh my god, I could hear her coming. She picked up the receiver.

The Truth Will Set You Free

'Hello?' There was an air of question and mystery in her voice.

'Oh, hi Yvette. It's only me. Sorry to get you out of the house.'

'Oh, that's all right. When that man came to the house and told me about the phone, I was there thinking who the hell is he?' She sounded so cheerful. I laughed with her nervously. I now had to get the conversation going. I had to bring it around to what I wanted to hear and not put words in her mouth. Just as I was going to start, there was a bleep in my ear.

'Oooo, what was that?' she asked.

'Oh, I was resting on the keyboard and it set off the alarm. Hold on a minute.' As she held on I quickly turned the tape over. Phew, that was close.

'Well, all I called for was just to say that I was sorry for all the upset and at the end of the day, you did win, but why did you deny that you did not say what you said?'

'Shoy, he did not ask me anything.'

'What do you mean? He did not ask you anything?'

'No. Nothing. When we got back here after I picked him up he just asked me what had been happening?'

'Yeah? And what did you say?'

'I said to him, what do you mean what has been happening? He asked me if we had had an argument today. So I said to him, no, and said that we just talked and that I had told you how I felt about him, but did not go into any great details with him. Anyway, Shoy, you said that you were not going to tell him what I had said.' I was getting very anxious now. She was not saying what I wanted to hear.

'Yeah, I know. But Yvette I was really annoyed by what you had told me and I wanted to hear from him whether or not he had actually said what you said he had said – understand?' I totally confused myself with that bit. But all I wanted was to be sure that the tape was taping and she was going to say what I wanted to hear.

'Yeah.' That was all she said.

'But at the end of the day, I actually twisted the story and told him that I was the one who received a phone call and I then told him more or less what YOU had said. Obviously not all of it because I could not remember it in detail, but I made sure that I included the bits that I wanted him to respond to. After that, he then asked if he could borrow my car.' Okay, now we were on the conversation that I wanted.

'Yeah, he called and never said a word all the way up until we got back to the house. Eh Shoy? Did you tell your mum that I was pregnant?' Yvette was pregnant again, but Lloyd was questioning whether it was his, Denny's, or someone else's.

'No. Me? Why?'

'Because your mum knows. She asked me.'

'No, my mum guessed, because she told me and I thought that YOU had told her.' Here we were again straying from the main event. 'Maybe, because you were leaving Mike there and you had told her that you had to go to the hospital, she put two and two together. You know what she's like. You can't hide anything!'

'Last night I thought 'Oh my god.' Although I like your mum and I get on with her, she can't keep her mouth shut.' How dare she say that about my mum, but that was another argument, one that I was not going to get in to today. As I paused to think, I had a glance at the tape to see how much I had left. There was not much, so I told her to hang on (again) and made out I was talking to someone who had walked into the room. That then gave me the opportunity to change the tape.

'Well, anyway, that's your problem!' I was going to have to be clever and bring everything around again. 'Anyway, Lloyd was well annoyed when he left me and he came back quite quickly, so I guessed he must have got a lift or turned back half-way over.'

'Yeah, he had me leave the kids and bring him back down to you, wait and then we went back to the house.'

'So he did not say anything about the phone call that I had made up? He did not even ask you about who said what?'

'He went into it a bit, but he did not say a lot. He just wanted to know what was going on between us. I told him again what I told you earlier, but I did say, also, that it seemed strange that you were saying one thing and he was doing another. There were all these mixed messages. He then asked me if I was sure that we had not been arguing and I said no. When we came back last night, he was all nice, and I was just left wondering – what the hell is happening? I also said to him that I told you that I did not want any more arguments; that I had had enough.'

'Mmmm. Well, that's another reason why I said I got the phone call, because I thought that if I said what you had said, then he was going to fly round to your house, mouth off to you and then that would be everything blown up again. All I wanted to know was if he had said it and if so, who to – you know?'

'Won't he tell you?'

'No. He denied it. He said he would never say anything like that to anyone because it is not true.' I purposely left bits out as I still wanted her to say everything for herself, but this was getting harder and harder.

'Well, when he came back last night, he would not tell me what had gone on at all.' I totally flipped and just chucked in my own line.

'Well, he just said to me that he had never said anything like that to anybody, and I just said that it was what the person told me. Who is this person, Yvette?' This was the leading question. If she answered this, it would put the person there with her and that was

Shoy
all I needed.

'Well, I can't say, but that is what they said.'

'What - the person rang you?' I was re-confirming what she had said to me the day before.

'Yeah?' I sucked my teeth in disbelief. She was not relenting. She would not name names, but at least she had confirmed that she got a call. But I was very close now, and not only to a conviction but also the tape was running out. Once again, there was a timely interruption and then our conversation resumed.

'He went on, right? Asking me what the person's voice was like. In the end when he said he was going and I could see that he was getting really upset, not wanting him to storm over to you, again, I said 'okay' and told him that it was not actually me who received the call - that it was you. With that, you can imagine the look he gave me and then he left after I refused to lend him my car. Half an hour later he's back.'

'Well, I found it difficult to know what to say, as we had already agreed that we were not going to tell him, so I did not know what the hell was going on at this point – you know?'

'Yeah, I know Yvette, but all I was thinking was how could he go and tell anyone that he was with me because I was sick – you know? That's what really got to me.'

'Yeah, but Shoy, even when I spoke to him, I kept thinking that he was not the sort of person to say that he would stay with someone just because they were ill and he gave me the impression that he always wanted to be with you for real. But then, on the other hand, I felt that part of him wanted to be with the kids and me and the other part of him was not sure at all. His brother even came and told me that he spoke to him about another girl that he was interested in but, because he was hooked on you, he just could not move on, and that also he really wanted to be with me and the kids, but again, because of you he could not do that either. I told him that if he wanted to be with you, then that is where he should be, but if he wanted to be with me and the kids, then that is where he should be, but he should not be between both of us like he is.' She was boring me now. She had so much bullshit to say. She suddenly screamed.

'What's the matter?'

'Hold on a minute, Shoy. I am watching this guy who is trying to

Shoy

hold his car back. Oh my god!'

'What? Has he crashed?'

'He has switched the engine off, but he must have had the handbrake off, so my car is parked right up in front of his and it is slowly rolling down towards my car and he is there trying to hold it back.' Side-tracked for a moment, she returned to the story, exactly where she had left off. She was good at that. She never lost track of what she was saying. 'Look, Shoy, Lloyd did not really go into anything last night, as I said before.'

'Yeah, you said. But I thought that originally he went to find out from you what was said and by whom? I thought that you told him the way the whole event went and he then came back and called me a LIAR.'

'Honest?' There was surprise in her tone.

'Yeah. He told me that you said you had not said any of the things that I had told him and that he did not believe me; that I had made it all up. I even asked him why he did not believe me and to that he just said because I don't. Why would you twist a story to protect Yvette? The way I see it, you have lied so much that you have now lost track of where you have got to with the lies.' At the end of the day, I twisted the story to protect you and that was all.

'Well, Shoy, that's what I have done all along – you know?'

'Yeah ……' She interrupted me.

'You see, Shoy, people have been so nasty saying bad things about you and I have been putting them straight on a few facts, especially as they don't know you, because a lot of things have happened to me and, if it was not for you, I would not have got through a lot of it.' I was rolling my eyes around. Her words were making me sick. I found it really hard to believe that she would defend me. Who was she kidding with her sentimental speech? Once again, I repeated bits of what I wanted her to confirm, again and again. I wanted it on the tape as many times as possible.

'Well, I can seriously say now, that I am not bothered any more by any of it ……..' She interrupted me again.

'I wish I could say that.'

'Say what?'

Shoy

'You know, that I am not bothered any more.'

'I tell you, Yvette, I really felt that I was going mad with all of this. I was beginning to think that I had made it all up.' Once again, she re-confirmed what had happened in great detail. I was loving every minute of it.

'I tell you, Shoy; I have been called a liar and just about everything else. You know, when I came and told you, I had held onto it for a couple of days.'

'What? It was not yesterday that you got the call then?'

'No.'

'Oh, right. What a mess. Anyway, he ain't coming to see me no more and that's that.'

'Are you sure?'

'Oh, yeah. I rang him at work this morning and all he said was that I lied, he is not going to see me anymore, and he hopes I have a happy life. I asked him if we could still be friends, but there was no answer to that, so I guess not. With that he said bye and I said bye and hung up – end of story.'

'Honest?'

'Honest.'

'You see, Shoy, I still don't believe that this is over. I don't think that he will give up on you that easy.'

'No. It is. You know what he is like when he feels he has been lied to?' With the conversation going around and around who had said what, somehow Wayne came in to the conversation. I was not expecting her to mention him. But I was all ears, and so was the machine.

'It is like where Wayne is concerned. I knew how he felt about your brother, but I did not realise that he was so jealous and how much he would get upset whenever your brother came over to see Mike. After a while I could not stand the atmosphere, so I just would not tell him whenever your brother came over. So that day when you let it slip that your brother had been up to the house, he went mad.'

'Yeah. Well I was sorry about that. I did not know, but these are

Shoy

part of the games that you play and I suppose after a while the games catch up with you.' With that, I told her I had to go.

I dashed out of the consulting room and back into the office. As I walked in, I looked at Carmel and all I said was, 'Oh yes. Caught, hook, line and sinker.' Now all I had to do was to convince Lloyd to come over to the house that night and I would set it all up for him to hear for himself. If this did not prove my innocence, then nothing would.

I called his workplace, not expecting him to come to the phone at all, but like Yvette, he was predictable.

'Hello?'

'Hi Lloyd, it's me. Look, I know that you don't want to talk to me because I have been a liar, but I have something that would, once and for all, show you that I am not the liar you make me out to be.'

'Look, Shoy, nothing you can say or do would ever make me believe you, all right? So whatever it is, don't waste your time.'

'Lloyd, please. Just come over tonight and I will prove it'.

'What can you have that will prove to me that you are telling the truth?'

'Well, if you want to know, you will have to come to the house and I am sure that once you see what I have, you will change your opinion of me.' He stalled. But I knew that I had fuelled his curiosity. He would be there.

'Look, Shoy, I am not making any promises.'

'Okay. Bye.'

Inquisitiveness got the better of him and he turned up at my workplace that lunchtime. He wanted me to tell him what this evidence was, but did he really think I was that stupid? This was my game now, they were playing with my rules, and he would have to wait. When I looked at him, I knew I had lost him. He had tears in his eyes and I so wanted to reach out to him and comfort him. He was still the gorgeous guy that I had fallen in love with, but he was a man with no home who was wandering aimlessly. He had to find himself for himself.

'Okay, as you are not going to tell me, I promise that I will come

Shoy

over. But I will only give you five minutes and if by then I am not satisfied, then I am off.'

As usual, I left work, collected the kids and as soon as I got in, I set up the transcribing machine, along with the tapes in the order they were taped ready for his arrival in my bedroom, so he had all the privacy he needed.

The kids and I were sitting in the living room watching TV when he arrived and let himself in. I completely forgot that he still had a key. As he walked in I could see that he had been crying and from the looks of things, a lot.

'Hi kids! How you doing?' The kids replied and continued watching the TV.

'Well, where is this thing that you are going to show me?' I walked past him and started up the stairs. He did not follow.

'Well, come on then.'

'What's up there?'

'Look, just come upstairs and I will show you. No tricks. What

The Truth Will Set You Free

I have to show you, well actually you have to listen to it, is set up in the bedroom.'

'Listen? What do you mean listen?'

'Look, just come on.' We walked into the bedroom and I showed him the equipment, explaining how to play, rewind and, fast-forward and change the tapes. Before he started, I thought I would ask him just one more time.

'Do you still think that I lied to you and Yvette was telling you the truth?'

'You know I do. Why you asking me that again. We had this discussion and you lost. Why can't you leave it at that?'

'So I gave you a reason to leave me in other words?' He did not answer. 'Okay, I will leave you in peace. Any problems, I will be downstairs. Just call me!'

'Who am I listening to?'

'If you are interested, start listening.' I turned it on, he put the headphones on and I went downstairs to be with the kids.

Shoy

He was taking ages and then he called me.

'Shoy?'

'Yep, just coming.' I answered. I stood at the door. 'What?'

'Shoy, please close the door.' I turned and closed the door, smiling to myself. It was touchdown.

'I am so sorry. Will you ever forgive me?' I looked at him and laughed.

'So now that I produce evidence for you, evidence that you, yourself can hear, you believe me.' I was pacing up and down the room in front of him with my arms folded my voice raised, raised as high as I could, not wanting the kids to overhear the conversation. 'Why the hell should I take your apology when you turned your back on me and called me a barefaced liar and chose her over me? Me, who gave up everything for you? Me, who gave up my family because they had taken Yvette's side in all of this? Me, who went through hell and got ribs busted and nearly died? Me, who would always consider you in most of my decisions to do with my life. Me, who you asked to marry you and go back to St Vincent

The Truth Will Set You Free

with you some day to run your family business – Eh?' I paused, but not for long. I did not want him to open his mouth just yet. He was listening to me now. 'Me, who loved you unconditionally, even though you proved time and time again to be spineless? But I could live with that because I knew that you loved your kids and wanted to be with them, and in an ideal world you would be. But to call me a liar, and dismiss me like dog shit under your shoes and now you expect me to accept your apology? Huh. Do you really think so? Well I will answer that for you – NO WAY. I want my key back and I want you out of my house. You go back to Yvette. You both deserve one another, but mark my words, you and she will never be happy. It may take a year, it may take ten years, but my true happiness will come and I will be there to see you want me after you have suffered at her hands. NOW GET OUT.'

He came towards me as if to hold me. I stepped back, opening my hand for my key. He slowly placed the single key in my outstretched hand. He was now openly crying and wiping the tears and snot that was running down his face. I moved to one side, opened the bedroom door and showed him out. He made his way down the stairs, said goodbye to the children and went out of the door. He walked out without closing the front door. I walked down the stairs, half expecting him to still be there, but as I reached the door I heard the iron gates screech open and slam

Shoy

shut. I closed the door.

I felt so good. I had done what I set out to do. I packed everything away and went back to my children. IT WAS OVER.

About The Author

Aandi Greenway is a 39 year old, first generation black British Caribbean, married to a serviceman. She has two children, three stepchildren and two step-grandchildren.

Her life has been over shadowed by sexual abuse she endured as a young child. As a teenage mother, she had to grow up fast, juggling education and work all under the watchful eye of her mother.

At the age of 36, she achieved her ambition becoming Air Cabin Crew for Britain's No1 Airline for which she had an article published with a worldwide distribution.

She has appeared on a TV game show, winning first prize. Appeared in video and on radio representing British Army families. This is her story.

Printed in the United Kingdom
by Lightning Source UK Ltd.
99671UKS00001B/10